AF600255

BUTINAGE

Butinage

The Art of Religious Mobility

YONATAN N. GEZ, YVAN DROZ,
JEANNE REY, and EDIO SOARES

UNIVERSITY OF TORONTO PRESS
Toronto Buffalo London

Toronto Buffalo London
utorontopress.com

ISBN 978-1-4875-0880-7 (cloth)
ISBN 978-1-4875-3899-6 (EPUB)
ISBN 978-1-4875-3898-9 (PDF)
DOI: https://doi.org/10.3138/9781487538989

Library and Archives Canada Cataloguing in Publication

Title: Butinage : the art of religious mobility / Yonatan N. Gez, Yvan Droz, Jeanne Rey, and Edio Soares.

Names: Gez, Yonatan N., author. | Droz, Yvan, author. | Rey, Jeanne, 1980– author. | Soares, Edio, author.

Description: Includes bibliographical references.

Identifiers: Canadiana (print) 20200402803 | Canadiana (ebook) 20200402862 | ISBN 9781487508807 (cloth) | ISBN 9781487538996 (EPUB) | ISBN 9781487538989 (PDF)

Subjects: LCSH: Christian life – Brazil – Case studies. | LCSH: Christian life – Kenya – Case studies. | LCSH: Christian life – Ghana – Case studies. | LCSH: Christian life – Switzerland – Case studies. | LCSH: Brazil – Religious life and customs – Case studies. | LCSH: Kenya – Religious life and customs – Case studies. | LCSH: Ghana – Religious life and customs – Case studies. | LCSH: Switzerland – Religious life and customs – Case studies.

Classification: LCC BV4501.3 .G49 2021 | DDC 248.4 – dc23

The open access version of this publication was funded by the Swiss National Science Foundation.

University of Toronto Press acknowledges the financial assistance to its publishing program of the Canada Council for the Arts and the Ontario Arts Council, an agency of the Government of Ontario.

Canada Council for the Arts
Conseil des Arts du Canada

Funded by the Government of Canada
Financé par le gouvernement du Canada
Canada

Contents

Acknowledgments

The seed for this research was sown back in the early 1990s, when Yvan Droz began studying the Kikuyu people of central Kenya. In his work, Droz observed links between urban migration and religious mobility (Droz 1999), leading him to propose the concept of religious butinage within the context of a discussion of the social practices of Kenyan Pentecostals (Droz 2000a, 2004). The concept was later developed by Edio Soares in his doctoral thesis (Soares 2007, 2009). In his own work, Soares systematized the concept and tested its coherence. Based on his ethnographic fieldwork in Brazil, Soares evoked the notion of *voisinage* ("neighborliness") as the fundamental logic governing butinage. Derived from the French verb butiner, which refers to the foraging behavior of bees and other pollinizing insects, the term was employed by Droz and Soares metaphorically to refer to the "to-ing and fro-ing" of believers between religious institutions. Both found that the employment of this biological metaphor corresponded, more than any formal terminology associated with "conversion," to the actual religious mobility of their Kenyan and Brazilian interviewees as manifest in their everyday practice. It is through these two case studies that a small research team began to form. In mid-2010, we launched a research project called "*Structures anthropologiques du religieux: Butinage et voisinage*," or Project StAR for short, under the direction of Droz as the project's principal investigator.* The project, financed by the Swiss National Science Foundation

* The project, which was centered around three countries (Kenya, Brazil, and Switzerland), was financed from 2010 to 2013 (project no. 100013–130340) and was then prolonged until early 2015 (project no. 100013–146301). The integration of additional fieldwork in Ghana, conducted in 2014 in the context of Jeanne Rey's postdoctoral fellowship at the University of Toronto, was made possible thanks to the support of the Swiss National Science Foundation (project no. 2GEP1_148656).

(SNSF) and run from the Graduate Institute of International and Development Studies in Geneva (IHEID), first focused on Kenya and Brazil and, upon its prolongation, incorporated two additional case studies: Switzerland and Ghana. Throughout the grant, the research team expanded to include Yonatan N. Gez (who joined in 2010) and Jeanne Rey (who joined in 2012).*

In executing the project, we remain indebted to a large number of people. First and foremost, we thank our many interlocutors in Brazil, Kenya, Ghana, and Switzerland, who have shared their stories with us. We also wish to thank the many colleagues and researchers who have followed this project and offered their advice. In particular, we wish to recognize Ari Pedro Oro of the Universidade Federal do Rio Grande do Sul in Porto Alegre and Hervé Maupeu of the research center Les Afriques dans le Monde at the Université de Pau et des pays de l'Adour. Additional thanks go to Samuel Owiwa and to Amir Atsmon.

In terms of institutional support, we thank the SNSF and the IHIED for their endorsement of the project. In Kenya, we thank the French Institute for Research in Africa (IFRA) and all its staff. Further thanks go to the Buber Society of Fellows in the Humanities and Social Sciences and the Harry S. Truman Research Institute for the Advancement of Peace – both of them at the Hebrew University of Jerusalem. We also thank Michael Lambek and the Centre for Ethnography at the University of Toronto.

Lastly, we wish to thank Jodi Lewchuk, Robin Studniberg, and the editorial team at the University of Toronto Press for their support throughout the book's production. We thank Carolyn Zapf for her thorough copy editing. Finally, we take the opportunity to appreciate the anonymous reviewers for their excellent comments on our draft manuscript.

* Due in part to this long timeframe, a portion of the material presented in this book is based on work already published elsewhere, albeit in earlier stages of analysis and less comprehensive than in the present volume.

PART I

Rethinking Religious Normativity

1 Introduction: The Mobile Religious Practitioner

James is an artist in his early forties. Originally from Kenya but well-traveled, he spends part of his time in East Africa and part of his time in Western Europe, where his wife is originally from. A Catholic by birth, James's religiosity has been characterized by inquisitiveness and exploration. When we asked him, sitting in a café in downtown Nairobi in 2013, about his religious identification, he paused and then said: "I don't know how you can tag me."

James's religious journey started in the countryside in western Kenya, where he was born into a large polygamous family. His village, he says, was dominated by the Catholic Church, to which his family belonged. During his childhood, the only alternative was a small Anglican community, "but it was not very vibrant." While his impressions of the Catholic Church were largely positive, James nonetheless had difficulties with what he perceived as the church's preoccupation with financial contributions. Dissatisfied with the church, James "lost interest in going to churches, slowly by slowly." He explained: "I went out … For quite a while I didn't move to another church, I just didn't go to church." Around that time, in the late 1980s, the neo-Pentecostal wave began sweeping across East Africa, and many of James's family members were converting. When he himself moved to Nairobi to pursue his artistic dreams, he too was drawn to the Pentecostal movement. Following a chance encounter at a bus stop with a group of youths from a growing Pentecostal denomination, James went to visit their Sunday service, which was held at a rented public hall. "When I visited the Pentecostal church, I found there is vibrant, young people your age, people are happy, there is dance, there is music, it is totally a different social setting, social religious setting, totally different, very very interesting. So without looking for the church I just found a church."

James stayed in his adoptive Pentecostal church for five years, and even though the church changed venue several times, he remained a committed worshiper and an active member of the youth ministry. Despite his individualistic tendencies, James enjoyed the sense of community and the youthful atmosphere, and for some time he felt that he fit right in. Gradually, however, he grew disillusioned and critical of the church. Of particular concern for him was the control that he felt the church had been exerting on its members in delimiting their social interactions. Most acutely for James, who was hoping to get married and settle down, that control implied "that you have to get a spouse from the church. So if you get somebody from outside, it's an issue." This challenge was aggravated by "class problems," as James noted that the congregants would "socialize according to rank," and that he, a struggling artist, was "cut off" and disregarded as a potential love interest.

Having left the church, James soon met his European wife, in whose company he migrated to her home country. In Europe, James tried a number of churches. On occasion, he attended Catholic Mass, and he tried participating in a local Pentecostal church, but was struck by the stark differences with the Pentecostalism he was familiar with from home. Eventually, he turned inwards and continued to explore his spirituality outside organized religion, praying and reading the Bible on his own. At the same time, he spent long days in libraries and later in online discussion groups focused on spirituality. He values his autodidactic learning, saying "there are things I have learned on my own ever since I have been in Europe, by just doing my own research, doing my own search, yeah. So I might not go to a church, but I still have beliefs, I still have my faith, yeah. But I have learned more things, more things even outside the church."

As the years passed, James and his wife have shifted back and forth several times between Europe and East Africa. Throughout these shifts, James was adamant in his spiritual thirst, but never became "a member of any group except artistic groups." In Nairobi, he has been occasionally going to an Indian temple in Parklands in order to attend their monthly events, where free food was being provided. While staying in Uganda, he discovered the Baha'i faith, and although he has had minimal contact with the religion, he attended their temple, where he enjoyed a free meal as well. He has never been to a mosque, but said he would be happy to go if invited. On occasion, he has paid visits to other Pentecostal churches, such as the one led by his brother Jim, whom he supports. Furthermore, one might assume, looking at James's dreadlocks, that he is a sympathizer of Rastafarianism, which indeed he is, although his acceptance of the teaching is selective. James is also interested in freemasonry and, unlike many Kenyans who recoil from the organization's alleged association with evil powers, James has been studying the subject as much as he can from afar. Explaining his selective adoption of different religious teachings, James said: "I am that kind of guy, I'm free." While recognizing the power of his religious upbringing, James proposed that, for him, religion is primarily about a personal quest for spiritual meaning, irreducible to institutional structures, which too often are about power and control. He concluded:

> [God] is not asking us to do anything, he just wants us to live a normal life, live with others, understand others, just a normal life, but just to recognize that he's God. He's not asking us to be a member, to call ourselves with a name, to look down on others, to be the correct ones, no, no, to consider ourselves we are Saved, and others no – from what? God saved the whole world, even Muslims will go in [to heaven]. (Interview with James, Nairobi 2013)

The Mobile Practitioner

While the details of James's case are clearly particular, his story is in many respects representative of the narratives we encountered in our ethnographic research in Brazil, Kenya, Switzerland, and Ghana. The majority of our interviewees have, like James, adopted a highly dynamic – if not quite as personalized – range of religious practices. At certain life junctures, these practices may overlap, possibly spilling over and fusing together in unexpected combinations. At other times, they may recede into the background – abandoned or merely dormant? – where they would be hidden from view and fail to register in observers' accounts. To complicate matters further, the differences that James reported between the Pentecostalism he knew from home and the one he encountered in Europe threaten to undermine the very idea of coherent and consensually stable institutional categories to which everyone can refer. Moreover, like the vast majority of our interviewees, James maintained a complex relationship with institutionalized religion, acknowledging and appreciating the value of his community and upbringing while remaining fundamentally suspicious of institutions and those at their head – citing, above all, concern with church hypocrisy and greed.

As such, James's story expresses much more than an individual religious biography. Our times – the early twenty-first century – appear to be marred in modes of polarization and radicalization: a deepening gap between political factions, divisions between the haves and the have-nots, and seemingly insurmountable tensions between people of different faiths. All over the world, we hear of retreat into ideological echo chambers, of rising nationalism-fueled walls, and of the automatic casting of another's conclusions as fake news. Paradoxically, the same mechanisms that ensure the global efficacy of such divisions are those that speak the language of connectivity – the global trajectory of technologies and ideas, coupled with global wealth, that allows for more physical mobility and opportunities than ever before. This tension extends to the realm of religion. The reader is no doubt familiar with Samuel Huntington's (1996) "clash of civilizations" hypothesis, for which religion serves as a central locus of identity. Such ideas strike a chord with a widely felt rise in religio-political fundamentalism: an anti-modernist stance that asserts a return to the "fundamentals" of faith, a trend that can be found in most of the world's religions.[1] At the same time, and even as some traditions emphasize rigidity in the face of modernity, many scholars observe that individual religiosity is becoming increasingly composite, with the rise of alternative spiritualities and syncretistic combinations prompted by globalization and processes of social atomization and personal meaning-seeking. To keep to the example of the "clash of civilization" debate, we note Amartya Sen's rejoinder to Huntington, in which the thinker rejected the premise of "the commanding power of a unique categorization along so-called civilizational lines, which closely follow religious divisions" (Sen 2006, 10). Rather than operating as a script that directs perceptions and action – a view that Kwame Appiah calls a "source-code fallacy" (Appiah 2018, 64) – Sen and others propose that personal identities are a meeting point between multiple identity aspects, whose complex intersection undermines a clear-cut identification between overarching ideology and personal identity. These ideas bring to mind earlier works such as that of Fredrik Barth (1983, 1984), who pioneered the view of individuals as internally diverse "universes of discourse" or "streams of tradition." Such streams include, among other things, ethnicity, gender, history and ancestry, religion, occupation and class, and settlement and lifestyle – all of which intersect in complex ways.[2]

All these concepts are made clear in the variety of practices designated as religious mobility, which render tangible the real-life limits of wishful notions about religious boundaries. Indeed, scholars note that, just as much as fundamentalism is a (selective) turn against modernity, it is also a (selective) turn against religious combinations. The struggle with modernist forces manifests not only in fundamentalist ideologies' traditionalist, backward-looking, and authoritarian orientations but also in a rigid resistance to ideas related to religious dynamism. Thus, for example, Almond, Appleby, and Sivan (2003, 17) define fundamentalism as a "discernible pattern of religious militance by which self-styled 'true believers' attempt to arrest the erosion of religious identity, fortify the borders of the religious community, and create viable alternatives to secular institutions and behaviors."[3] The idea of "preserving distinctiveness" (Haynes 1995, 8) and purity against mixing with other religious and political entities – a stance identified by Shaw and Stewart (1994) as "anti-syncretism" – is further noted by Prandi (2000, 24), who contrasts fundamentalism with syncretism as "two phenomena in a dynamic tension" and explains that "fundamentalism in general opposes any imposition of religious ideas from outside" and "reacts to meeting a new religion by a stiffening of observance of the letter of the law."[4]

This discussion, in fact, goes further back than the modern rise of fundamentalism and touches on the very heart of our conception of desirable identities. At least since the nineteenth century, the idea that identity and geographic stability is somehow superior to the changeability of mobility has been entrenched within mainstream European thinking (Gez et al. 2017). The theory of evolution and the burgeoning social sciences – archaeology, sociology, and anthropology – have been making various claims to the effect that human development throughout history has been shifting toward a more stable, sedentary life. Sociocultural evolutionary thinking (see, for instance, Morgan 1877) took for granted that the life of the sedentary farmer was largely an improvement over that of the hunter-gatherer or the nomad. Similarly, in popular culture, stability and fixedness have long been hailed as the hallmarks of a more mature, "developed" state of being.[5] Other strands of thinking have joined in to reinforce this intellectual bias. The creation of the nation-state encouraged the propensity for both stable identities and sedentariness. The marriage of (ethnic) identity with (bounded) territorial organization, which is constitutive of the organization of the modern state (Gellner 1983), resulted in cross-border mobility being designated as potentially suspicious (see Schnapper 2001). Similarly, in the realm of individual psychology, the ideal of stability was confirmed through viewing individuals as possessing a core self – an idea inspired, in part, by Judeo-Christian notions of an indivisible soul – that is either coherent and consistent or aspires to be so.

Against the identity-flattening risk of religio-political fundamentalism, it is important to recognize practitioners' actual complexities, contradictions, and ambivalences (Schielke 2012). All of that, we argue, is embodied most clearly in the context of religious mobility. For example, it has been suggested that conversion is not "just" about theological conviction or pragmatic advantage-seeking, but rather is a complete human "passage" that encapsulates "a quest for human belonging" and negotiates "a place in the world" (Austin-Broos 2003, 2). To give a specific example, some scholars argue that, historically in the United States, the trope of "conversion" has been abstracted well beyond its purely theological meaning and was central to the fashioning of American identity (Wilson 2009). Far from ideas about fundamentalism and possibly a counterweight to them, this trope pointed to an ongoing process of "pluralized commitment to modes, mores, and vocations to beatitude," which "can open up a language of possibility, metamorphosis, transregional migration, [and] cultural unsettling" that is "unstable, open-ended, and world-shattering" (3). While the notion of conversion can have a ring of dogmatism, such ideas show how the term can just as easily be used to counter fundamental rigidities.

Going back to our interviewee James, we can begin to see how his peripatetic religious journey can be read not only as a theological quest for "truth" but also – and primarily – in terms of making and remaking of the self as embedded in a broader sociopolitical reality, responding to and renegotiating culture and personal identity. At the same time, the allusion to the American spirit and the trope of conversion further draws attention to the individualistic aspect of religious mobility, as we have indeed observed in James's case. While here, too, context is key, the modern idea of religion as noncoercive draws attention to issues of choice and agency, as people exert their free will in navigating a landscape of religious possibilities and their individual experiences thereof. As Appiah (2018, 39) proposes, "people may join churches and temples and mosques and announce sectarian identities, but when it comes to the fine points of belief, it can sometimes seem that each of us is a sect of one." The notion of "sect of one" invites us to think of religion in private terms. This idea is best captured by what, based on an interviewee called Sheila, has generically been termed "Sheilaism" (Bellah et al. 1985, 220–1), but could assume as many names and variations as there are people on the planet.

While this line of argument in favor of full-fledged personal religions has an intuitive appeal, it also raises substantial challenges by underplaying the formative role of religious rules and local culture. Thus, for example, while James's discourse emphasized religious freedoms, his journey was no less shaped by social expectations and calls for conformity. At various junctures, James was confronted by pastors, family members, and fellow congregants who tried to keep him on the straight path of institutional commitment and criticized him for his supposedly arrogant individualism. To call James's religion "Jamesism" may fail to give due consideration to the regulative role of his environment. In this respect, James's trajectory of mobility between East Africa and Western Europe brings to mind the often-cited suggestion that the idea of personalized religion mirrors uniquely Western ideals of individual autonomy and division between the private and the public sphere. In the present work, thanks to the examination of four case studies, three of which are in the Global South, we put this hypothesis to the test. Seeking, as a methodological approach, to avoid assumptions about the supremacy of either individual autonomy or social rules and structures, we developed heuristic sensitivity attentive to the interplay between three factors: individual latitude, formal religious-institutional traditions, and local cultural norms. We argue that bringing these three factors together, while recognizing their unavoidable intertwinements and built-in tensions, can provide a comprehensive look into the complex dynamics that make up the religious landscape.

From this focus on the interplay between three factors follows a recognition of religion as changeable, both over time and across place. Such flexibility can be read as healthy adaptability, if only because "if scriptures were not subject to interpretation – and thus to reinterpretation – they wouldn't continue to guide people over long centuries. When it comes to their survival, their openness is not a bug but a feature" (Appiah 2018, 56). Whether a bug or a feature, the changes undergone by various religions and by the cultures that host them raise questions about how scholars ought to conceive of and articulate the subject at hand. Since the period of the Enlightenment and the proliferation of deistic views concerning natural religion, Western thinkers have been trying to identify generalizable, universal components associated with religion. However, contemporary scholarship has shown the limitations of many such attempts. Terms such as "believer," "faith," "conversion," and even "religion" itself are so common that we sometimes forget they are loaded with (mainly Western) history and (mainly Christian) connotations. As Graham Ward argues, "what is understood by *religio* changes with time and place" and "even in those places dominated by western European languages the use of the term is bound to specific cultural politics" (Ward 2006, 179; emphasis in the original). Such understandings promote normative expectations, which may at times be contested but nonetheless introduce biases into our thinking. Thus, for instance, Talal Asad (1993) criticizes Clifford Geertz's (1973) definition of religion as emphasizing belief as a "state of mind," an approach that makes sense in the theological context of (post-Reformation) Christianity but can hardly lay claim to universality.[6] Asad (1993, 2003) goes on to criticize the very division between religious and secular realms as a late Western development that sets all religions in the same category – and apart from the normative secular space (see Fountain 2013).

Another case in point is the notion of belief, which has been strongly tied to the modern understanding of religion at least since Edward

Burnett Tylor's well-known nineteenth-century "minimum definition" of religion as "belief in spiritual beings" (Tylor 1871, 383). Later scholarship, however, has been quite critical of such emphasis on belief, which has been suggested to serve as a false universalization based on Eurocentric perspectives and Christian emphasis on creed (Lindquist and Coleman 2008), while simultaneously pointing to the concept's vagueness and polysemy (Pouillon 1979; Sperber 1982). For example, Needham (1972, 108) proposes that belief as a phenomenon "appears to be no more than the custom of making such statements." Drawing attention, among other things, to how certain languages offer "no verbal concept at all which can convey exactly what may be understood by the English word 'believe'"(37), Needham makes the case for belief as a linguistic construct rather than a universal characteristic of human experience.

The question of bias and the (in)adequacy of concepts may not occur to the majority of believers, or even to most producers of academic scholarship whose research focuses on the (Christian) Global North and above all on the United States and Western Europe. By contrast, there is substantially less scholarly work on religious identity and mobility within the Global South, to which terms and models developed with respect to particular Western contexts and histories are too often carelessly applied.[7] Indeed, we agree with Henri Gooren's lament, in the context of a discussion on models explaining religious mobility, whereby, "unfortunately, there are almost no instances of these models being applied to the 85 percent of the world population living in the other continents [that is, not Western Europe or North America]" (Gooren 2010, 41). This marginalization of perspectives from the Global South is particularly striking in light of how the center of gravity of key religious traditions, most notably within Christianity, is said to be shifting toward the Global South (see, for example, Jenkins 2002; Norris and Inglehart 2004). Scholars have shown how often-ignored perspectives from the Global South may lead to quite different, surprising, and potentially radical corollaries (Comaroff and Comaroff 2015). In particular, long-standing intertwinement between indigenous and Abrahamic cosmogonies has created modes of fluidity and hybridity that do not resemble the Abrahamic ideal sedentary practitioner. Rather, the study of religious identity in the Global South is, more often than not, a study of in-betweenness and flux (Premawardhana 2018), with emphasis on real-life pragmatism and religious, cultural, and geographic negotiations.

This discussion leads us to the perspective put forth in this book. In the introduction to James's religious biography, we quoted him as saying "I don't know how you can tag me." This comment is understandable considering James's complicated relationship with institutionalized religion and the fact that his religious identity does not fall into neat preexisting categories. This book can be understood as our attempt to rise to James's challenge. Our key argument is simple: religious identity often extends far beyond exclusive institutional ideal-type members and generates fluid, circumstantial, and somewhat personalized religious identities. Along these lines, and away from stigmatizing preconceptions about religious mobility, we propose rethinking the religious practitioner as fundamentally mobile.[8] But while considering religion from a highly personal perspective, we find that such variations are not fully divorced from institutional injunctions and social expectations. This basic observation is certainly not new and has been recognized in the anglophone, francophone, and lusophone literature that forms the basis of our theoretical exploration, with special indebtedness to the work of anthropologists. What we hope will be particularly enlightening in the present work is our attempt to present a systematic, gradual unpacking of this line of argument, firmly grounded in dialogue with multisited ethnographic data. This gradual unpacking and recourse to a refined scholarly toolkit allows us to account for a range of mobile religious practices that often pass under the scholarly radar, and will eventually help us to rethink formal religious identities through the consideration of de facto practice.

In this respect, the present volume converses with and expects to contribute to scholarship in both religious studies and anthropology of religion. While the former, as we show, still tends to conceive of religious practice/identity as static, the latter, though more cognizant of the pervasiveness of religious mobility, largely struggles to offer a systematic conceptualization thereof and a conceptual alternative that can challenge the prevailing paradigm. Oftentimes, we note a gap between scholars' – primarily anthropologists' – documentation of religious identities and practices as inherently dynamic and their reproduction of the static standpoint through their conceptual language. Our work thus sets out to provide a systematic consideration that will reflect, through both theorization and a conceptual toolkit, what anthropologists have long been documenting. Beyond the specifics of religious mobility, our elaborations also set out to offer a modest contribution to broader questions regarding the inherent dynamism of human identity.

Aware of the many pitfalls toward which this line of argument could lead us, we proceed with care, and delve at length into topics that have often been swept aside in favor of a broad, at times vague, recognition of religious dynamism, such as questions of religious motivation, the limits of mobility, circularity versus succession of practices, and the ongoing relevance of past practices. All of this exploration is grounded in our four case studies, whose presentation takes up the book's middle section. Spanning three continents and multiple cultural and linguistic spaces, the case studies offer a range of distinct contexts – religious as well as socioeconomic, cultural, political, and so forth. This comparative perspective allows us to expand our observations beyond any particular instance and to make the case whereby everyday religious mobility is in no way unique to any particular country or region. Indeed, religious mobility amounts to much more than – as some utilitarians would have it – modes of coping and "getting by in the Global South." Showing how Brazilians, Kenyans, Ghanaians, and Swiss all have a propensity for religious mobility – marked though it is by significant differences – allows us to move toward more general statements. The case studies, which were intentionally limited to Christian-dominated contexts (see the methodological introduction to part II), thus elucidate the three-tier interface mentioned earlier between individual propensity, institutional scripts, and social context and norms. At the same time, as the purpose of our case studies is mainly illustrative, we were careful not to overwhelm the reader with elaborate historical and political particularities. Rather, wherever these details struck us as having particular relevance, we guided the reader further using external references.

The idea of exploring and fleshing out categories associated with dynamic religious identities may appear paradoxical. After all, academic paradigms may fix themselves into a rigidity that undermines the very fluidity that one seeks to grasp. This challenge is real and daunting, and may indeed explain the incompatibility that we observe between scholars' recognition of diffused religious identities and their willingness to commit to concrete, applicable models explaining the variations that they observe. Indeed, dynamic perspectives give us a picture that is much less clear-cut and much more fuzzy. The challenge at hand raises significant questions with regard to concretizing and capturing the vicissitudes of religious identity from an inherently dynamic standpoint. How much should we try to pin it down before we undermine the very dynamism of the phenomenon in question? This core question echoes all through the structure of the book, which offers a gradual theoretical unfolding and to which we will turn later in this introduction. First, however, we present the reader with a central concept, one that will accompany us throughout the book: the metaphor of religious "butinage."

The Butinage Metaphor

The French term "butinage" derives from the verb *butiner*, which shares the same root as the French word *butin* (loot) and has its origin in the Middle Low German word *būte* (to trade, share, or loot). Until the sixteenth century, the verb *butiner* thus had the meaning of "sharing that which has been caught." During the seventeenth century, the term began to assume its current meaning, which refers to the action of bees visiting flowers in search of nourishment for themselves and their hive. Through their butinage, bees also nourish their environment, because by transporting their "loot" (*butin*), they facilitate the reproduction of plants through pollination. More plants means more "*butin*" to share and also more bees to engage in butinage.

It was these images of dynamism, foraging, collectivity, and processing that sent Droz and Soares to propose the metaphorical employment of the term to refer to the unfolding of everyday religious mobility. As Soares wrote in his book on religious mobility in Brazil, "just like bees, the practitioner engages in butinage from one 'religious denomination' to another (re)creating meaning, whose 'scent' is ever-particular and renewed" (Soares 2009, 20; our translation). Like the bees in constant motion between flowers, so do religious practitioners or "butineurs" lend themselves to multidirectional mobility: "The practitioner does not simply 'pass' from denomination A to denomination B and then to C. Far from it, they never cease to 'commute' from A to B to C, and then again to A, then C, then B, and so on. The result is a continuous to-ing and fro-ing, in which the practitioner articulates different religious contents within a single religious practice" (54–5; our translation). As every beekeeper knows, bees' foraging activities are neither circumstantial nor seasonal; rather, constant motion is their default state. Their motion, therefore, is full of intention, direction, urgency, and a sense of purpose: a potent, dramatic image with which to counter that of the unremittingly sedentary churchgoer.[9]

By recognizing the possibility of "commuting" between multiple centers, the butinage perspective is able to account for both what we may call diachronic and synchronic mobility. Diachronic butinage corresponds to the traditional notion of exclusivity of affiliation and may be associated with an itinerary of conversions or a "conversion career" (Gooren 2010). Considering diachronic butinage implies questioning the life trajectories of the butineur and observing patterns of religious practice across life moments of special significance (for example, romantic breakups, the death of a loved one, geographic migration, coming of age, starting a family and having children, climbing up or down the socioeconomic ladder, and so on). Are there phases in which people commonly tend to be more mobile and others during which they tend to be more sedentary? Can we detect patterns of mobility away from their childhood religious traditions? By contrast, synchronic butinage relies on the idea of simultaneous religious practices, which may be limited to a specific religious territory (such as the Pentecostal universe) or to a broader religious tradition (such as a self-identified Christian who participates, throughout a single week, in Anglican, Catholic, and Pentecostal services).

Thinking in terms of butinage, with its emphasis on individuals' flexible and potentially rich religious identities, allows us to better understand and balance national statistics, which show that the number of members joining new religious movements (NRMs) does not necessarily correspond to the number of people said to depart from the historical churches. It allows us to observe the "*manière de faire*" (De Certeau 1980) within religion and to document practices that too often go unnoticed: occasional shifts and visits from one denomination – or, to use a more neutral term, "religious form" (Gez 2018)[10] – to another, participation in religious events without formal affiliation, religious exposure through the media (which we will later term "religious zapping"), or mobility across multisited kinship structures, such as will be presented in chapter 5 on Ghana.

So far, the reader is at risk of suspecting that we are advocating for a view of the religious practitioner as an unrestrained agent who freely flouts institutional authority at will by conjuring an idyllic image of a carefree bee buzzing and foraging in boundless meadows of attractive churches-as-flowers. This conjecture, however, would do little justice to our approach, and indeed, we are even apprehensive of going as far as Hervieu-Léger did with her notion of "pilgrim religiosity," which she characterizes as "voluntary, individual, mobile, non-normative or weakly normative, adjustable, and external to the routines that govern the daily lives of the individuals concerned" (Hervieu-Léger 2001a, 90; our translation). Instead, we recognize that butineurs are not all of the same ilk: some develop a taste for more exclusive affiliations, while others are insatiable butineurs keen on adopting whichever religious practices are available to them.[11] Furthermore, the butineurs themselves do not tell the whole story. The Abrahamic religious traditions, on the whole, have a tendency to privilege sedentary religious identities by setting stigmatizing dichotomies between believer and unbeliever, and leaving little room for "deviations" and in-betweenness (Laplantine 2003). Here again, while theologies are not deterministically binding, we agree with Rambo (2003, 214–15) that, "whatever one's opinions concerning the validity and value of theology, theology often plays a pivotal role in shaping experience and expectations regarding conversion. Moreover, theology constitutes part of the 'DNA' of the conversion process for people existing within a particular religious tradition."

Indeed, as Mahmood (2005) rightly suggests, we cannot simply expect the undoing of the weight of religious socialization. Moreover, such socialization may go beyond what we may narrowly consider to be religious injunctions. As our conception of butinage seeks to strike a chord between individual choice and the regulative power of religious and social tradition, a word of clarification is in order concerning the distinction between religious regulations and social norms. While we should not automatically assume religion to be equated with tradition, culture, and ethnic identity (Roberts 2016), we also should not isolate butinage from a practitioner's socioreligious context. Indeed, individual practice is embedded within social norms as much as it is embedded within formal religious-institutional expectations (Geertz 1973, 126). While the case can be made, in some situations, whereby what we refer to as religion originated in social norms that overlapped with ideas of ethos and worldview, the institutionalization of religion, especially in the West, has given rise to specific theological or sociological aspects that deserve scholarship in their own right. As recent years have seen a growing interest in bottom-up perspectives to religious practice that emphasize practitioners' own agency, often through focus on rational choice, it is important for scholars to avoid downplaying the palpable force of social and religious traditions, whose regulative powers reward conformity while exerting pressure to stem deviance. The practitioner does not operate in a void, and local customs and expectations have a major bearing on people's religious action. Accordingly, the butinage metaphor draws attention not only to the act of foraging itself, but also to the dynamic relations between three key objects: the "bee" itself (the mobile practitioner), the visited "flowers" (religious institutions), and the "hive" (sociocultural environment). This three-tier nexus is central to our proposed perspective and will therefore be returned to again and again throughout this volume. In particular, thanks to our multisited comparative ethnography, the three-tier nexus allows us to reflect on the role of local social norms in their bearing on actual religious practice. Just as importantly, this three-tier perspective offers a word of caution against generalizing all members of a social group, geographic space, or religious community.

One more word of clarification needs to be said about our choice of butinage as the notion standing at the heart of our inquiry. Our purpose is not to do away with theologically loaded terminologies, but rather to promote a shift toward a more comprehensive and inclusive perspective. First and foremost, we propose to consider religious mobility as a fundamental way of being. No longer should we regard belonging to this or that denomination as the "norm" for practitioners, as expected by religious authorities within the Abrahamic traditions; instead, the "norm" might be found in religious butinage, whose organizing principle is that of polymorphous, fluid mobility. Accepting the enduring fact of mobility – if only as an exercise in shifting perspectives – opens the door to a particular set of questions: How may we be able to capture and "map out" dynamic religious identities? What are the social codes, if any, associated with such mobility across different social contexts, and what are the social consequences and penalties for such mobility? How frequently does our subject of inquiry move and within which range or possible patterns, and what might the motivation for their mobility be? What are the relations – possibly tensions – between practitioners' stated religious identity and de facto practice? Lastly, how does the perspective presented in this book help to understand the contemporary challenges *for* religion (secularization), as well as those posed *by* religion (fundamentalism)?

The choice of a metaphor does not ignore the language employed by local actors. Followers of traditional religions in Kenya or Ghana, for example, may not speak of their own belief systems in terms of "denominations." Instead, as we will see in the respective chapters in part II, communities adopt their own changing jargon with which to conjure up an image of their religious landscape and its particular features. The choice of the "neutral" metaphor thus eases the alignment of different cases with less concern for a normativity bias. At the same time, we do acknowledge that the notion of butinage itself is a terminological imposition on our interlocutors. While we noted that the language is intuitively relatable – for example, Romildo Ribeiro Soares, founder of the International Church of God's Grace,[12] wrote: "Truth be told, I would have loved to be a birdlike pastor; one Church today, another tomorrow, and so on incessantly" – the application of the terminology of "butinage" to religion was something of a *terra nullius*. Thus, while the notion of butinage allows for a certain synthesis of disparate idioms, we acknowledge that our interlocutors have not been the ones to introduce it.

This acknowledgment, in turn, points to the broadness of the metaphor as both a strength and a limitation. The metaphor is deployed as a heuristic tool, with the intention of directing the reader's gaze toward a particular, often-neglected horizon, transcending scholarly lacunas, and rethinking core questions. It goes without saying that the intellectual exercise of thinking about religiousness with the help of butinage does not constitute an attempt to force the biological representation of the bee world – which is also, after all, a form of social construction – on religious practices and to apply social biologism. Rather, the obvious gap between the metaphoric and literal designations of butinage serves as a reminder that the metaphoric language may be qualified or even abandoned at any time so as not to fall into the "honey trap" – pardon the pun – of seductive language.

Above all, the core simplicity of the notion of butinage makes it a starting point and a basis for a number of conceptual elaborations. Locking steps with our four case studies and drawing on empirical data, we systematize and theorize these elaborations in the third part of the book. There, we proceed from the metaphor toward an increasingly refined scholarly toolkit, a theorization that takes us back to the original Greek conception of the notion of "theory" as associated with observations and travel (Tweed 2006). One important development is the idea of a typology of butineurs, that is to say, a dynamic continuum of ideal types, which, drawing on the metaphorical language, invites reflections on a spectrum ranging from the "polyfloral" butineur (an avid, limitless, peripatetic practitioner) to the "monofloral" butineur (a model loyal church member). This typology also allows to consider the case of "monochrome" butineurs, whose mobility is inscribed within a clear religious universe. The question of delineated universes of mobility we further explore using another notion, that of "territories." Territories, we explain, are hypothetical, personalized "cartographies" of conceivable and legitimate religious mobility.

Another direction in which we develop the notion of butinage later in the book is in relation to the question of religious motivation. Recognizing epistemological and other challenges associated with determining people's motivation, while acknowledging that religious choice-making is not always based on rational action, we propose rethinking motivation through the consideration of three intertwined conceptual categories or "logics": practical logic, social logic, and inclinational logic. Avoiding the reduction of mobility to singular "reasons," we instead show how acts of mobility reverberate concomitantly along these three registers. Yet another elaboration of the basic idea of butinage that emerges later in the book relates to the constellation of multiple synchronic practices. As we show time and time again across our four case studies, practitioners often adopt an inclusive stance and may maintain multiple long-standing relations with a number of religious traditions. This synchronicity raises questions regarding the arrangement and management of their multiple practices. As we will demonstrate, practitioners largely maintain an implied hierarchy between these multiple practices: a single center of belonging surrounded by – and over time, possibly eclipsed by – secondary or peripheral practices. Linking this basic distinction with our notion of the three logics helps us to understand the center and the periphery as potentially complementary. To be somewhat schematic, the center grants access to member-only practical and social attractions, while granting an anchoring sense of belonging, and secondary practices quench practitioners' thirst for exploration, while offering complementary, visitor-only practical and social attractions.

These additional conceptual developments show that, despite its usefulness, the metaphor of butinage is above all a heuristic tool. As such, and much like Wittgenstein's (1922, 6.54) image of the ladder, it might be disposed of once the intended objective has been reached. Indeed, toward the end of the book, we set aside the notion of butinage and return to the concept of religious identity. Building on the accumulative conceptual elaboration developed throughout the preceding chapters, we then propose a prism called "religious repertoires": a model through which we can map the dynamism of inclusive individual religious identity and the interplay not only between central and peripheral practices but also between present and former – yet still relevant – ones. Drawing on our core empirical observations and on the work of Pierre Bourdieu and Ann Swidler, we show that the notion of religious repertoires revolves around the notion of familiarization as its organizing principle.[13]

The Structure of This Book

Earlier, we presented the reader with a core challenge: how much might we be able to say about religious identities, once we understand them as inherently dynamic, without reifying and effectively undermining the very fluidity being described? The challenge of developing an integrated perspective on religious mobility, which would combine individual, institutional, and social factors and ensure its applicability to a wide range of cases – including some in which suspicion toward formal religious membership is widespread – can lead to casting all clear-cut theoretical frameworks as potential straightjackets. This tension has guided us in laying out the structure of the present volume and in its division into three parts. The book unfolds in a gradual progression from the openness of an encompassing metaphor to its increasing refinement and elaboration, through dialogue with specific case studies, regarding emerging questions and challenges.

We thus begin by offering our basic argument concerning religious identity as inherently dynamic (part I), continue with an illustrative discussion of our four country case studies (part II), and eventually return with an ever-refined set of observations that culminate in the presentation of the religious repertoires model (part III). This structure implies a reading experience that is not necessarily limited to linearity, and while the three parts converse and shed light on one another, parts of the book may be read in isolation. Thus, for example, readers interested in the broad case to be made in favor of rethinking religious identity beyond rigid categories of conversion will find plenty to engage with in the first part. Readers interested in specific regions may jump to the second part and, in particular, to one of our four country case studies. Lastly, the third part may appeal to informed readers who ponder over a specific theoretical question or – in the case of the religious repertoires model – look for a tangible template to draw on. What follows is a breakdown of the content of each part.

The book's first part – "Introduction: Rethinking Religious Normativity" – includes, in addition to this introductory chapter, a chapter outlining the state-of-the-art scholarly debates in the study of religious mobility and our purported contribution thereto. In line with the multisited comparative approach, which draws from anglophone, francophone, and lusophone universes, this chapter dialogues with schools of thought drawn from within these three linguistic-academic realms. The chapter begins with a critique of the notion of conversion – which has long been central to, at times synonymous with, religious mobility – as largely insufficient, and continues with a discussion of existing scholarly alternatives, dwelling in particular on the notions of syncretism and lived religion. With this presentation, we set the scene for the journey ahead, having pointed to key scholarly trends and lacunas, and oriented our own position vis-à-vis our conversation partners.

The second part – "Case Studies" – consists of four chapters, each dedicated to everyday religious mobility within a single country/region. We begin with a short methodological introduction, in which we reflect on our ethnographic experience both individually and collectively. In the first chapter of part II, we discuss our work in Brazil, where we first elaborated the concept of butinage (chapter 3). We then move on to two anglophone African case studies – Kenya and Ghana (chapters 4 and 5) – and conclude with the case of Switzerland (chapter 6). To be clear, none of our case studies lays claim to absolute representation on a national level. Indeed, while the case studies drew on nationwide data and scholarship, our own ethnographic exploration within each case focused on designated (urban) areas: the city of Joinville in south Brazil, the cities of Nairobi and Kisumu in central and western Kenya respectively, the city of Accra in southern Ghana, and the city of Geneva and its vicinities in francophone western Switzerland.

Each of the chapters in the second part follows roughly the same pattern: a general introduction of the local religious landscape, followed by a presentation of key themes that emerged from our ethnographic data. Such association between themes and case studies is, however, far from exclusive, and, as we note through frequent cross-case referencing, themes highlighted in one chapter are likely to have also featured in the other three case studies, if less prominently. Indeed, we chose to dedicate each case study to the highlighting of a particular theme. Thus, for example, the centrality of neighborly ties in stimulating religious mobility is explored in the chapter on Brazil, but is also applicable to the other case studies. Similarly, the Kenyan case focuses primarily on questions of trust in religious leadership; the Ghanaian case explores religious mobility through the prism of other forms of (spatial, educational, social) mobility; and the Swiss case grapples with the manifestations of religion and spirituality in a context where the category of religious membership has fallen into disfavor. By adopting such a comparative perspective – attentive to both commonalities and differences – across our case studies, we are following our key proposition to read religious mobility as located at the crossroad between the institutional, the personal, and the social-contextual. Our attempt to understand local ethos, values, and logic related to religious practice in our four case studies thus helps us to build a comprehensive set of insights that we will then use in the book's third and final part.

The third and last part – "Beyond the Metaphor" – offers a synthesis and tentative path for systematizing our theoretical innovations as extracted from the data, with the aim of offering the reader a well-wrought, practical toolkit. Chapter 7 is dedicated to understanding the relations between practitioners and religious forms. Early in the chapter, we offer a typology of ideal-type butineurs – that is, practitioners of butinage – ranging from the sedentary monofloral to the borderless polyfloral. This typology is followed by a section on the notion of "territories," which refers to practitioners' hypothetical, discursive range of possible practice. In the next section, we introduce our notion of three "logics," or prisms, through which religious mobility can be studied without recourse to problematic interpretations of motivations.[14] Using those ideas, the final section considers the presence of multiple, concurrent practices and the idea of a hierarchy – and possible complementarity – between them. Chapter 8 continues our synthesis and proposed toolkit by bringing together various strands to suggest a methodical vision of religious identities as inherently dynamic and capable of encompassing a multiplicity of voices and tensions. This idea, which relies on the organizing principle of familiarization, is presented through our innovative religious repertoires model. This section is followed by a conclusion (chapter 9), in which we sum up our key findings and propose possible paths for future research, reconnecting to the questions with which we started off. In the appendix, we present the English version of our interview guide, which was used throughout our research alongside parallel versions in French and Portuguese.

2 Religious Mobility: Current Debates

Since the late nineteenth century and the emergence of academic research into religious mobility, the field has offered a range of informative debates regarding the significance, causes, frequency, and appropriate terminology with which to understand this phenomenon. In this chapter, we take a step back from the butinage metaphor to offer an overview of key scholarly debates, which we present with a critical eye toward Eurocentric, Abrahamic conceptions of religious affiliation and the often-imprudent attempt at their universalization. This critique, which we began developing in the previous chapter, relates to such challenges as the Abrahamic fascination with membership exclusivity, the inadequacy of the notion of religion-as-belief, and the many challenges related to the generalization of the concept of conversion as the foundational template for religious mobility. Régis Debray wrote, summarizing how such European ideas penetrate our thinking:

> It is as if our tradition of thought has maintained, ahead of history, a Platonic ideal of religion, of some monotheistic essence, that has made itself flesh more or less imperfectly, here and there. We hypothesized a particular historical case, detaching it from its specific place and time ... This archetype is carved from the idea of revelation, which has forced the inclusive world of beliefs into that exclusive world of a single Truth. This strange short circuit between the logic of ideals and the logic of conduct has normalized an idea that would have otherwise been seen as barbaric or idiotic to a Chinese, a Japanese, or an Indian: the idea whereby having one religion prevents one from having another. (Debray 2005, 33–4; our translation)

The limitations of Western Abrahamic models of religious identity as laid out by Debray and others had become increasingly clear as the twentieth century advanced. Since the mid-twentieth century in particular, alternative, inclusive, and accumulative models have been gaining prominence, reinforced by the explosion of alternative religious forms and by contact with Eastern traditions, whose different conceptions of religious belonging is alluded to in Debray's words. Indeed, while Abrahamic faiths have often come to regard conversion as an anathema and a cause for severing ties to a practitioner's past, non-Western religions largely show greater flexibility and inclusivity.[1] Similarly, research into NRMs showed that, while some require a radical reorganization of a person's core identity and worldview, others have only "limited institutional elaboration" (Meintel 2007, 158), laying no claim to exclusive religious ownership over the believer.[2]

The chapter begins with a historical survey of trends related to the application of the notion of "conversion," being the most common term associated with religious mobility. As we reject what we consider to be an over-application of the term and instead propose a set of alternative terminologies – above all, the notion of religious butinage – we find it important to dwell on this key concept at some length. In the process, we also set the critical groundwork for the search for alternative conceptions. This discussion is followed by a section in which we contrast the exclusivism of conversion with another strand of literature focused on religious combinations, and on syncretism in particular. In the third section, we present some of the literature's proposed solutions to account for everyday religious mobility and the often-minute dynamism that makes up actual religious identities. Here, we make extensive reference to the "lived religion" approach, which has provided invaluable inspiration for our own theoretical contemplations.

The Conceptual Limitations of Religious Conversion

The systematic academic treatment of religious mobility began toward the end of the nineteenth century. Early research on the topic was dominated by theologians as well as psychologists.[3] Probably the best known among these scholars is William James (1902), whose classic book *The Varieties of Religious Experience* continues to inform conversion studies today.[4] Still, it is widely accepted that such early studies were, on the whole, overly descriptive, methodologically flawed, and lacking in theoretical conceptualization (Heirich 1977). Some scholars thus subsume this early phase under "the old paradigm" (Richardson 1985; Hood, Hill, and Spilka 2009). Shaped after the Christian Pauline "road to Damascus" model, this paradigm is characterized by an understanding of conversion as a sudden transformative experience associated with a mental disposition toward sin and guilt, often coupled with mental disorders. The practitioner's role is seen as passive, as they respond to a "calling," be it from a higher being or from their own subconscious. Yet, despite its intuitive appeal, this characterization of the so-called old paradigm has been subject to criticism (Granqvist 2003). Indeed, some early scholars have actually considered the possibility that conversions may not always conform to the Pauline model, for instance, by unfolding gradually and not resulting in a fundamental rupture, and may also happen in people of "sound mind."[5]

In line with our interest in appropriate terminologies, it is interesting to note that some early scholars already felt limited by the dramatic implications of the notion of conversion and experimented with supplementary concepts. Elmer Clark (1929), for example, proposed the notion of "regeneration" (see Lang and Lang 1961), which referred to the enthusiastic adoption of a belief system that had previously been abandoned or used to be merely marginal in the person's life. Another example is that of Arthur Nock (1933), who suggested an interesting distinction between conversion and adhesion. While, for Nock, conversion implied – in line with its etymological origin – a "reorientation of the soul" (6–7), adhesion denoted a state of participation in religious groups and rituals without such spiritual transformation. In that sense, Nock suggested, adhesion becomes a "useful supplement" rather than a "substitute" to former affiliation, with the adherent having "a foot on each side of the fence."

Another important early contribution are the findings of several early psychologists, who suggested that conversion is most likely to occur during middle and late adolescence. Later scholars have for the most part confirmed these claims, although the common age has been pushed up somewhat into late adolescence and early adulthood.[6] Scholars have been far less unanimous, however, when it came to agreeing on the root causes of such shifts. Over the years, speculations regarding early age conversion "have ranged from psychoanalytic notions of increased libidinal energy, via a humanistic psychology emphasis on self-realization, to more sociological explanations in terms of re-socialization processes" (Granqvist 2003, 173).

The 1950s saw the advent of what some have called the "second wave" of conversion studies (Snow and Machalek 1984, 178). Still dominated by psychologists, studies concentrated on "brainwashing" and "coercive persuasion" models. This focus was largely inspired by the experiences of American prisoners of war during the Korean War and was mainly applied to the study of conversion to NRMs and so-called cults, which were gaining visibility at the time, mostly in the United States.[7] According to such models, new converts are subjected to coercive means and deprivations that strip them of previous identities and neutralize their willpower while reprograming them to accept the group's beliefs, creating deep psychological dependency in the process. So radical and effective is the transformative hold of such mind-control techniques over converts that extricating the person would require fundamental "deprograming." In later years, as the brainwashing model fell into disfavor, religious psychologists offered other interpretations, such as the compensatory model. Building on John Bowlby's (1969, 1973, 1980) attachment theory, this model takes religion, and in particular the notion of God, as a form of compensatory attachment substituting for absent parental figures.[8]

The 1960s and 1970s saw a significant increase in the study of conversion, especially from a sociological angle, with the primary focus being on social deviance.[9] Lofland and Stark (1965) presented an influential seven-step model known as the "social drift" model, which takes into consideration both predisposing conditions and situational contingencies. In this process, individuals who experience personal strain and tension, and who define themselves as spiritual seekers, gravitate toward new religious groups through their "affective bonds" with existing members. Later social scholarship, inspired by new studies that examined the role of social structures in sustaining a religious worldview (for example, Berger 1967a), has moved toward developing comprehensive conceptions of conversion, taking into consideration the wider socialization of converts (Long and Hadden 1983). Such an approach acknowledged the role of particular social systems and networks such as family and community, which influence choice-making related to affiliation, disaffiliation, and conversion.[10]

The "brainwashing" model in its various forms, on the one hand, and the Lofland-Stark and other social deviance models, on the other, capture two distinct approaches to religious conversion. The former adopts a passive, deterministic perspective, often highlighting personal psychopathological tendencies among converts, while the latter adopts an "agent-centered" approach focused on converts' active volition (Richardson 1998; Long and Hadden 1983). More generally, the division between these perspectives indicates what is still the main divide between the scholarly opinions on conversion today, namely, the divide between the psychological and the sociological schools of thought (Granqvist 2003).

Regardless of the school of thought and its views on conversion, the term "conversion" is premised on the idea of a transition whose end result is the complete abandonment of the old and its supersession by the new. Thus, according to Diane Austin-Broos (2003), the notion of conversion – whose unidirectionality she captures through the notion of "passage" – should be set apart from religious syncretism and bricolage, on the one hand, and from absolute cultural breach, on the other.[11] The idea of radical transition is also assumed by the "conversion career" approach, developed by Richardson and Stewart (1977; see also Richardson 1978) and later elaborated by Gooren (2010). This approach allows for a nuanced, comprehensive study of individual changes in religious affiliation throughout the life cycle, taking into account personal, social, institutional, cultural, and contingency factors. However, as this approach singles out particular religious affiliations, examining them one at a time along a lifelong timeline, it is at risk of omitting significant interrelations between concurrent affiliations and religious influences, including latent influences by affiliations that were formerly held openly.

As such, the employment of the notion of conversion poses three main challenges. The first challenge lies with the particular, often-negative connotations that are associated with the concept. This negativity is closely related to the fact that, up until the 1970s, the social sciences were dominated by an outlook by which religion was considered antiquated and destined to fade by the bright light of modern science and progress. In this respect, scholars' choice between conversion theories – all of which offer but limited answers – is telling of their own biases: disciplinary, religious, moral, or political.[12] We ought to remember that conversion theories have developed within particular American and European political contexts and, as such, might not necessarily account for conversions in certain contexts in the Global South, where greater religious pluralism – to employ a gross generalization – renders conversion more "complex and heterogeneous" (Gooren 2007, 347).[13]

The second challenge has to do with methodology and epistemology (Hood, Hill, and Spilka 2009). If conversion is "a radical reorganization of identity, meaning, life" (Travisano 1970, 594), then how may we determine and qualify such change? Relying on so-called objective indications, such as formal membership records, is not without flaws. Indeed, not all religious movements understand membership in quite the same way, nor do they and their followers agree on the importance thereof, as we will see in the third part of the book. Moreover, such an indicator might prove too vague to capture the nuances of changing degrees of religious involvement. From an institutional perspective, declaring that someone is or is not a member of a given religious group can easily overlook various forms of actual engagement (Snow and Machalek 1984). Similarly, conversion narratives may be problematic as sources of reliable information. Touching on the fundamental tension between memory and linguistic reconstruction, on the one hand, and actual experience, on the other, these narratives might easily be "tainted" by posterior reconstructions of events. This "tarnishing" might in part stem from implicit social pressure on the narrator to conform to a "normative" conversion paradigm.[14]

The third and most fundamental challenge has to do with conceptual adequacy. This challenge, which is the key focus of this chapter and has already been noted, acknowledges the limitations of the concept of conversion to account for nuanced, accumulative, or mundane forms of religious mobility. Anthropologists of religion have been at the forefront of acknowledging the limitations of the exclusive categorization of religious belonging.[15] For example, Michael Lambek's (2002) study in Mahajanga, Madagascar, tells us how children from a single family may undertake different religious practices, a divergence that draws on the conflicted spiritual guidance of their ancestors. But while most agree that a strict conception of the Pauline paradigm of conversion is seldom applicable, there is a divergence in response to this challenge, most fundamentally regarding the legitimate use of the concept, in a qualified form, to suit suboptimal cases. This divergence we can see, for example, in Buckser and Glazier's (2003) edited volume, *The Anthropology of Religious Conversion.* In the introduction to the book, and in anticipation of the complex geometries of mobility from across the world that will soon follow throughout the fourteen case studies, Austin-Broos defends the use of the term "conversion" by arguing for an expansive understanding thereof. Conversion, she argues, does not have to be reduced to a singular moment or experience, "paranormal or otherwise," but is rather "continuing and practiced" (Austin-Broos 2003, 9) and does not "involve a simple and absolute break with a previous social life" (2). Being a gradual passage, Austin-Broos proposes that the study of conversion should pay attention to the constitution and reconstitution of "social practice and the articulation of new forms of relatedness" (9). Such emphasis on porous and fluid mobility is also described by Attiya Ahmad (2017), whose book on engagement with Islam among female South Asian domestic workers in Kuwait carries the intriguing title *Everyday Conversions.* Here, the apparent tension between the two words appears to be intentional, as it effectively captures the tension between the gravity of conversion in Islamic theology and the actual cultivation of Islamic sensibilities by the women under study in the context of their ordinary interactions.

While we understand scholars' interest in saving this widely used term from marginalization, we believe that, in light of the preceding discussion, salvaging its use in an attenuated form is highly problematic. While we do not believe that the term "conversion" should be completely shelved, its application must be mindful of its invocation of a fundamentally institutional perspective that perceives mobility in absolute, uncompromising terms. In light of the limitations of this image, we look for alternative concepts and conceptions. We begin this search in the next section by invoking the case of religious combinations and syncretism.

Religious Combinations and Syncretism

If the notion of conversion assumes, as is commonly accepted, the complete abandonment of one tradition and its replacement with another, then the notion of syncretism stands for the seeming opposite: a combination of two or more religious traditions or practices and their mergence. Historically, and in many circles still today, such combinations have been treated as something of a corrupt version of an original, essential religious message. Such attitudes result in possible stigmatization of such terms and may lead to their use in a derogatory manner, especially among the custodians of religious traditions. This disparagement, in turn, raises genuine concern about the ability to "conceptualize cultural mixture" (Stewart 1999, 41) in a nonjudgmental manner, even though beliefs about "purity" of cultures and religions are largely fictional.[16]

In recent years, syncretism and related terminologies – such as "creolization," "bricolage," and "hybridity" (Canclini 1998) – have enjoyed growing scholarly appeal, primarily in reference to observations made in societies in the Global South. Many such societies were rendered fundamentally diverse by their colonial heritage, as colonizers brought with them and superimposed new cultural layers but were unable to eradicate previous layers. At the same time, and today more than ever before, the experience of cultural syncretism can be observed as an omnipresent "natural human response" (Berk and Galvan 2009, 544) to the rise of new, multiple orthodoxies. Such experience, together with the basic recognition that all cultures are essentially syncretistic, has boosted the term's scholarly appeal by recognition that syncretism is "normative rather than exceptional" (McIntosh 2019, 114). At the same time, some scholars wonder whether the broadness of the term might not undermine its actual explanatory value (Kirsch 2004, 706) – if indeed "all religions have composite origins and are continually reconstructed through ongoing processes of synthesis and erasure" (Shaw and Stewart 1994, 7).

A good starting point for understanding syncretistic work is found in the writing of Roger Bastide. In his study of Afro-Brazilian religions, Bastide (1960, 387, including footnotes) uses the terms "magical syncretism" and "mosaic syncretism" in reference to the pragmatism enacted by

Afro-Brazilian bricoleurs as they face their range of religious options and shift back and forth between Afro-Brazilian and Christian cosmologies. Such shifts are made possible by the syncretistic traits of Afro-Brazilian churches such as Candomblé, Umbanda, and Macumba, which introduce additional practices rather than demand their members to convert. Writing on Candomblé, Bastide observes that the simultaneous participation of the "black" in both the (Christian) world of the "whites" and the world of Candomblé tells less about the practitioner's ambivalence than about the disconnection between the two worlds:

> When a member of Candomblé affirms their Catholicism, they are not lying. They are both Catholic and fetishists. The two are not opposed, but separate ... Candomblé is part of an African world; Catholicism is part of a Brazilian world. They are both true within their own respective worlds, but between them there are only connections. (Bastide 1955, 499; our translation)

Pedro d'Oxum Docô, a "Father of Saint"[17] from the city of Porto Alegre (southern Brazil), offered an updated image for such religious coexistence by proposing that a good *Batuqueiro*[18] is also a model Catholic who goes to Mass in the morning and in the evening seeks *Saravá*[19] at a Batuque ceremony (Oro 2009). An illustration of that practice is found in the composition of Afro-Brazilian *terreiros*, where we find at least two alters: a Catholic one and an African one (known as *pegi*). Within these spaces, social relations do not necessitate synthesizing the two worlds. Real life, however, is even more complex, with institutions, on the one hand, and individuals, on the other, carrying the marks of their multiple registers of religio-cultural influence, often unconsciously. As we can see, religiousness may present itself in several places at the same time, with the believer taking an active part in the multidirectional reshuffling of various practices. In short, rather than adopt a new faith through conversion, the believer may invigorate their faith through circulation, articulating that which offers spiritual meaning, improves social ties, and, perhaps, yields material benefits.

A key question with regard to syncretism relates to the compartmentalization of multiple cosmologies – Bastide's notion of mosaic syncretism – and the articulation of relations between them. Bastide himself recognized that "the term syncretism is justified, but if no further explanation is then provided, it risks giving rise to confusion. It is not about mixing, but rather, like in role playing, it relies on an exchange of roles, depending on which segment of reality one participates in" (Bastide 1955, 500; our translation). By and large, the concept of syncretism is thought to assume that the dual (or more) religious cosmologies that have come together are reconcilable and can together show coherence in belief and practice. To the extent that the different systems are in tension, it is assumed that their clashes demand resolution, and the state of syncretism is "intrinsically temporary" as the conflicting meanings will eventually merge and be assimilated into a single coherent worldview (Pye 1971). But the process of linking together such disparate strands is an engaging one, which requires what Patricia Birman (2001, 1996) calls "syncretic work." In her studies on Afro-Brazilians at the Pentecostal Universal Church of the Kingdom of God, Birman emphasized that recurring transitions across traditions requires internal and external negotiation:

> In fact, the movement of individual passages between services constructs a constant range for dialogue, where we find social and symbolic mediations and mediators that make the said conversions possible. This dialogical space is necessarily somewhat fluid and syncretistic, for it is constantly subject to reinterpretations by believers and nonbelievers, by converts and skeptics. This space can therefore be conceived as a "passage" in the broadest sense and includes redefinition of borders; symbolic exchanges and syncretistic elaboration; and innovations and inventions which, to some extent, can force changes on the religious services concerned. (Birman 1996, 90; our translation)

Implied in Birman's words is the idea that people are concerned by apparent inconsistencies in their practice and seek to "make sense" or otherwise reconcile their partaking in multiple cosmologies. Yet, such assumptions of desired coherence have attracted critique as external scholarly impositions. As Johannes Fabian argues, "exaggerated expectations regarding the logical consistency and coherence of belief systems often lead to elegant but potentially misleading descriptions" (Fabian 1985, 139; see also Gellner 1974). Such critique is captured in Janet McIntosh's notion of "polyontologism." Originally growing out of her observations among the Giriama people of the Kenyan coastal region, McIntosh makes the claim for her ideas to likely be applicable "to numerous sites in Africa and beyond" (McIntosh 2019, 112). Among the Giriama, McIntosh has observed a concurrent engagement with both traditional and Muslim forces of divine power. Acknowledging her interlocutors' recognition of the mystical potency of multiple sets of cosmological forces – hence their ontological reality – she coined the term to account for the concurrent, parallel acceptance of incommensurable systems of belief. She writes: "Religious plurality is not about reconciling Islam and Giriama Traditionalism into a new, systemic whole, but about drawing on both religions while continuing to mark them as distinct.

More than one religion may be used, but they are juxtaposed rather than blended" (McIntosh 2009, 188). Following McIntosh, Devaka Premawardhana (2015, 46–7) notes that the notion of polyontologies is akin to "what computer scientists call toggling or multitasking, what linguists call code switching, and what psychologists call cognitive shifts." His own research among the Makhuwa people of northern Mozambique supports McIntosh's concept, in particular with regard to the drawbacks of identifying mobility with clear-cut rational reasoning and coherence (Premawardhana 2018).

McIntosh's thought-provoking ideas invite scholars to reexamine their own taste for coherence – anchored, perhaps, in Western Enlightenment ideas of rationality and Christian ideas about "faith" as undergirding religious practice. The idea that the logical reconciliation between systems of belief is a "neglected" (McIntosh 2019, 117) aspect of Giriama reflections draws attention to the risk of scholarly imposition of categories on our interlocutors.[20] At the same time, the application of McIntosh's ideas also has its limitations: her case, she acknowledges, is one in which traditional Giriama beliefs are closely intertwined with identity politics, leaving open the question of whether the same would apply with regard to self-chosen religious systems that do not contain a strong ethnic or political identification element.

Yet another question is raised by these ideas: Where, if at all, should we draw the line between exclusionary mobility – conversion or other – and syncretistic combination? This question is not an easy one, as many scholars have noted the fluidity between the two. David Stoll, for example, has suggested, with regard to Evangelical churches in Latin America, that the term "conversion" may be construed as misleading because, "despite the teleological thinking surrounding the term 'conversion,' a missionary premise that has often been accepted unconsciously by scholars, it would be a mistake to assume that most people who attend Evangelical churches are converts and that becoming an Evangelical is a one-way, irreversible process" (Stoll 1993, 8–9). This example is striking as it brings to mind how the Evangelical and Pentecostal movements, which have become notorious for their intolerance toward other traditions, often do recognize that, in reality, their members uphold additional practices (Smilde 2007). Indeed, conversion to born-again Christianity is often considered an "additional conversion," in which the new convert "turns toward" Pentecostalism without necessarily renouncing their former practices.[21]

We thus see that, while in its popular usage religious mobility implies the total abandonment of one cosmology in favor of another, many practitioners actually engage in a type of "infinite circuit" (Velho 2003), in which they do not necessarily repudiate anything. In such circumstances, multiple religious practices can become omnipresence and not easy to disentangle. The actual extent of overlap and influence across practices is complex and far from straightforward. In light of this fact, we turn in the next section to ask the following question: What, then, can we actually say about everyday religious mobility in all its variations?

"Lived Religion" and Everyday Religion

In Erving Goffman's (1961) classic study at an American psychiatric hospital, he drew a useful distinction between normative and typical roles. A normative role ("primary adjustment") suggests straightforward conformity to the organization's demands, while a typical role ("secondary adjustment") "usually reveals those behaviors or arrangements through which the participant attempts to obtain rewards not thought proper by the organization while still appearing to play his/her role sincerely" (Ingram 1982, 138). Asserting their individual agency, actors engaging in secondary adjustments position themselves "somewhere between identification with an organization and opposition to it" (Goffman 1961, 320), forming what Goffman calls the organizational "underlife."[22] Such underlife, he suggests, is particularly prosperous in "free places," which are spaces or moments where institutional discipline tends to relax and secondary adjustments flourish relatively unhindered. Demonstrating the applicability of Goffman's insights to a religious case study, Larry Ingram (1982) observes the bustling underlife of a Baptist Church in the southern United States. Ingram suggests that one possible reason for a widespread underlife is that formal church positions involve a variety of duties, many of which are defined with imprecision, thus straining the line between primary and secondary adjustments. Secondary adjustments, he notes, may also be "structurally generated" (149), resulting from a clash between several valid normative roles, as in the case of female choir members who, as dedicated mothers, attend rehearsals with their infant children. Ingram also identifies several "free places" that exist both temporally (for example, between Sunday school and Sunday worship) and spatially (for example, the restroom as a hiding place). Echoing Goffman, Ingram muses that it might be in the institution's best interest to turn a blind eye to much of what takes place in such gray areas as a way of ensuring member retention (Ingram 1982, 150).

In the decades since Goffman's study, scholars have been showing increasing interest in the imperfect application or enforcement of institutional rules and the resulting gap or "slippage."[23] As Gerald Berk and Denis Galvan argue, "rules are not so much ambiguous (that is, constraints that permit more than one course of action), as they are partial guides to action, because life – experience – always overflows their authority. This means that rules are incessantly corrigible, always open to syncretic recombination" (Berk and Galvan 2009, 549). In the case of religion, this tension has been enjoying growing attention under the banner of "lived religion," sometimes also referred to as "everyday religion."[24] Wade C. Roof defines lived religion simply as "religion as experienced in everyday life" (Roof 2001, 41). Following Mary Catherine Bateson, Roof suggests that lived religion can be seen as a kind of improvisation in the way that it "amounts to a creative refocusing of religious resources, often in response to a mishap or a new set of challenges" (Roof 2001, 133). Focused primarily on individual practitioners, the lived religion perspective approaches individual religiosity comprehensively, leaving room for experiences outside of formal institutional settings. One example, offered by Meredith McGuire (2008, 7–8), is that of an unaffiliated American interviewee, who regards organic gardening as her daily "worship service." In our own work, we recall the case of our Swiss interviewee Zara, a pianist by profession, who at the time of our interview was not practicing religion in any formal sense but described playing music as her way of communicating with God. Such individual spiritual expressions demonstrate that, despite the appeal of institutional channels, the religious tends to overflow normative categories of affiliation and worship.[25]

For the researcher, the lived religion perspective is primarily a starting point. Its emphases include concentrating on religion in ordinary daily lives and outside formal religious settings; recognizing the embeddedness of religion within the wider range of social practices; emphasizing practice over dogma; considering questions of identity performance; and keeping one's mind and definitions open to personal variations. The approach is particularly useful for considering religion in coping with life's challenges, such as in the context of urban volatility and hardships associated with socioeconomic aspirations (Orsi 1997). More specifically, the lived religion perspective can be contrasted with the institutional perspective, whose scholarly dominance has already been discussed. While the institutional perspective prescribes exclusive affiliation, the lived religion perspective recognizes people's tendency to uphold flexible and broad religious identities. Whereas the institutional perspective emphasizes the importance of formal membership, the lived religion perspective shows that people tend to maintain complex relations with the religious forms with which they engage and even develop suspicion toward them, as we indeed discovered in several of our case studies. Another difference has to do with the application of rules. While an institutional perspective prescribes certain manners of conduct and worship, lived religion, rather than seeing these rules as binding, recognizes the possibility of applying them in sometimes-creative ways through diverse forms of butinage. As McGuire asks, "what if we think of religion, at the individual level, as an ever-changing, multifaceted, often messy – even contradictory – amalgam of beliefs and practices that are not necessarily those religious institutions consider important?" (McGuire 2008, 4).

Many scholars working on religion have pointed to the need to articulate the relations between the institutional and the lived religion perspectives. Indeed, as one researcher argues, religious practice cannot be dissociated from rules and doctrines that set limits on a person's religious practice and imagination (Orsi 2012). Far from considering the individual practitioner as a fully atomized arbitrator of their religious practices, beliefs, and belongings, the lived religion perspective addresses the interplay between traditions and the embedded practices that are not fully determined by them. For instance, Nancy Ammerman (2003) discusses religious identity as negotiated between "public narratives" and individual "autobiographies." Similarly, Hervieu-Léger considers religion to be operating as a "chain" that links past, present, and future, thereby bringing together individual meaning-making and the "legitimizing authority of a tradition" (Hervieu-Léger 2000, 83). As she suggests, modern society has experienced a deep reworking of practitioners' relations to tradition, to the effect that they are now freer than ever before to choose which of countless traditions they wish to invoke.[26] The dialectic relations between actor and institution are pertinently articulated by Penny Edgell, who refers to religious establishments as inculcating a "cultural repertoire" that contributes to the shaping of individual identity and equips practitioners with a range of potential action:

> Research at the intersection of lived religion and institutional analysis helps us to get past the idea that the analyst must choose between understanding religion as operating on the surface (as tools that people use to solve problems or position themselves strategically) or as being deep (formative of preconscious or automatic habits and dispositions) ... [R]eligious institutions produce cultural repertoires that may be employed strategically as tools to solve problems, but that may also influence individuals in deep ways by providing cultural models that inform initial, rapid, automatic forms of cognition, including the making of moral distinctions. (Edgell 2012, 255)

In this section we presented some of the literature on everyday religion, which has drawn attention away from institutional perspective and emphasized a more agent-centered outlook. Needless to say, the two perspectives are intertwined: the "continuing tension between the individual's sense of identity and the impositions of the organization" (Ingram 1982, 140) beg for a comprehensive, complementary approach. While a lived religion perspective legitimizes the examination of actors' religious behavior in their own terms, recognition of the institutional perspective enables the acknowledgment of shared categories that, though sometimes essentialist, standardize the discourse and make it comprehensible and transferrable, and allow for a scientifically significant articulation of generalized assertions.

Conclusion

From conceptions of conversion to syncretism to everyday religion, scholarship on religious mobility is characterized by terminological unrest, with researchers continuously on the lookout for creative metaphors with which to conceptualize socioreligious boundaries and their blurring and possible collapse (for example, Chanson 2011; Tweed 2006). Again and again, researchers have been testing new and alternative concepts, most of which met with little consensus.[27] While some of these concepts certainly overlap, their very evocation attests to dissatisfaction with the notion of conversion and the challenge of capturing the nuances of de facto religious mobility (Long and Hadden 1983).

A key question revolves around the place of what Samuli Shielke and Liza Debevec (2012b) call "religious grand schemes" in individual religious meaning- and decision-making. As these authors, inspired by Michel de Certeau, propose, the study of everyday religion seeks to overcome the dichotomy between high (or orthodox) and popular (or heterodox) culture, without marginalizing either. Indeed, Schielke and Debevec insist on the commanding power of religious grand schemes:

> Religious grand schemes can be so powerful because believers locate them outside their lifeworld to grant them the purity and certainty which life can never have. This allows them to be evoked to navigate the complexities of life: the horizons, the social relations, the promises, the pressures, the necessities, the desires, the fashions and the discussions that together make up in a given moment what is important, what is possible, what can and what needs to be done and thought. (Schielke and Debevec 2012a, 10)

In other words, moving beyond a straightforward conversion paradigm does not imply studying individuals in isolation, but rather involves recognizing the contradictions, ambivalences, and inconsistencies between scripts and practices that make up people's actual religious lives. Rather than keeping to either individual or institutional perspectives, we may seek the "intersection of lived religion and institutional analysis" (Edgell 2012, 255). In exploring the interface between the two, we agree with Berk and Galvan in their argument that "action always takes place in relation to prior rules and practices, which serve not as guides or constraints, but as mutable raw material for new action" (Berk and Galvan 2009, 544).

And yet, despite their intuitive usefulness, ideas about such "intersections" have been struggling to translate into systematic and comprehensive approaches and methods. This situation is hardly surprising considering that such preoccupations are relatively recent and only gained prominence toward the 1990s. In addition, the lived religion perspective easily gets mired in the trap of relativism: if self-fashioned practices and beliefs, such as organic gardening and piano playing, are recognizably religious, would it be possible – if at all necessary – to systematize this diversity within applicable categories?[28] Indeed, the fact that lived religion represents open-ended, improvised religion in action that is (somewhat) unconfined by normative prescriptions sets significant challenges for the researcher. What else might we be able to say to generalize and possibly systemize the interface between the individual and the normative? In particular, how might we "reconceptualize institutions as not prior to, exogenous from, or determinative of action, but as the raw materials for action" (Berk and Galvan 2009, 575)? In our own individual research (Gez 2018; Droz 1999; Rey 2019; Soares 2009), we began to articulate some answers. In the next part, we turn to look at these variations within our four national case studies. Through discussions of the case studies both individually and in relation to one another, we begin to flesh out a nuanced set of generalizable observations.

PART II

Case Studies

Introduction to Part II: Methodology

This work is based on a comparative multisited ethnography conducted in Brazil, Ghana, Kenya, and Switzerland (Marcus 1995). In this introductory section, we discuss our choice of the four case studies and present our work process and methods.

The choice of the four case studies stemmed from a subtle balance between comparability and difference.[1] On the side of comparability, the selected case studies all represented an allegedly similar religious orientation, with all being thought of as predominantly Christian. At the same time, however, local contexts showed the variety of expression of this Christian focus, either through a tendency to combine between Christian and other practices or through varying degrees of commitment. The manner in which these four case studies reflected a multiplicity of engagements with a predominantly Christian heritage – socially constructed and individually practiced in line with geographic, historical, linguistic, economic, and cultural differences – thus allowed us to explore the de facto plurality behind a seemingly similar religious tradition. In addition to these core considerations, the choice of case studies was also influenced by a secondary practical consideration of our team's prior research expertise: Soares in Brazil, Droz in Kenya, and Rey in Ghana. The choice of Switzerland was in line with the project's institutional affiliation with the Graduate Institute in Geneva and our own familiarity with the Swiss case as scholars and lay observers. The Swiss case was further chosen as a Global North counterpart to the other case studies, drawing attention to the influence of the European heritage of secularization as well as to state-level economic prosperity on individual engagement with religion. Due to these wider ambitions, the Swiss case is presented last and is slightly longer and more comprehensive than the other three.

In this respect, and recognizing the pros and cons of "anthropology at home," we diversified between cases in which the principal researcher was perceived as a local, as a clear foreigner, and as a mixture of both – a combination that led to interesting insider-outsider dynamics. In Joinville, Soares explored his own hometown, as did Rey in Switzerland. In Ghana and Kenya, however, our team members stood out as clear outsiders, as "white" Western scholars. It is interesting to reflect, in this respect, on how scholarly integration into the host society may influence analysis and even data. As anthropologists have long since recognized, the scholar's position vis-à-vis the studied community constitutes a trade-off. In most cases, scholars agree that, while an insider may find it easier to establish trust with his interlocutors, an outsider would have an advantage in developing reflexive distancing and critical perspectives (Coffey 1999; Corbin Dwyer and Buckle 2009; Headland, Pike, and Harris 1990).

In addition, we soon noted that socioreligious, historical, and linguistic differences implied different manners in which we were approached in the field. In Brazil, for example, most interlocutors did not simply agree to be interviewed, but were keen to profess their faith and offer their personal "testimony" – a Christian term that implies a moral obligation and a religious duty. In Switzerland, by sharp contrast, the very word "testimony" would chase away most people, who try to avoid being cast as "fanatic" religious adherents to religions of whatever persuasion. But while typical Swiss interviewees preferred to perceive themselves as free from obligations to religious institutions, they would nonetheless be willing to "secretly" broach the topic and its wider social representations. In fact, as we propose in the chapter on Switzerland, our Swiss interlocutors approached the topic from a distanced position, as something of a social taboo. "Nobody ever asked me about my religious practice," said one of our interviewees, before wondering: "Am I a believer then, just like others?"

This difference in approach to religion manifested in the very use of language. Our four case studies relied on multiple languages, including English, French, and Portuguese. Language and its latent baggage have a bearing on discourse in ways that are difficult to disentangle and are powerfully intertwined with specific cultural contexts. One relevant example is found in the case of the term "*crente/croyant/*believer." In Brazil, the term is often associated with the Assemblies of God; thus, in a country where Catholicism has so long dominated the religious landscape, the *crente* is something of a dissident. In some quarters, the term's negative connotations have persisted, to the extent that even members of the Assemblies of God may shy away from using it. But while one may not encounter many self-professed *crentes*, one is likely to know plenty of religious "brothers" and "sisters." This terminology, in some sense, resembles the situation in Ghana or Kenya, where the term "believer," most commonly associated with the born-again movement, has something of a puritan ring and is not well thought of outside the realms of strict Pentecostalism. Instead, the omnipresent concept of born-again Christianity, often associated with the notion of "salvation," renders the dichotomy between being born again and non–born again a central and intuitive form of Christian classification among Kenyans and Ghanaians, a classification that is not easily translatable into other contexts where this terminology is uncommon. In Switzerland, both the terms "believer" and "religious brother/sister" offer little appeal. Many do not see themselves as carriers of a religious heritage, Christian or other, and actually consider themselves as being outside the basic paradigmatic dichotomy between believers and nonbelievers. Indeed, for the Swiss, the very term "believer" brings to mind bygone times of (imposed) religious dominance. When our Swiss interviewees were asked if they regarded themselves as "believers," they tended to respond with indecisiveness – "perhaps, maybe, I believe in something, but..." – seldom offering an unequivocal answer. Another example concerns the very connotations associated with the term "religion." As we show, in Switzerland, the term is often associated with Christian – Catholic and Protestant – beliefs and is regarded as something of a constraint. Religion is understood in terms of outdated, constricting life prescriptions, associated with blind and often-mindless repetition, and deemed superstitious and suspicious. Many Swiss interlocutors spoke of their rejection of "religion-as-obedience." Instead, they proposed that religion is one social institution among many, linked to structures of power and control. Those who "too frequently" attend services at their local cathedral or mosque (for the critique is hardly limited to Christianity) are suspected of fanaticism. By contrast, in Kenya or in Ghana, more than in Brazil and certainly more than in Switzerland, such critique is mostly directed at secularism. In these two countries, secular people are widely associated with moral questionability and hedonism, and can even find themselves suspected of witchcraft and accused of being in league with the Devil. In short, our respective fields presented not only a breadth of languages but also a breadth of sociolinguistic connotations.

This wealth of perspectives and even terminologies was brought to bear on our research approach and methods. Our data gathering hinged on ethnographic methodology built around a core of in-depth, semi-structured biographical interviews and on participant observations in places of worship, oftentimes at the invitation of our interviewees whom we have accompanied. Indeed, in many cases, interviews and participant observations went hand in hand, as we accompanied our butineur interlocutors through their religious itinerary before asking for a confidential interview (Soares 2007). Some, indeed, we met in their place of worship for the first time. Such combination of spoken interviews and observations permitted us to compare discourse and practice – an important point out of which we extracted key observations explored in the last part of this book. In collecting our data, we followed the principles of grounded theory (Glaser and Strauss 1967; Olivier de Sardan 1995) through an iterative process that allowed us to combine empirical collection with the (re)elaboration of research hypotheses and theoretical construction.

Interviews were based on a semi-structured interview guide (see appendix). The guide consisted of six categories of questions that aimed at mapping out the interviewee's religious biography and itinerary – past, present, and hypothetical. The guide adopted an open approach to religious practice, including media-based consumption and private practices. The interview also addressed the interlocutors' religious comfort zone, as it were, with the intention of developing a "religious cartography"' – an idea that we return to later in this book. Interviews were mostly conducted in public locations such as cafés, but a minority were conducted in people's homes, inside religious compounds, or elsewhere. They lasted, on average, around one and a half hours, but varied greatly, ranging from thirty minutes up to three and a half hours. In the interest of anonymity, we have changed the names of all interviewees, as well as some of the places of worship included in the study. While recognizing the importance of conveying to the reader a solid grasp of the interview's context, in the interest of privacy we sometimes changed information regarding personal details (for example, profession, specific locations).

Responding to the large scope of the field, in tracing interviewees – the same as in conducting participant observations – our rule of thumb has been to attain diversity in interviewees' personal profiles and backgrounds. For this aim, we considered factors including age, gender, socioeconomic level, professional and educational backgrounds, family status, neighborhood of residence, ethnic origin, and, last but not least, religious affiliation. Actual methods for identifying interviewees combined chance encounters with active measures. We also employed snowball sampling, but avoided overreliance on it, lest it should bias our data. In some cases, we approached random people in the street or in a variety of public spaces (such as shops, offices, bars, markets, parks), while in other cases we were approached by passersby who were curious about our activities (Soares 2009). While mainly relying on such neutral-space encounters, in a minority of cases initial contact was made during our habitual participation at places of worship – a fact that may have created some selection bias. Indeed, while we tried, through our diversity of methods, to minimize such bias, it is unlikely to have been eliminated altogether. Our research is likely to have been more appealing to interlocutors from an extensive mobile background and propensity for mobility to begin with, while at times, we may have unwittingly been drawn to dig further around sensational mobility stories. Aware of that limitation, we refrained from making a clear-cut conclusion based on statistical samplings, sought to triangulate our findings based on multiple stories, and shied away from the mere anecdotal.

Overall, we conducted 70 interviews in Brazil, 87 in Kenya, 23 in Ghana, and 40 in Switzerland.[2] Upon transcription, interviews were coded using a computer-assisted qualitative data analysis software (CAQDAS), a process that allowed us to identify internal trends specific to each case study as well as to explore transversal themes across case studies. The use of a shared set of categories of analysis thus facilitated cross-site dialogue and comparison. The identification of such shared categories proved particularly important considering the concurrent application of multiple languages. Working closely together as a team, over the project's five-year period we held frequent meetings in which we employed reflexivity to question the comparability of the data collected and the epistemological rupture with dominant conceptions of religious mobility. These joint sessions were similarly dedicated to sharing and crossing our respective data, identifying points of (dis)similarities, and discussing fruitful avenues for comparison and theorization.

In order to lend ourselves to new conceptions of religion – indeed, possibly to an epistemological rupture (Bourdieu, Chamboredon, and Passeron 1973) – we trod carefully when it came to conceptualizing what people actually mean when they conceive of religion and religious practice. Throughout our interviews, we were careful to leave it to the interlocutor to define what constitutes the religious for them. Indeed, while we relied on the common Christian heritage of the four case studies as a starting point, we made it clear to every interviewee that we had no preconception or moralizing interests, and should not be confused with either missionaries or advocates of secularism. In chasing the religious, and in line with the lived religion stance discussed in the previous chapter, we tried not to limit ourselves to formally sanctioned moments and sites. Indeed, this open stance toward how religion is to be defined and lived has been – to resonate with a Christian image – our guiding star.

3 Neighborliness as a Driver for Mobility in Brazil

"So many religions! The more there are, the more you practice" – thus say many Brazilians including, in particular, the inhabitants of the city of Joinville, located in the southern state of Santa Catarina. Indeed, with more than six hundred places of worship and a wide array of doctrines for a little over half a million inhabitants, Joinville is not short of religious traditions. With such diversity, rich individual religious itineraries also emerge. In fact, it was in Joinville, and in particular in the neighborhood of Paranaguá-Mirim – located in the southeastern area of Joinville and home to some 25,000 residents – that the notion of religious butinage emerged in the course of long ethnographic fieldwork (Soares 2007, 2009). This chapter explores the highly mobile behavior of the people of Joinville and the logic on which their behavior hinges. We propose that, in Joinville, practitioners' practice largely revolves around social logic and, in particular, around social ties within their immediate neighborhood.

Fieldwork in Joinville built on and benefited from the long experience that Soares had of the area. In his work, Soares combined an insider and an outsider perspective: Joinville was his native city, but he was returning there after a long stay in Switzerland, where he had moved in the late 1990s. Soares's intimate knowledge of the area helped him to develop a detailed religious cartography of the city (Soares 2007, 2009) and to establish meaningful rapport with local interviewees, some of whom he came back to visit regularly over many years, first as a PhD student and later in the context of Project StAR.[1] Throughout the project, two other members of the team – Droz and Gez – joined Soares for shorter fieldwork stays in Joinville and Porto Alegre.

The Circularity of Practice

The practice of religious butinage, as presented earlier in the book, treats visits to multiple religious denominations as normative. Like a bee, the practitioner "hops" or "butines" from one denomination to another, forming an ever-renewed reworking of the "perfume" released through such pollination. In Brazil, a country whose religious landscape has historically been shaped by multiple encounters between European, African, and indigenous spiritual traditions, such religious combinations – as well as other cultural conjunctions – are widely tolerated. Throughout the twentieth century, Brazil has seen a steady decline in the hegemony of the Catholic Church, long considered a unifying force linked to national identity. With this erosion, the country's religious diversity became more overtly manifest. Non-Catholic religious forms, such as various Afro-Brazilian movements and Spiritism – a religion based on the teachings of Allan Kardec – have gained vast popularity and visibility, as have various Protestant Christian churches. Thus, for example, since the mid-twentieth century Brazilian Pentecostal churches, such as the Universal Church of the Kingdom of God and the God Is Love Pentecostal Church, have won immense success at home and abroad, with countless congregations and missionary activities all around the world.

As an emblematic celebration of this wealth of Brazilian religious culture, we may think of Riobaldo, the protagonist of João Guimarães Rosa's famous novel, *The Devil to Pay in the Backlands*, which takes place in the southeastern state of Minas Gerais. Let us recall Riobaldo's words before turning to meet some of our Joinville interlocutors who, just like Riobaldo, never miss an opportunity to supplement their religious practice:

> What I firmly believe, declare, and set forth, is this: the whole world is crazy. You, sir, I, we, everybody. That's the main reason we need religion: to become unmaddened, regain our sanity. Praying is what cures madness. Usually. It is the salvation of the soul. Lots of religions, young man. As for me, I never miss a chance. I take advantage of all of them. I drink water from any river. In my opinion, just one religion isn't enough. I pray the Christian, Catholic prayer, and I take refuge in what is certain. I also accept the prayers of my compadre Quelemém, according to his doctrine, that of Kardec. But when I can I go to Mindubim, where there is one Mathias, a Protestant, a Methodist: they reproach themselves for their sins, read the Bible out loud, and pray, and sing their beautiful hymns. It all calms me down, allays my worries. Any shade refreshes me. But only for the time being. I would like to pray – all the time. Many persons do not agree with me; they say that the true religion is only one – exclusive. That's an idea I detest. There is a colored woman, Maria Leônica, who lives not far from here, whose prayers are famous for their potency. I pay her, every month, to say a chaplet for me every blessed day, and a rosary on Sundays. It is worth it, it really is. My wife sees no harm in it. And I've already sent word to another one to come to see me, a certain Isma Calanga, of Vau-Vau, whose prayers too, it is said,

> are of great merit and profit. I'm going to make the same kind of deal with her. I want to have several such on my side, defending me before God. By the wounds of Christ! Living is a dangerous business. Longing too ardently for something good can be in some ways like wishing for something bad. (Rosa 1963, 10–11)

Rosa has put the matter clearly for us: Riobaldo drinks water from any river. One religion, one prayer is not enough for him; he must have many, all of them, and at the same time. Not only does one practice not negate another, but they are actually mutually reinforcing. Riobaldo is aware that "many do not agree and say that the true religion is only one," but he brushes these reproaches aside, motivated, as he suggests, by the desire, within such a perilous life journey, to have many religions "on his side," "defending him before God." Searching for such assurance, he conveniently and unapologetically traverses religious traditions: Catholic, Protestant, Afro-Brazilian, Spiritist, and others.

In everyday Brazilian life, this religious inclusivity is expressed through various common phrases, such as "all religions are good"; "it is more interesting to practice several religions at once"; "other religions are just as powerful, or even more so, than mine"; "religion allows us to meet people and strengthens ties between us"; and "the more religions I practice, the more I exist." Such views are commonly held by Joinvillians. Among them we find Léo, a forty-year-old man, Protestant by origin and Catholic on occasion, who often prays with the Evangelists and the Spiritists:

> When I pray to God – and I pray often – I do not think of any church in particular; I pray to God. The religious heads – the pastors, the priests – all speak of the same god. If he is everywhere, then so am I … I was baptized Lutheran, I was confirmed in the Catholic Church, and I married a *crente* [Pentecostal believer] at the Foursquare Church, my wife's church. Over time, through my colleagues at work, I got to know Allan Kardec's Spiritism, which I like very much. I am like that, there's nothing you can do, I pray a little bit everywhere. (Interview with Léo, Joinville 2012; our translation)

Léo's inclusivity is representative of many of our Brazilian interviewees. While Léo is at times skeptical of his own practice – "it is worth what it is worth," he says – he persists with his peripatetic approach. Whatever this practice is worth for him, it seems to always be worth something.

Conducted in 2010, the latest Brazilian national census (IBGE) attests to the growing number of butineurs in the country.[2] Among Evangelicals, the number of practitioners who claim to have no fixed religious denomination has risen from 4 to 14 percent, or four million individuals, within only ten years (Gois and Schwartsman 2011). This increase means that a growing number of believers see themselves as religiously mobile and refuse to be confined to a single denomination. To some perplexed observers, they are known as *desigrejados* ("churchless," in the sense of being institutionally unconfined). Of course, statistics are a problematic instrument for gaging religious mobility, due to their clear-cut classificatory and exclusivist nature and absence of further clarification: *desigrejados* might be nonbelievers, agnostics, or dedicated butineurs. And yet, these national statistics do offer some indication that butinage – an approach at least as old as Riobaldo's statement, back in the 1950s: "In my opinion just one religion isn't enough." (Rosa 1963, 10) – is on the increase.

If we are unsatisfied with examining religious practices merely by their normative prescriptions ("I am Catholic, I therefore pray the Catholic way") and would rather listen to the voices of practitioners and their actual engagements, we see that these go well beyond the scripted range of religious activities. This was the case with Léo and is also the case with thirty-one-year-old Maria, Catholic since birth and Evangelical through neighborly ties:

> I go to Mass every Sunday. I am Catholic. But when I have time, I also pray with Rosa and Lurdes, my friends who are *crentes*. One goes to the church God Is Love, and the other to New Life Church. With Rosa, at her God Is Love Church, I like speaking in tongues. With Lurdes, at New Life Church, I like the biblical readings. It is all good for me. (Interview with Maria, Joinville 2010; our translation)

Another interviewee, Dona Conceição, formally a Seventh Day Adventist, shared similar views:

> If we search for God, we find Him without a shred of doubt ... When I experience stress, when I am in need for moral support or simply to feel the soothing presence of God, I visit a church different from my own. I meet God elsewhere; he always speaks to me outside of my church, using a person I do not know. "You who sit here in the pew" – someone calls me without knowing me, she might be a church leader, a pastor, an assistant. She would know nothing of my life, of my suffering; she is a stranger to me. She might know nothing, but God knows! You see? (Interview with Dona Conceição, Joinville 2010; our translation)

Dona Conceição's perspective is not unique. From her words to those of Riobaldo, Léo, and Maria, there emerges the first trait of religious butinage. Butinage is not a simple meander between denominations, but a continuous circular commute between religious traditions, which somehow coalesces into a single comprehensive practice. And while the residents of Paranaguá-Mirim are not bees, they still accumulate sacred pollen: from time to time, they may go to Lord Pereira's to have their spirits massaged; every other Sunday, they may go to the Catholic Saint Joseph Community; they might regularly visit the Spiritist Society, Light of the Orient, to study about the origin and destiny of spirits; and, when the occasion lends itself, they may drop in for a special service at the God Is Love Church. Such behavior is equivalent, by analogy, to a kind of religious ubiquity, which is embedded in a fundamental theological tenet: like in Kenya and Ghana, "God" – however understood – is omnipresent, hence the practitioner may travel and stand before Him just about everywhere. It is precisely the logic of this omnipresence, which implies continuity and inclusivity, that urges us to think in terms other than those of religious conversion. We can propose that, instead of thinking in terms of double (or triple, or more) religious affiliations, the butineur's religious identity is "redoubled" and reinforced through different practices. But far from being in the hands of fate, such personal trajectories are influenced by multiple logics and transcend the principles and scripts laid out by the different religious institutions. Indeed, in Joinville, individual practitioners self-fashion the boundaries between religious traditions and denominations, but often keep them quite fluid – after all, a popular saying suggests that "the house's own saint performs no miracles." Groundedness in specific religious traditions and openness toward further mobility may be found in equal measure:

> Every time I pray to God some more. I first prayed with the Catholics, with my daughter – who now goes to the Quadrangular Church [the church of the interviewee's mother-in-law]. Then, as my Catholic "reflection group" recommended, I went to pray with the Evangelicals at the Assemblies of God and the Foursquare Church. Today, I pray to God at the Baptist Church, where I go with my neighbors, Dona Consolação and Zé. But still, when I hear God calling, when I am anxious, I go elsewhere. I go wherever the door is open. I consider myself "Catholic-Apostolic-Christian." (Soares 2009, 219; our translation)

Combining diachronic and synchronic narratives, this last interviewee demonstrated how butinage is an ever-shifting journey between multiple religious universes and systems of institutionalized practices, somewhat like Bastide's (1960, 387) earlier-mentioned notion of mosaic syncretism. Unlike the synthetic work of bricolage, butinage consists of largely distinct practices, each with its own designated time and space. The practices between which the butineur circulates maintain their distinctive nature, as well as their institutional referents. By inscribing the religious within the field of everyday practice, with its emphasis on practical considerations, social ties, and production of meaning, the notion of butinage is part of a larger effort to identify the religious beyond the parameters set by institutions. Free from normative prescriptions, religious mobility thus seems more like a way of life than a social constraint. We are rather far from the idea of rational, individualist practice, wherein practitioners choose that which they crave from an assorted religious supply – which is always disjointed and therefore constantly in competition – spread across the shelves in the enormous contemporary religious supermarket.

Territories and Bridges

If we go beyond the façade of formal institutional discourse, we may find that nearly every religious institution in Joinville would have wished for exclusivity, investing as it does in emphasizing its uniqueness and distinction. Such distinction ranges from the most general of differences, such as the structure of the place of worship (dimensions, color of the façade, furniture, and seats), to more specific elements, such as liturgical objects and choice of formal attire. But it is primarily in how the practitioner comes into contact with the supernatural that distinctions are felt. Although many would claim that all places of worship direct themselves to the same ultimate divinity, no two places of worship pray in exactly the same way. Some emphasize individual prayers, and some focus on communal chants; some pray at the top of their voice, arms raised to the sky, while others meditate solemnly in a serene and quiet environment; some encourage dancing, while others specialize in speaking in tongues. In short, in Joinville, when it comes to entering into relations with "God," each place of worship and every individual have their own preferences. This pluralistic reality is epitomized in a popular saying "*cada macaco no seu galho*" ("every monkey has his own branch").

Later in the book, we will offer a systematic examination of the concept of territory, inspired by the work of Ronaldo de Almeida (De Almeida 2004; De Almeida and Monteiro 2001). For now, it suffices to explain that, by religious territories, we refer to either personal notions or collective conventions that set certain religious traditions in proximity and apart from others. A religious territory tends to be fairly porous, and butineurs may pass between practices within the territory without encountering substantial outside challenge or feeling great discomfort or disloyalty. This notion, with its conceptions of proximity and dissimilarity, helps to explain our observations in Joinville. For example, we observed how the Assemblies of God and the Universal Church of the Kingdom of God distinguish themselves through their specific conception of the Holy Spirit. This seemingly minor theological difference is responsible for the production of two well-defined religious territories, distinct enough to challenge practitioners' mobility. Indeed, the smallest change makes a big difference. Thus, thinking in terms of territories, we can begin to identify that, even in Joinville's pro-mobility environment, there are limitations to butinage:

> Today, I am Evangelical, practitioner at the Assemblies of God, but my family is still Catholic. I have always prayed as a *crente*: I visited the Baptist churches of Belém, God Is Love, and Only the Lord Is God. And it all suited me well – there is only one God! All? Nearly all, because I could no longer pray at the Universal Church – this is a church that has distanced me from the brethren. (Interview with Gabriel, Joinville 2012; our translation)

In addition, religions of African or Eastern origins form their own territories, which can be considered as separated from the Christian domain. Clearly, some territories are more open than others in terms of the circulation of practitioners. A *Macumbeiro* (practitioner of Macumba – an Afro-Brazilian religion) would cross over without too much difficulty to join a Catholic or Evangelical Church, whereas an Evangelical practitioner of the Assemblies of God would have more difficulty in attending an Afro-Brazilian *terreiro* or *centro*.[3]

> Me, my mind goes like this: if a given place of worship is not a church or a denomination, it must be a sect. My mind thinks like that, there is nothing I can do about it. And I would add that, even had I not been a *crente* of the Assemblies of God or of Catholicism, I would not go to a Spiritist center. (Interview with Pedro, Joinville 2012; our translation)

Pedro's words demonstrate the limits of religious mobility even in an environment accommodating of butinage. Furthermore, by suggesting that "if a given place of worship is not a church or a denomination, it must be a sect," he demonstrates how the internalization of formal institutional categories and boundaries – which create the legitimate territory where one "butines," as we will see in the chapter on Kenya – are taken into account when devising individual religious trajectories. However, Pedro proposed that he would gladly visit other Pentecostal services that follow a similar theology. At the same time, participating in a Catholic Mass might be ruled out for some Pentecostal butineurs, as in the case of Maria, a Catholic who became a *crente* at the Assemblies of God after passing through God Is Love and Foursquare Church, all of which argue that the living spirit of God cannot be seen through images of dead saints:

> Catholics believe in images, they pray to the image of the dead. Saint Mary, Saint George, Saint Peter, Saint John, and many others were people of faith, of great faith. John was a saintly man, nothing more. A man of great faith, just like the rest of Christ's apostles. Through his faith, John made miracles. However, he made them when he was alive. As a man, he is dead and, like all the dead, he awaits the day of Final Judgment. Jesus is the only one who has not died. It is, therefore, only the living spirit that is able to help us. It is to the living that we must turn and not to the dead – or even worse, to the plaster figures. (Interview with Maria, Joinville 2005; our translation)

The cases of Gabriel, Pedro, and Maria all demonstrate the theological and social boundaries that operate as a wedge between different religious traditions, with consequences for individual practice. However, to the extent that people are indeed motivated by theological consistency, we can consider, together with Birman (1996), how seemingly incommensurable religious universes can share points of confluence that facilitate individual crossover. These points of confluence, which Birman terms "bridges," are symbolic elements identifiable across otherwise-disparate religious universes. As an example, Birman considers spirit possession as a locus of symbolic overlap between the Pentecostal and Afro-Brazilian universe(s):

> Indeed, in this church – the Universal Church of the Kingdom of God – we find a variety of symbolic ritual activities that act as bridges between the two religious systems, to the extent that the activities have the same source: possession services. While they might be subject to different interpretations, the two are placed in constant dialogue. These activities facilitate passages between one form of worship and another, as well as the symbolic harmonization by individuals located halfway between the two systems, whether they are designed to create ruptures or continuity in the face of existing religious choices. (Birman 1996, 93; our translation)

In his work in Joinville, Soares identified many bridges between otherwise separate religious territories. For example, he noted the similarity between the ritualistic descent of the Holy Spirit among Pentecostals and the experience of trance among Afro-Brazilians. The case of José, a Pentecostal pastor, is illustrative in this respect. José, Soares observed, "does not open his head wide for the Holy Spirit to enter and act upon and through him. Instead, José opens his heart. He does not speak either Fon or Nagô, but through glossolalia, he speaks a language just as strange as those of the African spirits" (Soares 2009, 174; our translation). Soares went on to describe the enactment of José's interreligious combinations:

> José has no drum, and the audience does not stomp their feet at the rhythm of the religious chants, which succeed one another as the "Daughters of the Saint" attempt to attract the attention of their entities. José, however, has his guitar and the clapping of his assistant. This is how they invoke the Holy Spirit to come down and touch their hearts. One descends on them from the heaven, while the other, the Orixá, comes from Africa. As they live so far away, it requires noise – sometimes a lot of it – for them to hear the call of their believers. Some play the drum, others the guitar; all sing and dance. Some chant old songs, others make up their own. Some dance in their place while clapping their hands, whereas others move about in their dance while stomping their feet around the *pegi*. Whatever one does, the call is often heard, and the spirit comes to those who invoke it: to some, it offers counsel; to others, it recites biblical texts. But to all, it is the very fact of its presence that matters most. (Soares 2009, 174; our translation)

The need to establish bridges between incommensurable theologies is clear to many Joinvillians. The dominant socioreligious ethos in Joinville – as well as in Kenya and Ghana – endorses the legitimacy of religious combinations because, after all, "*a placa de igrea não salva*" ("the church's label saves no one"). Such are the views of Dona Clara, a Catholic, and Seu Pedro, an Evangelical. Dona Clara declares: "When I pray to God, there are no more churches … It is a wholeness communicating itself to everybody! A church is the heart of people and not just a building." For Seu Pedro, different religions share an essence that trumps all differences: "There is only one experience, and we all practice a single religion regardless of our religion." On the level of representation, religious butinage lends itself to Birman's notion of bridging, as there is only a single god who is the same for all, regardless of the individual's formal religion – a view that, incidentally, is also very common in Kenya and Ghana. On the level of practice, be it ritualized or not, we find this core idea in phrases, gestures, prayers, and objects that cross religious boundaries and define territories.

Butinage and Neighborliness

What is the role of social ties in prompting religious butinage, and do these ties help to bring together formal religious categories and self-fashioned itineraries? Dona Flor, formally a Catholic, gave the following account, in which she reflected on her struggle with cancer:

> The flesh is weak ... I have not had any strength left. I nearly died of cancer. I lost the ability to speak. I whispered. I struggled to stand up and walk. I sighed more than I breathed. The doctor gave me six months to live, no more than that. I was dying slowly. But, just before the priest could say the last rites, I decided, against all odds, to go back home. I did not want to die in a hospital away from my loved ones. I wanted, at the very least, the warmth of Laudelino, my husband, and the compassion of my children and the kindness of my neighbors. I have many neighbors ... Protected – I feel myself protected at home when I am surrounded by my own parents and friends – I prayed in every way: I prayed to the Catholic God with my charismatic friends of the Saint Luzia Community, and I prayed to the Evangelical God with my *crente* neighbors of the Assemblies of God. They sure have beautiful hymns there ... With them, I have prayed to the spirit of the Lord. And I have seen it! It is pure light ... but you have to believe in it to see. (Interview with Dona Flor, Joinville 2005; our translation)

Dona Flor always prays as a Catholic, but she cannot resist an invitation from her *crente* neighbor to accompany her to the Assemblies of God. It was at her neighbor's church that she eventually found healing. She had not left the Catholic Church – indeed, she is proud to be part of it, but she never misses an opportunity for a *crente* prayer at her neighbor's house. Putting her trust in her neighbors, Dona Flor demonstrated how social and practical logics come together in the context of a quest for healing.

A different case demonstrating the combination of social and practical logic within the context of healing involves Dona Euvira. With her husband struggling with cancer, she made a vow that, if he regained his health, she would follow him and join his Church of Jesus Christ of Latter-Day Saints. True to her word, upon his recovery she indeed left the Catholic Church and joined her husband at his church. Dona Euvira's loyalty, however, has not been reserved to her husband but was also extended to her neighbors:

> Here, in the neighborhood, religion is very present, and we don't talk too much about it: to each their own religion. There are the Evangelicals, the Catholics, and even those who visit the Spiritist centers. I don't really like this Spiritist thing. However, as neighbors, we are all the same – my neighbors are good people – and it is to my neighbors that I turn when I am in need of anything at all, and I love them very much. So when there is something special in the church, I invite my neighbors to come along – we

> often go together. The reverse is also true – I accompany them to their place too. It is normal to join your neighbor, isn't it? (Interview with Dona Euvira, Joinville 2012; our translation)

Another interviewee, a sworn butineur named Seu José, shares the same sentiment, emphasizing how butinage is closely intertwined with neighborly obligations:

> That which makes all the difference is the relations between neighbors and the respect that it implies. To tell you the truth, what keeps me separated from my neighbors in terms of religion is what brings me closer to them as neighbors. When there is a neighbor who baptizes a child, for example, we all go to his church regardless of its name. At any rate, the religious label does not save anyone. I am a Catholic, but as a good neighbor, I also visit the Evangelical churches – Assemblies of God and Foursquare Church – and the Spiritist centers. (Interview with Seu José, Joinville 2014; our translation)

We can see, then, that there is something in neighborly relations, something perhaps as sacred and important as personal conviction, that widens the frontiers of institutionalized religion. Revolving around social logic but intertwined with practical considerations, personal preferences, and institutional injunctions, this neighborliness is central to Joinvillians' social identity.

To understand this supremacy of social ties for butinage in Joinville, we note the importance of the uniquely Brazilian concept of "*jeitinho*." *Jeitinho* refers to the reliance on interpersonal relations to get by and respond to life's various challenges. According to Da Matta (1983; see also Fauré 2012), *jeitinho* is a social practice intended to solve conflicts and create original alternatives for each problematic situation, while rendering the decision-making processes more flexible. To give a concrete example, the power of *jeitinho* might let a person off without a fine after a parking violation when the passing policeman finds out that the offender is a member of the same religious congregation. *Jeitinho*, then, might manifest in the bending of formal rules in the name of social ties and their own accompanying imperatives. Importantly, the concept of *jeitinho* thus demonstrates how the centrality of socialization cannot be isolated from the wider struggle to "get by" through both material and spiritual means.

Similarly, in Paranaguá-Mirim as in the three other case studies, institutionalized religions represent only one dimension of religiosity and must be thought of in conjunction with social imperatives and actual lived religious experiences. We may consider the case of Maria, a practitioner at the Assemblies of God. She does not like images, which are forbidden by Pentecostals and Evangelicals. However, in the name of her friendship with her Catholic neighbor who keeps an image of the Virgin, she finds a *jeitinho* – an arrangement – that allows her to smooth things out and pray together with her neighbor despite these differences. The neighbors will pray together – with or without the Virgin. Neighborly ties nourish butinage, which in turn supports neighborliness.

Maria's example also shows how, for the people of Paranaguá-Mirim, mobility does not only take place within formal places of worship, but is also likely to occur even within their own homes. In the home, each and every one of the neighborhood's popular saints may have their place. Under a single roof, we might find images of the (black) Virgin, the sword of Saint George, portraits of Imanjá (the spirit of water) and of Saint Benedict, and a statuette of the Buddha. Moreover, due to the emphasis on social logic as central to butinage in Joinville, the home is always ready to welcome in new saints introduced by a neighbor. Thus, to reconcile the rules of the houses of God with those of churchgoers – the former exclusive, the latter inclusive – a *jeitinho* is needed: a bridge of neighborliness that overcomes institutional boundaries.

Conclusion

In this chapter, we considered religious butinage in the Brazilian city of Joinville. It is not incidental, perhaps, that the term "butinage" was first developed in Joinville. The religious field in Brazil is diverse and ever expanding. As the examples of our interlocutors suggest, butinage is a common practice, and its territories can be wide and broad, sometimes almost indiscriminate, as it is commonly held that all religions contain some grain of truth and even that they are related and mutually reinforcing. While Brazil has been a breeding ground for some of the world's most successful Pentecostal churches, with their widely exclusive – at times aggressively so – theological ideas, it is interesting to see how the majority of our Joinvillian interviewees were relentlessly keeping their religious territory wide and porous, with the help of an occasional *jeitinho*.

Such acceptance of butinage in Joinville demonstrates a significant point: for the residents of Paranaguá-Mirim, religious butinage does not constitute a temporary phase, a particular moment of religious or personal crisis, but is rather the common way of conducting oneself from one day to the next in relation to all matters religious. There is, our interviewees agree, nothing tragic about the butineur's religiosity. Their religiosity is not at risk of being stigmatized as unstable, loose, or floating, as might be the case in Kenya, for instance. Quite the contrary – the butineur is widely understood as a dedicated believer, supportive of and supported by neighborly ties, who insists on accumulating practices through engaging in religious combinations that are in no way perceived as dubious. Moreover, it is through the very act of shifting back and forth between practices and influences – complex movements that are full of improvisation – that new religious paths emerge. In understanding this tendency, we again emphasize how butinage in Joinville is first and foremost relational, as the social bond precedes the act of religious passage. It connects, rather than isolates, the practitioners and their social environment. Kinship, neighborliness, and religious circles all combine around joint practices. In Joinville, we are far from an individualist religious world, wherein practitioners transition by creating for themselves – and themselves alone – a bricolage of religious combinations.

Importantly, the Brazilian case reminds us how butineurs are not passive subjects overtaken, like simple consumers of religious goods, by the strong currents of socioeconomic trends. Rather, they act – rather than react – upon their surrounding socioreligious environment. Our Joinvillian interviewees are active subjects who reposition themselves within the religious sphere as a way of giving meaning to the socioreligious system to which they belong. At the same time, however, the Brazilian case invites us to think beyond the autonomy of individuals and to embrace the complexities of relational networks and their inherent logics. Indeed, in considering the local socioreligious ethos, we emphasized the centrality of neighborly networks, putting the focus primarily – but not exclusively – on the social logic. As an emblematic element in religion, visits to neighbors' places of worship is central for accumulating meaning within the practice of butinage. It is a way of doing things that implies reciprocity. Visiting someone is an invitation for a future visit, as we will see in the next chapter, which will focus on Kenya. In this sense, religious butinage is not so much an accomplishment as it is a process, and not so much a solution as an attempt. It is in-between and in-betwixt, a production rather than a product. To engage in butinage is to take an active role in shaping the religious – and social – environment.

4 The Kenyan Case: Dynamism and Precariousness

The very idea of religious mobility as prominent across sub-Saharan Africa is, in and of itself, not new and is demonstrated again and again in the literature. Scholars have long discussed the fluid nature of African religious affiliations both in precolonial times and following conversions to Christianity and Islam (Ranger 1993). Indeed, despite the break with the past implied by the notion of conversion, it has been noted that, across Africa, conversion "does not happen once and for all but is constantly taking place through historical processes at different levels of a particular society" (Aguilar 1995, 536). At times, the very notion of conversion as understood in the Abrahamic tradition does not adequately translate into local languages – a fact noted by Premawardhana with regard to his Makhuwa interlocutors in Mozambique and by Droz, following Valeer Neckebrouck, with regard to his Kikuyu interlocutors in Kenya (Premawardhana 2018; Droz 2002b).[1] So much has the anthropological literature on religion in sub-Saharan Africa become accustomed to acknowledging religious identities to be in a state of flux that many scholars have come to expect it. Thus, for instance, Thomas Kirsch (2004, 699) notes that he was not surprised by the high frequency of mobility among his interlocutors in southern Zambia, as they moved around between multiple Christian churches and traditional practices: "This high mobility in religious affiliation and the tendency to be simultaneously engaged in a variety of religious forms did not surprise me in itself, because practices of this kind have already been described in much of the literature on sub-Saharan Africa."

Such understanding serves as the starting point of this chapter and the next one, in which we describe and draw lessons from everyday religious butinage in urban Kenya and Ghana respectively. We begin by discussing the case of Kenya, looking in particular at mainstream Christianity. Kenya is a predominantly Christian country, with more than 80 percent of its population professing Christianity. Moreover, Kenyan Christians tend to be highly practicing, expressing their religiosity through regular participation in services, home fellowships, and outdoor "crusades," and infusing the public sphere with their faith. Indeed, the Kenyan urban setting is particularly vibrant, as churches both traditional and new vie for following. The explosion of the neo-Pentecostal wave since the 1980s and the liberalization of the religious market as part of the gradual return to democracy in the 1990s and early 2000s have left a strong mark in the form of countless new churches "cropping up" or "mushrooming." For the cynics, some of these churches are motivated by ulterior interests: accumulation of economic means (including land) and amassing personal power. Between these new and old denominations, as well as outside this Christian universe, one finds a large degree of individual to-ing and fro-ing. In particular, the city of Nairobi, Kenya's capital and economic, political, and cultural hub, is the heartland of the country's religious fervor.

Urban Kenya – our fieldwork focused on the cities of Nairobi and Kisumu – thus presents two features that are seemingly in tension. On the one hand, urban Kenya is characterized by a certain institutional hegemony, wherein to be an engaged member of a church is the norm and to be a non-practitioner is regarded as unusual, or – as Christian Kenyans would often say – "funny." On the other hand, urban Kenya is also characterized by a common tendency toward dynamic religious butinage. To this tension between institutional authority and individual agency, we can add a third factor, namely, the socioreligious ethos. It is this implicit system of values, and the social discourse that underpins it, that influences, for example, the definition of some religious forms as legitimate while others are regarded with suspicion and considered as "no-go areas."

Research in Kenya was conducted by Gez, with the support of Droz, as part of Gez's doctoral project. Fieldwork was conducted over an accumulated period of about a year in 2011 and 2012 (Nairobi) and 2014 (Kisumu). In order to allow for in-depth study of an expansive urban landscape, Gez focused on several neighborhoods and places of worship. Thus, in Nairobi, he concentrated most prominently on the Kibera slum (lower class), Kilimani and Ngong Road ([higher] middle class), and the city center (mixed). While he visited events organized by dozens of churches, he developed close ties with several specific denominations – interviewing their leadership and studying their institutional structures. Most of his interlocutors, however, were lay practitioners and were identified using a mixture of the snowball method, mediation of gatekeepers, and reliance on chance encounters. Thus, his interviewees include church attendants and congregants but also various service providers, local acquaintances, and people approached in city parks. In identifying interviewees, Gez sought to maximize diversity and minimize the risk of a selection bias, while also aiming at the center of the bell curve with the intention of accurately representing mainstream Christianity in Kenya today.

We begin by introducing the Kenyan religious landscape before moving on to discuss some of the main themes of religious mobility that arose from our research in Kenya. We dwell on the elements that have presented themselves most consistently throughout the research, focusing on three in particular: the hierarchical distinction between membership and visits; the prevalence of return mobility; and the precariousness of the religious landscape itself, as seen through common schisms and scandals.

The Kenyan Religious Landscape

From the late nineteenth century until its independence in 1963, the territory to be known as the Republic of Kenya was under direct British colonial rule, which introduced rapid breaks from traditional social systems.[2] Prior to British occupation, societies in Kenya were for the most part comprised of small social units, which had no unified government or a single standardized language. The religious in precolonial Kenya was hardly differentiated from the social, the political, and the moral. Contrasting that precolonial period with the significant hold that Christianity seems to have in Kenya today, Derek Peterson (2004) registers the first reactions of laughter and bewilderment among the Kikuyu people of central Kenya upon listening to the early European missionaries. According to Peterson, the missionaries appropriated Kikuyu traditions and terms to their own understanding of religion in order to enter into a comparative dialogue and show the superiority of the Christian faith.

Since independence, religion – and Christianity in particular – has been accorded a special status, which it has retained throughout the country's multiple crises. Like many countries, Kenya has seen the incorporation of religious symbolism into the heart of its national ethos. The English version of Kenyan's national anthem, for instance, starts with the words "O God of all creation/Bless this, our land and nation," and formal state oaths are taken in God's name. However, the importance of religion in Kenya goes well beyond such symbolic references. Dating back to colonial times, religion has established itself as a key player, tightly linked with politics and commanding a powerful lobby. Through their involvement in the country's "nation building," religious institutions have carved out a unique status for themselves. Schools, hospitals, and other services have remained in the hands of the churches after independence and up to the present day. In this respect, the inadequacy of post-independence state provision helped entrench religious institutions' autonomy (see Piot 2010). Today, according to Paul Gifford, the Catholic Church, the biggest single church in Kenya, is probably the country's "most significant institution" (Gifford 2009, 56). Such de facto institutional privileges are potentially in tension with the formal and legal emphasis on freedom of worship and protection from religious coercion, as guaranteed in the 1963 constitution and reaffirmed in the 2010 revised constitution.[3]

Indeed, beyond being a predominantly Christian state, most Kenyans also perceive their country as a Christian nation, with religion playing a paramount role in the national ethos. The country's four presidents – Jomo Kenyatta, Daniel arap Moi, Mwai Kibaki, and Uhuru Kenyatta – have all worked hard to establish a devout Christian image for themselves, with their religious commitment enjoying vast coverage by the Kenyan media. Other Kenyan politicians similarly try to appeal to religion in order to muster support. As Hervé Maupeu observed some years back, "every Kenyan member of Parliament knows that his election is often won in the church square" (Maupeu 1991, 262; our translation). More recently, Damaris Parsitau, commenting on Kenya's growing "Pentecostal Constituency," argued that Pentecostalism has accumulated a "critical election mass that can easily be mobilized by its influential leaders" (Parsitau 2008, 15). Without being overly cynical concerning politicians' religious persuasions and intentions, we should consider Gifford's (2009) argument that a pious Christian guise has been a convenient decoy for members of the corrupt elite, as it offers a veil widely regarded as virtuous behind which they can act with impunity and eschew accountability. Indeed, we may wonder about the alleged conversions to born-again Christianity by such questionable figures as Kamlesh Pattni, the architect of the large-scale Goldenberg fraud, or Maina Njenga, a senior figure in the Mungiki vigilante movement (Maupeu 2014; Kavulla 2008; Gifford 2009).

Today, Christianity holds a privileged place in the Kenyan national ethos. According to the country's 2019 census, Christians form about 85.5 percent of Kenya's general population.[4] Other statistics show that, unlike places where religious affiliation tends to be merely nominal, Kenyans live out their religious identity through active practice. One poll showed that Kenyans tend to perceive themselves as highly religious, with 88 percent (85 percent of men and 90 percent of women) arguing that religion is "very important" in their lives (Afrobarometer 2011). Another survey had 80 percent of Kenyan respondents claiming to attend church at least once a week and 64 percent saying they participate in religious groups at least once a week (Pew Research Center 2006). In both categories, Kenya ranked highest among the ten countries under question.[5] To the extent that such statistics are reliable, they indicate that, notwithstanding recent transformations – including, perhaps, a drop in religious conviction or formal affiliation – religiosity remains prominent in Kenya.

While the total number of churches in Kenya is hard to gauge, it is possible to tally those that have been registered. In a widely cited newspaper article from 2007, Kenya's Attorney General Amos Wako stated that there were 8,520 registered churches in Kenya, with 6,740 more applications pending and 60 new applications being filed every month. Wako was also quoted as saying that the Registrar General's department was "overwhelmed" and facing difficulties processing the increase in requests for registration made by new churches (Ndegwa 2007, 6). According to Julius Gathogo (2011, 2), by 2010 there were about 10,000 registered churches in Kenya and many more being processed, causing a huge backlog. These numbers do not include, of course, the many churches that, aware of this backlog or simply willing to take their chances, have not even attempted to register.[6]

In line with the common division of the Pentecostal movement into three waves (Freston 1995, 2004; Anderson 2010), the antecedents of the Kenyan movement included the missionary Pentecostal churches of the early twentieth century and, later, the growth of Pentecostal churches in Kenya's urban areas between 1950 and 1980 (Maxwell 2002, 18–20; Droz 2000a). A favored country by missionaries since colonial times, Kenya has in recent decades seen considerable presence of American Evangelists, who contributed significantly to the transformation of Kenyan Christianity through the propagation of charismatic liturgy, the importance of achieving salvation by becoming born again, and the gospel of prosperity. As John Lonsdale tells us, "in the 1990s Kenya had 1,300 of them [Evangelical missionaries], an astounding figure, twice as many as any other African country, and a second missionization none would have foretold in 1963 [Kenya's year of independence]" (Lonsdale 2002, 184). According to Gifford (2004b), the total number of foreign missionaries around those years was even higher.[7]

Dominant in this respect is the rise of neo-Pentecostal churches, sometimes known as Third Wave Pentecostalism, which has been the most significant development in Kenya's religious landscape. Neo-Pentecostalism can be characterized by a number of elements (Anderson 2004). First, it tends to paint the world in dichotomous terms, as a spiritual battlefield between demonic and godly forces (Marshall 2016). Second, it tends to emphasize financial prosperity and overall success as the claimable right of every "true" believer. Third, it is marked by an entrepreneurial spirit, which leads to the employment of corporate-like models of operation, use of the media, and a crossover into politics. Fourth, it is geared toward a circulation of ideas, leaders, and commodities and has an international orientation. To these elements we may add that neo-Pentecostalism tends to be geared toward urban areas, an orientation made possible by the movement's flexible modes of operation and its embrace of modern technologies (Parsitau and Mwaura 2010; Togarasei 2005).

Since the 1980s, neo-Pentecostalism has been taking root in Kenya, eventually going hand in hand with the gradual liberalization of the airwaves and the press throughout the 1990s, which suited the Pentecostal appeal to technological modes of mass communication. This liberalization also included permission to develop new churches, mainly independent of the Pentecostal stock, many of which emerged as a result of splinters and secessions due to leadership struggles and scandals involving financial or sexual misconduct. The (neo-)Pentecostal family of churches is highly heterogeneous and offers substantial challenges to those seeking to define it (Anderson et al. 2010). The situation is further complicated by the fact that many believers are themselves indifferent or even opposed to the term "Pentecostalism" or are simply confused by it (Corten and Marshall-Fratani 2001). For example, a study ordered by a leading independent denomination, Nairobi Pentecostal Church, has shown that, despite the church's name, its congregants are divided as to whether their church actually counts as Pentecostal or not.[8] The rise of (neo-)Pentecostalism has, above all, been identified with the diversification of the religious market. With the movement's emphasis on the gifts of the Holy Spirit, we note a shift from pastoral training to individual charisma, with countless new entrepreneurs, including so-called self-professed pastors, prophets, and healers, entering the scene. Some of these new practitioners may be accused of straddling the imaginary line between "legitimate church" and "illegitimate sect." As one commentator mentioned with dismay, some erroneously claim that "church leaders need only the Holy Spirit to lead the church" (Olando 2012, 16). Several of our interlocutors also intimated similar apprehensions, arguing that "to become a pastor nowadays, all you need is a Bible and a suit." As Ruth Marshall writes with regard to the Nigerian Pentecostal context, "while various forms of institutionalized accreditation exist, pastoral authority is represented as inhering in a personal call from God; anybody with a vision can start a church, a fellowship, or a mission, and they do" (Marshall 2009, 12; Corten and Marshall-Fratani 2001, 5).

Indeed, while the changes in Kenya's religious landscape have been greatly influenced by the advent of the neo-Pentecostal wave, its impact goes well beyond. The transformation of the landscape as dominated by the Pentecostalization process – which also includes the advent of charismatic strands within traditional Christian denominations – has been described by Peter Oduor in a cover story published in Kenya's leading newspaper, the *Daily Nation* (Oduor 2013). The article's starting point is that "from the 1970s to date, what was and what is are now worlds apart," begging the question: "How did the church in Kenya get so BIG?" (capitalization in the original). Trying to account for what he regards as a dramatic transformation, the author points to the rise of "individual Evangelical churches," which offered a loosening up of the liturgical rigidity characteristic of mainline institutions and created a shift toward "free, flexible, and open forms of worship." Up-and-coming pastors became more down to earth and free in their demeanor – "gone is their insular nature and in its place is an emancipated man of God. Suave, debonair, and well versed in any issue under the sun." This new brand of middle-class, young, educated pastors have opened Christianity to new technologies and modern musical styles. Their success and independence allows churches to be treated like private enterprises, with large and sometimes-paid staff and investments in "secular" business ventures. Substantial funds are directed at media outlets – with Christian publishing houses and magazines as well as gospel radio stations and TV channels abounding.

These changes, Oduor argues, appeal mostly to the youth, who have risen in "the past few decades ... to be the largest group of churchgoers."[9] In their attempt to court the youth, churches are flirting with what has traditionally been considered a secular lifestyle. Thus, the gospel music scene has changed dramatically, and artists and their songs "do not look like gospel songs and artists anymore. They are lively, carefree, and with little restraint ... The songs are easy, the language is Sheng,[10] the performance is heated, the videos are flashy, and the marketing aggressive." Yet another attraction of the new churches is their specialization. Oduor suggests that, whereas in the past church was just about "scripture, songs and offerings" centered around Sunday service, churches today are well-oiled businesslike institutes, which are active all week round, offering anything from marriage counselling, to specialized family services, to programs for orphans and widows, to hospital visits. There are specific ministries for women, men, teens, youth, and the elderly. As Oduor concludes, nobody "is left out." Oduor also stresses the growing power of individual lay believers. As he points out, "before, people went to church, but now the church has come to the people." In addition, this new brand of church leaders and church structures is characterized as much more democratic in nature. The new leaders "consult the congregation through discussions and meetings. They give out questionnaires; What would you want changed in the Sunday service? Which visiting preacher should we invite for the Supper Sunday?"

While Christianity is a privileged point of reference, Kenya also has religious minorities. Its Muslim population is substantial if often marginalized, and it also has several minorities of Indian descent (Adam 2015). On the whole, borders between religions tend to be maintained, and it is rare to find people who perceive themselves, for instance, as both Christian and Muslim. Religious mobility, we will show, tends to take place within a prescribed territory – such as normative Christianity or, even more narrowly, born-again Christianity. A partial exception can be found with regard to the rich religious traditions contentiously referred to as African traditional religions (ATRs).[11] By being embedded in actors' traditional roots and enjoying greater flexibility, ATRs may coexist or be mixed with other religious engagements in relative harmony (see, for example, Ellis 2011). Kenyans may follow customs associated with their ethnic group's traditional religion, including consulting traditional healers. However, in line with the hegemony inherent in the notion of territory, these instances tend to be underplayed. People tend to hide traditional practices and beliefs, especially in urban settings (which are presented as sites of modernity), as these practices and beliefs have become associated with traditional life and have been demonized by the church. Many religious rituals are site-specific and make sense within a setting of ethnic cohesion, which is not easily found in the city's multiethnic environment. But even if engagement with traditional practices is restricted in urban settings, the ubiquity of circular migration between rural and urban settings means that traditional religions may be "deactivated" only temporarily and reintroduced upon practitioners' return to their rural home.

For the present discussion, therefore, several insights may be drawn regarding the Kenyan religious landscape. First, religion is deeply embedded in Kenyan culture. Even though there might be signs that atheists and agnostics are on the rise,[12] (Christian) faith is still the norm, as is the idea that everyone should be affiliated with a congregation. Thus, even though freedom of worship is cherished, in practical terms some religious conformity is socially expected. Second, religion's prominence within the national ethos helps explain its significant presence in Kenyan public life. From street preachers through school chaplains to the national fascination with religious scandals and rumors, the presence of religion should be recognized within the larger social system with which it is intertwined. Third, and relatedly, urban Kenya's booming religious market needs to be recognized within the political context of the democratization and liberalization process of the 1990s and early 2000s. The overflow of requests to register new churches and the minimal state mechanisms set in place to oversee this explosion mark a new stage in Kenyan Christianity. Fourth, as we will see later, the Kenyan religious landscape is characterized by a great precariousness (schisms, scandals) that reflects on the mobile practices of individual religious believers.

Hierarchy in Practice: Members versus Visitors

Early in our research in Kenya, we noted the common use of a certain parlance and a set of concepts when referring to religious matters. One popular conceptual distinction has been drawn between "membership" and "visits." This distinction, we found, is so widespread that it was used by almost all of our interviewees across the denominational board. It points to what we propose to be a loose structure of hierarchically compartmentalized elements within a person's religious identity. "Membership" can be considered as the "center" or "pivot"[13] of religious practice and belonging, which usually – but not always – corresponds to official institutional recognition. By contrast, "visits" represent any number of secondary practices, either one time or protracted, beyond membership. This distinction indicates the possibility of maintaining several concurrent religious engagements – something that, as we have seen, is often neglected in scholarly work. As we shall propose in this section, this duality points to relations of both hierarchy and complementarity between the two categories, and this basic distinction corresponds with the common makeup of religious identity in Christian Kenya.

Let us first consider the term "membership," by which our interviewees refer to an individual's principal belonging to a particular congregation or "home church." The term is often used loosely to point to the center of the practitioner's religious belonging, even when not backed by formal membership status. Indeed, some of our interviewees have stressed the distinction between "member" (or "member by profession") and "legal member," whereby only the latter includes official institutional registration. Many congregations, and certainly the more established ones, have designed methods for identifying members, for instance, by keeping membership lists and distributing formal membership cards. While such methods have reached many churches both large and small, others lack clear membership procedures and criteria, relying instead on devotion and consistency as a way of gaging membership. And yet, not all practitioners see membership with the same degree of importance, as was the case with Rose, a thirty-year-old interlocutor who, despite having worked for one of Nairobi's largest Pentecostal congregations for several years, has never bothered to become a member – partially due to lack of interest and partially due to her difficulty in meeting the criteria for membership.[14] Indeed, religious institutions do not all hold membership categories in the same esteem, while individual practitioners themselves may opt – for any number of reasons, or simply due to disinterest – not to become formally registered. As can be expected in a predominantly practicing Christian country, long-standing church membership – whether formal or informal – is regarded as socially laudable and has come to be associated with stability, commitment, and perseverance, qualities that are particularly noteworthy against the backdrop of Kenyan's socioeconomic fragility and crisis of trust (Gez and Droz 2015).

A telling practice in this regard is the affirmation of de facto membership through the offering of tithes, which is common across the denominational board. One interviewee explained: "I believe it is only in your church that you can give [tithe], because you want to see your church grow, you want to see things moving in your church, and you can never be a member in several churches at once." Indeed, the choice of where to tithe has pronounced social implications, as it is usually a constitutive indication for membership affiliation. Moreover, by making membership in more than one church financially strenuous, hence something to be avoided, this type of offering has an added regulative effect on membership patterns. This effect is supported by a general social delegitimization of multiple affiliations, which – like in the case of non-practice mentioned earlier – is cast as "funny." Considering the sometimes-concealed tensions that already exist between churches in their competition over membership, such regulation through tithing may play a pacifying role. It is imperative, most Kenyan interviewees argue, for a person to be well grounded in a single church.[15]

In line with the general perception concerning multiple affiliations, Kenyans generally regard shifts between memberships with caution; when considered excessive, such shifts are frowned upon as a sign of instability and bad character. While the doors of the church are wide open for new members to join, concerns that people might switch church in order to escape their evil deeds lead some church leaders to go to the extent of demanding an admission interview and even a release letter from the leader of the person's former congregation as a precondition for admitting prospective members. This negative attitude is encapsulated by the widely employed derogatory term "church hopping." The term is associated with not being serious in one's faith and even being a troublemaker, a behavioral pattern that supposedly explains frequent mobility.

But although such changes of membership are looked at with suspicion, Kenyans tend to emphasize their religious freedom. This tension is handled through the employment of a second, highly common and very broad category of religious engagement – church visits. In formal terms, church visits refer to a one-off attendance at services or events organized by another denomination. Visits of this kind, often made in response to an invitation by a friend or a relative, are a common practice and – like the notion of "neighborliness" discussed in the context of Brazil – can be seen as a manifestation of solidarity that bears important consequences for consolidating and expanding a person's social networks. When visiting a weekly service, congregants might inform or even ask permission from the pastor of their home church, a practice indicating the carefully maintained hierarchy between membership and visits. While Kenyan Christians acknowledge the value of commitment to a single church, visits to other churches also enjoy widespread legitimacy and do not normally strain the visitor's reputation.

At the same time, in Kenya's loose religious parlance, the term "visits" can also imply a prolonged and substantial engagement with another religious denomination. Used in such a way, the term can refer to any secondary or additional practices beyond the individual's church membership, while emphasizing the hierarchy between practices. Thus, for instance, a person may persistently attend early morning fellowships (Morning Glory) at a location more convenient than their home church, or attend a series of sermons on a particular subject, all the while referring to these as "mere visits." By this use of the term, visits can be misleadingly diminutive – one outcome being the diffusion of tension surrounding membership. Importantly, while shifting membership is regarded as potentially problematic, visits are widely held as positive and enriching experiences. Even cases of prolonged, ongoing "visits" can be thought of as acceptable, or even socially and spiritually virtuous, as long as a clear hierarchy is kept and the "visitor" is firmly anchored in a home church.

While every visit holds a potential for change in membership, our interviewees showed a different standard for delimiting their territory in reference to visits and membership. While most said they would be willing to visit most churches and sometimes even non-Christian places of worship, they clarified that they would "only go there for a visit," whereas they would only consider membership in a limited range of churches. The term "visit" thus implies expansion and exploration and allows practitioners a way of asserting their religious latitude and assuaging concerns about engagement with new religious forms. The fact that visits are an established social institution that largely follows familiar protocols

(Gez and Droz 2017) helps legitimize such explorative tendencies, subsuming them into a familiar paradigm based on reciprocity and solidarity. In trying to understand why boundaries are more porous for visiting than for membership, we can refer to the different roles each category serves. For instance, one of the important aspects of church membership is found in the creation of a welfare-like support network, a crucial aid in light of the hardships and uncertainties faced by Nairobi's lower classes. In that sense, the importance of membership can be felt especially during moments of crisis and distress. Visits, on the other hand, belong to a time when a person steps outside the familiar and the secure, responding to friendly invitations and signaling that social solidarity between friends and family overcomes institutional differences. For the daring, it can even be a moment of playful experimentation with alternative identities. Membership and visits are, in this respect, complementary.[16]

To illustrate the importance of the interplay between membership and visits, consider the story of Zacharia, a Nairobian from the Kibera slum in his mid-twenties, who told us about a scandal that nearly led to a schism in his Pentecostal church. His denomination was especially strict, and the chief pastor, obeying the teachings coming from the church's headquarters in the United States, was enforcing a doctrine whereby congregants were forbidden to visit other churches, own a television set, or preach the Word of God outside of official events orchestrated by the church. Having expelled some congregants for breaking these rules, the pastor was faced with an internal rebellion that led to a significant dwindling in the size of the congregation. The overseas leadership, disappointed by the pastor's inability to maintain his flock, replaced him with another, who was more open and offered greater freedom to his congregants. Zacharia concluded that this change in attitude succeeded in bringing people back, and today, several years after these events, the church has allegedly regained its former size.

This story illustrates the enactment of the dual membership-visit identity structure, wherein practitioners willingly accept their groundedness in a single church in the form of membership, while at the same time regard their freedom to extend beyond their single affiliation as an inalienable right. Even in a strict church such as Zacharia's, people insist that they should be allowed to adopt a somewhat inclusive religious identity that leaves a window open for secondary engagements and experiences outside the fold.

In understanding the implications of this membership-visit dual logic, we focused on personal interests and interpersonal solidarity. However, we conclude this section by reflecting on the consequences of mobility for the transformation of the religious landscape itself. For this purpose, we stay with Zacharia and consider another episode at his strict Pentecostal church:

> [One time,] we were told to lead the Praise and Worship [and we introduced a new song, and the church leaders said], "That one is new." But then we sang it because it was nice. [The] people of the church were moved, even the pastor was very very happy of that song, it was good itself. So he told us, "Where did you learn that song?" [We answered, "We learned it] somewhere else, we went somewhere else, we saw those others, they were presenting it, so we were inspired, we have to know it, so we practiced it, so we knew [the song]." (Interview with Zacharia, Nairobi 2011)

Zacharia's example of a Christian song learned in another church during a visit – but brought in and eventually celebrated at his home church – touches on a question worth pondering, namely, the question of the "honey" produced by the bee-like work of butinage. Beyond its bearing on personal and social ties and on the institutionalized religious field itself, engagement in butinage, as managed through the dual prism of membership and visits, offers a basis through which to consider the channels of cross-fertilization of borrowing and adopting external ideas.

Return Mobility

It is by now clear that Kenyan practitioners often shift in their degrees of practice. In common speech, a range of terminologies is dedicated to describing uncommitted practitioners, a language that often conveys disdain. Thus, for example, a non-practitioner may be regarded as "unchurched," a terminology that, through negation, emphasizes that which is correct and normative. A non-committed churchgoer may win the label of a "backbencher," an unflattering designation in a Pentecostalized environment where religious participation is expected to involve much more than passive attendance at Sunday services. Even less flattering is the notion of "backsliding," which denotes a retreat from active religious engagement, especially in the case of born-again Christians. In a universe where salvation is largely construed as a unidirectional vector – "you cannot lose your salvation," explained one interviewee – a backslider is seen as having walked away from salvation, attracting contempt but keeping alive the hope for eventual realization and return. Ridden with guilt, backsliders might indeed repent and find their way back to the bosom of the Lord, only to fall from grace once more in a recurring cycle that is highly recognizable among Kenyan youth.

The discussion on weakening religious commitment and the prospect of return to a former religious state has its antecedents as early as the beginning of the twentieth century, when scholars studying religious mobility – their term of choice being "conversion" – recognized the possibility of reverting back to a former (ir)religious condition and/or sinful state, acknowledged through such categories as "regeneration" and "backsliding" (Clark 1929; James 1902; Nock 1933). An early piece by Edwin D. Starbuck (1899), recognized by William James as "the only statistics I know of, on the subject of the duration of conversions" (James 1902, 257), found that, among the Evangelical church members studied, 93 percent of women and 77 percent of men had been backsliding to some extent compared to the time of their conversion.

In the contemporary literature on Africa, the prospect of return mobility is often implied in the emphasis on religious dynamism and on the ongoing circulation between two or more religious cosmologies (McIntosh 2009). As Mario Aguilar suggests with regard to the Waso Boora people of northern Kenya, conversion from ATRs to Christianity is not necessarily unidirectional and may well "include processes of reconversion to religious practices socially present in the eras preceding the world religions" (Aguilar 1995, 526; Premawardhana 2018). But where, if at all, do we draw the line between complete "reconversion," weakening commitment, or "backsliding" and ongoing religious circularity? Following our distinction, in the previous section, between members and visitors, we argue in favor of a clear category of "return mobility,"[17] as relating to a practitioner's primary affiliation. Such return mobility is demonstrated, for example, by Frans Wijsen in his condensed presentation of one of his East African interviewees: "I was baptized a Catholic. When I married a Muslim, I became a Muslim. Then, when we had to educate our children we sent them to a Catholic school and I became a Catholic. Now my children are grownup, and I have become a Muslim again" (Wijsen 2007, 176). Such contextual diachronic religious mobility, related to location, status within the kinship structure, and educational projects echoes the situation of several of our interviewees in Kenya as well as in Ghana, as will be explored in the next chapter.

The idea of return to a once-dropped religious denomination may seem counterintuitive. Why would someone choose to go back to a tradition that they have left – some even use the term "outgrown"? Indeed, there is great appeal in thinking of religious mobility in terms of progression. "Conversion careers" are intuitively understood as diachronic movements to evermore suitable religious contexts. The framing of conversion narratives, which is deeply affected by formal doctrines and teachings, may portray the past in negative terms, for example, as a condition of birth that time and spiritual growth have rendered irrelevant (Stromberg 1993; Wuthnow 2011). And yet, in our Kenyan fieldwork, we encountered plenty of instances of return mobility that suggest it is a common feature of Kenyans' lived religion. Thanks to our use of biographical narratives, we noted that, among our eighty-seven Kenyan interviewees, over 40 percent recounted an instance of return mobility throughout their religious itinerary.[18] Here, building on the former section's distinction between membership and visits, we may draw another distinction between two groups. First, there are those who have experienced return mobility in terms of their primary practice – that is, reverted in their membership to a denomination that they had once left. This group included seventeen (about 20 percent) of all Kenyan interviewees. A second category includes those interviewees who described having left a religious form that was once their primary practice, but eventually renewing ties with it as a secondary practice. This category, in which return mobility is framed in terms of visits, included twenty-three (about 25 percent) of all Kenyan interviewees. Of the total number of interviewees, four reported instances of both primary and secondary return mobility. In addition, two interviewees admitted that they were contemplating return mobility, but had not yet made up their minds. It thus emerges that mobility to a once-abandoned denomination is a common practice in Kenya, or at least in the country's urban centers.

The choice of the term "return mobility," like that of "circular mobility," evokes a spatial, geographic image, and it is indeed to the field of migration and mobility studies that we are indebted for this name.[19] Instead of assuming a unidirectional vector and the abandonment of past practices and ties, the returning religious itinerant articulates new bridges and religious links and, in the process, raises questions about the relevance of their religious past that may otherwise seem invisible. While our research shows that the line between circular and return mobility can be fine – mainly when it comes to borderline cases involving secondary practices or visits – we also note the usefulness of this distinction, above all in the case of returning after a long time to a once-dropped religious membership. A paradigmatic case of return mobility, for example, would be that of Stephanie, a twenty-year-old student and member of Nairobi Pentecostal Church (NPC), who moved to Nairobi Chapel for six months together with her sister – following an invitation from her sister's friend, whose father was a pastor there – before deciding to reestablish herself in her old church.

In trying to understand the appeal of return mobility, our contention is that, far from the image of a radical conversion, practitioners often maintain a sense of continuity before and after the mobility sequence, a fact that facilitates their eventual return. Indeed, we can cite numerous cases where religious change did not necessarily entail rupture with the practitioner's old life and social ties. After religious change, their family and friends may remain committed to their former affiliation, providing a basis of continuous ties that would accommodate return. As religious mobility is primarily a solitary activity (as opposed, for instance, to collective geographic mobility within the family unit), it is true that, once a religious form has been jettisoned, the social environment with which it was associated may nonetheless continue to exert its relevance. In this sense, it is important to recognize the external circumstances and pressures that may induce religious mobility: migration, marriage, professional career, and similar factors. We argue that such induced mobility can result in an artificial discontinuation of one religious form and the embrace of another, even as past religious engagements continue to maintain their allure. The jettisoned religious past may thus lie in waiting for a new constellation of circumstances conducive to its eventual reemergence. The proposed link between external inducement and eventual return can be explored by appealing to three common Kenyan instances propitious to religious mobility: aggressive evangelization and peer pressure, marriage/divorce, and geographic mobility.

Let us start by looking at aggressive evangelization and social pressure. The Kenyan urban setting is full of evangelists – professionals as well as lay people – trying to win people over. While some operate in the name of a particular church, others simply seek to get people to accept salvation and become born again. Indeed, it is not unusual for Pentecostal Kenyans to keep note of the number of "souls that they have saved," taking pride in high numbers. At times, people may feel that they knuckle under because of social pressure in accepting religious change. In the absence of deep conviction and considering the continuous appeal of their previous affiliation, they might assume this new identity superficially and temporarily, later casting it aside or otherwise maintaining a different backstage behavior. Indeed, many of our Kenyan interviewees suggested that too great an emphasis on evangelization and peer pressure has caused them to accept salvation half-heartedly and later to recant. While getting saved is typically presented as a profound personal decision, sometimes made in response to a life crisis, many accept it under more mundane circumstances.

In particular, it is common to get saved in high school, an experience often associated with social pressure and aggressive evangelization. When we asked Julie, a university-educated career woman in her late twenties, whether she sees herself as a born-again Christian, she answered: "No, but I should, huh?" She told us that every week in church, when her pastor announces an "altar call" – an invitation to approach the podium for congregants to get saved – her legs get heavy, and she cannot get herself to respond. In a detailed account, she recounted how she felt she had been "forced to get saved" by her high school peer group. Traumatized by the experience and by the religious hypocrisy she encountered among the school's saved students, she drifted out of Christianity and only recently began renewing her religious commitment. A fifty-year-old interviewee called Miriam offered a more benign account, telling us how, back in high school, she and her friends accepted salvation "because it was the 'in' thing." Having been brought up Catholic, Miriam drifted out of born-again salvation, but later renewed her commitment to born-again Christianity within her husband's African Inland Church (AIC). We may also mention twenty-year-old Gabriella, who, having recounted similar experiences during her school days, described the tension, even chasm, between the social expectation to project a born-again identity and actual behavior and values, which results in inevitable pretense. Having been saved a handful of times herself, the bemused Gabriella also told of a young, rugged man who used to come every Sunday to her NPC home church. Smelling of alcohol, this young man would be the first to raise his hand and respond to the altar call – week after week. As another interviewee concluded, taking a more philosophical stance, salvation should not be understood in terms of a life-transforming moment but rather as a journey, saying that "we are always getting born again."

We have suggested that, while practitioners may shift to another religious form, the unchanged and familiar religious environment from which they depart may continue to beckon them back home. This trajectory can be demonstrated by the case of marriage and divorce or, more broadly, relationships and breakups. It is customary in Kenya, in the case of interdenominational marriages, for the wife to follow her husband to his church.[20] This practice is framed in biblical and traditional patriarchal terms, the argument being that, just as the bride moves to her husband's household, so should she make his congregation her home. Family values being high on the church agenda, this move is regarded as important for reasons of domestic bliss and especially with regard to bringing up children, who should "know one church," to employ the language used by Kenyans. Overall, our female interviewees showed a willingness to follow this custom, but sometimes expressed resignation in the face of the uncertainties that it would entail. As Laura, a twenty-five-year-old unmarried woman, explained, "the Bible says that, as wives, you should be subject to your husbands. So, like, [if] my husband tells me that you have to be in my church, so I think I will just pray about it and ask God for the right way, yeah. I don't know what I can do about that, yeah [laughing]." Another interviewee, Alexandra, a forty-year-old married woman, told us how, having been brought up Catholic, she later married a Presbyterian man and shifted to his church. In fact, Alexandra's commitment to her new church was such that she ended up being employed by the church, albeit in a lay position:

> I got married to a Presbyterian, and I had to get to my husband as the head of the house and to follow him ... I am a faith-based person, so being the head of the house, I followed him. So it is not everybody who would do this, and I am comfortable with it ... So if it [the Bible] says – woman, you are under your husband, so I go this way. Do you understand me? This is faith-based, doing things according to the Bible. (Interview with Alexandra, Nairobi 2012)

By following custom and leaving her home church, at times reluctantly, the wife dissociates herself not only from a set of familiar dogmas and practices but also from the community in which she was brought up, which includes her family and friends. Shifting to a new denomination, she would often feel the break with her former religious affiliation to be artificial, and it would be accompanied by mixed feelings. Despite moving, the woman might still feel attached to her former church and indeed is likely to re-engage with the jettisoned affiliation, if only by participating in special functions in response to invitations. In addition, when visiting her family members back home, she might accompany them and visit her old church. Moreover, in the event that the marriage failed, the woman would have to decide whether to remain in her divorcee's denomination or return to her former religious home. Here the example of forty-five-year-old Maureen proves enlightening. Having divorced her Catholic husband, for whom she had shifted her affiliation from the Pentecostal church of her youth, Maureen returned to her previous church, NPC. In her case, the return was accompanied by frustration with the Catholic Church's denunciation of her divorce and her subsequent stigmatization. By contrast, at NPC she felt accepted despite being a single mother. To show that dilemmas of return in the context of relationships are not unique to women, we can also consider the case of thirty-five-year-old Leonard. Leonard was born and brought up Catholic, but followed his girlfriend to her Pentecostal congregation, Deliverance Church. The couple later broke up, but Leonard was happy enough at Deliverance and, despite the disapproval of his staunch Catholic family, decided to remain there. Later, however, he met another girl, this time a Catholic, who tried to convince him to join her back at the Catholic Church. He explained: "She insists. Like, 'You are Catholic, why did you go? Then you [should] come back.' She says she doesn't want to go to me, because the one who moved should come back … Our family is Catholic, and she is like … 'It is also your church.' [So it] is not like a church [that] I don't know."

Perhaps the most popular kind of induced mobility is associated with geographic relocation, above all that between the village and the city. For years, scholars have been recognizing the importance of religious circles in helping people cope with the challenges of urban migration by providing networks of collective support (Roberts 1968). In the field of African Studies, significant networks of economically motivated migration, such as in Southern Africa (McDonald 2000) and West Africa (Cordell, Gregory, and Piché 1996), tend to involve individuals who are intent on eventual return. In Kenya, where rural and urban worlds closely interlink and lend themselves to frequent mobility (Droz 1999), it is not uncommon to maintain religious identities that are diffused but at the same time geographically well demarcated. Thus, a person may take part in their family's traditional religious practice when staying at their rural home, but while in the city they would maintain a different affiliation, without this duality posing a substantial threat to the integrity of their religious identity. Even thoroughly urbanized Kenyans tend to maintain ties with their rural origins, returning to their *shamba* or countryside plot from time to time. The rural home is where a person may eventually retire or retreat, in case life in the city becomes unbearable, but it is also a living testimony to their ethnic roots. That home remains a gathering point for the wider family, bringing together those who stayed and those who migrated. In his work on the Kikuyu people of central Kenya, Droz showed that religious migration often goes hand in hand with geographic migration, taking the form of "multidirectional displacement" (Droz 1999). Internal migratory practices obey a circular logic, with families and individuals shifting between – and relying on – different socioeconomic "islands," forming what Droz and Sottas (1997), following John Murra (1981), have termed a "vertical archipelago."

In our research, we often observed such compartmentalization of the separate worlds of urban and rural life, noting that the shift to the city may be accompanied by a change in the makeup of an individual's set of religious practices. Reasons for this change may vary from the unavailability of familiar denominations to willful attraction to other religious forms. For some, the load of urban breadwinning and the temptations of secularism associate urban migration with a process of distancing themselves from religion altogether. Even so, by going back to the village – for a festival or a family gathering, to take care of a sick relative, or to look after their *shamba* – people often involve themselves with family practices and former religious traditions. While this return mobility might be presented in terms of the limited worshiping options available in the village and as a sign of respect toward family, it is a testimony to the ongoing relevance of the person's religious history, even when it has been formally abjured.

Thus, Daniel, a twenty-five-year-old staunch Pentecostal, told us that, when visiting his village in western Kenya, he joins his extended family at the Catholic Church, which he had formally left as a teenager. Similarly, Tina, a thirty-five-year-old Presbyterian of Catholic origin, told us that, "during the Easter holiday, I normally go to Catholic if I am in the rural area where my parents are, I would join them and go to Catholic." Thirty-five-year-old Christina gave an overview of this internal division by comparing Pentecostal churches – which are most active in the cities – with mainline churches, with which most Kenyans associate their religious roots:

> Pentecostalism is creeping into every church, and now in Nairobi, there are people who, for example, at home they are Anglicans [and when] they come to Nairobi they are Pentecostals. They find it comfortable, because their friends are going there. But they are still Anglicans when they go to the village. So you find somebody may have two churches and active in both [depending on where they are located at a certain time]. (Interview with Christina, Nairobi 2012)

The high rate of return mobility raises interesting questions regarding the unfolding of religious identity over time. In particular, it undermines the idea of disengagement and the supposed irrelevance of the religious past, leaving us to wonder to what extent the past is ever truly gone. Indeed, instances of return mobility show that what may seem like a rupture with the past is often temporary, partial, or superficial. To understand the full extent of people's religious identity, we must therefore combine the exploration of present practices with an acknowledgment of actors' religious history. This, in turn, begs a methodological reflection, forcing the scholar not only to rely on current practices but also to register and account for the relevance of the seemingly bygone. We shall return to this challenge in chapter 8, "From Religious Mobility to Dynamic Religious Identities," when discussing the idea of religious repertoires.

To conclude, in this section we examined the prevalence of return mobility in the lives of Kenyans from several angles. We have shown how, in many cases, and notwithstanding the discourse on freedom of worship, religious mobility is not wholly voluntary in the sense of involving a disembodied actor, but should rather be understood within a larger frame that includes social norms and external pressures. We have suggested that Kenyan Christians often maintain an inactive yet relevant attachment to former engagements and affiliations. Moreover, we showed how, beyond the level of practice, return mobility can be understood within the particularities of the Kenyan socioreligious context through such popular features as aggressive evangelization, patriarchal patterns of religious change upon marriage, and circular rural-urban migration.

A Precarious Religious Landscape: Scandals, Schisms, and Sects

The diversification of the Kenyan religious landscape is often celebrated as a manifestation of Kenyans' freedom of worship. Such diversity, however, is also cited as having a dark side. In this section, we dwell on several challenges that emphasize the fragility of the Kenyan religious landscape, which we shorthand as "the three S's": scandals, schisms, and sects. By bringing up these points, we are certainly not implying that Kenya's religious landscape is hopelessly fragile and corrupt. Rather, because of the wealth of data on the question of institutional precariousness emerging from our research in Kenya, we found this chapter to be the most suitable place to develop this topic. Later on, we expound upon these observations and generalize them beyond the specifics of any single country case study. In doing so, we shall explore the connection between concern with institutional trust – often circulated by rumors – and religious mobility. While significant, this connection is in no way straightforward: at times, religious scandals stimulate mobility for a disillusioned flock or even force it due to institutional collapse. Conversely, hair-raising stories about the deviations that hide in other places of worship are sometimes enough to deter people from leaving their own religious safe haven. Yet a third outcome of such institutional misgivings might be a stay-at-home attitude to religion, which we have termed "church zappers" after the safe-distance spectatorship of Kenyan televangelism that is common within this group (Gez 2018, 189, 273; Gez et al. 2017, 149).[21]

The Kenyan religious landscape is replete with scandals – that is, stories of inappropriate conduct whose discovery disrupts institutional confidence.[22] Such confidence is essential to the emotional connection and sense of moral guidance so closely associated with religion, and its erosion has consequences both for the individual and for society as a whole (Gez and Droz 2015). In Kenya today, the term "hypocrisy" is often used in the context of religious behavior.[23] A feeling that "something has gone wrong" with Kenyan Christianity is widespread, and "tuning in" to

Nairobi's "sidewalk radio" – to borrow Stephen Ellis's (1989) term – of popular tales and rumors, one encounters stories and aphorisms that suggest a gap between past and present, for instance, by suggesting that preachers today "preach water and drink wine," that they are "wolves in sheep's clothing," or that they are "out to fleece the flock" since "churches nowadays have become a business." More than a merely descriptive statement, this last saying implies a popular sentiment whereby, to cite one of our interviewees, "the prosperity gospel has gone too far," and Christianity is now compromised by economic interests (Gathogo 2011). Thus, a typical comment by a newspaper reader suggests that "the last decade has witnessed an explosion of prosperity churches where the Bible is used to rob innocent Kenyans of their hard-earned cash" (To the Editor 2012, 14).

So widespread is the concern with such deviant religious behavior that it is even widely discussed from the pulpit, with religious leaders competing to distance themselves from "M-Pesa pastors."[24] Thus, for example, in 2010, Nairobi's popular Mavuno Church, which primarily targets urban youth, conducted a survey in order to detect issues its congregants were grappling with concerning their faith. Later that year, the church ran a series of sermons addressing the themes raised by the survey. One theme that was highlighted by many church members was religious hypocrisy. In a sermon that drew much interest and carried the provocative title "Why Are Christians Hypocrites?" (Mavuno Church 2010), the church's lead pastor, Pastor Muriithi Wanjau, acknowledged that inconsistency between a pietistic façade and actual behavior is widespread in Nairobi and causes many to lose faith in, and even to reject, organized Christianity. The pastor criticized the behavior of religious leaders, saying:

> I imagine most of you heard of a pastor who was preaching the gospel on Sunday and was involved in sexual liaisons during the week, or who was stealing and embezzling church money during the week, or who only got into this position of preaching because they wanted to amass power, personal power, for themselves. No wonder then that many have said: "I could never become a Christian – they are just a bunch of hypocrites." (Mavuno Church 2010)

It might be illuminating to expand on one such typical high-profile scandal, which combines three common, unbecoming motifs: misappropriation of funds, sexual misconduct, and hyperbolic promises of miracles. The scandal, which exploded in mid-2012, followed the coming forth on national television of a sex worker from the Nairobi neighborhood of Embakasi called Esther Mwende, who accused the lead pastor and televangelist at Fire Gospel Ministries, Pastor Michael Njoroge, of hiring her and other girls to give false testimonies of miraculous healings. Mwende's "healing"' – she pretended to suffer from a twisted jaw – was done live on the televangelist's program (NTV Kenya 2012a). In the original NTV coverage and its follow-ups, the televangelist's healing session was played alongside Mwende's televised confession, causing a huge stir and public outcry. In fact, the story generated so much popular interest that a special DVD containing NTV's original coverage began circulating in the informal video markets. According to one vendor we spoke to in the slum of Kawanguare, the DVD became a hit and was soon sold out. In the aftermath of the scandal, voices abounded demanding strict regulations in order to rein in such "M-Pesa pastors."

The scandal was unusual in its persistence in the Kenyan public eye. When, a year after the story first erupted, we discussed church regulation with one of our Kenyan interlocutors via email, he wrote back with concern:

> Actually, if you are successful in registering a church, I think it ends there. Unless there is a problem in the church, there is no institution, governmental or non-governmental, that follows you. That is why funny things happen in churches. By the way, do you know that that pastor of Fire Ministries is still pastoring? No one monitors what the church and its leadership does!

Not long before receiving this electronic comment, in April 2013, we noted a journalist's remark referencing the story (Kinuthia 2013, 17). Moreover, many of our interviewees, even as late as 2014, referred to the story, indicating that even in the fast-paced world of Kenya's religious and political scandals, the Fire Gospel Ministries exposé has become something of a symbol that has left its mark on people's minds. Indeed, it is a story that brought forth with particular force the question of vetting church leaders and inspecting religious institutions, and came to epitomize all that is problematic about the uncontrolled spread of Pentecostal churches in the technological age.

Stories of religious misconduct are often circulated by word of mouth. Of the many that we have heard, we offer two illustrations. First, let us consider the story told by Miriam, a Nairobi family woman about fifty years old. Miriam's story was framed as a warning against associating with the wrong kind of religious institutions, and it involved an old university friend called Sarah, whom Miriam presented as beautiful and intelligent. According to Miriam's dramatic story, Sarah fell in love with a Nigerian man who was involved with a branch of Winners' Chapel in Mombasa.[25] Sarah followed the Nigerian to Mombasa, got saved, and "joined full ministry" at

Winners – that is to say, left her old job in order to dedicate herself to the church full time. But what seemed at first like a legitimate Christian choice soon turned out – according to Miriam – to be a dangerous sect:

> In Mombasa, that is where she got hypnotized, because that is where they were told [that] when you serve a man of God you are serving God. So the girls used to have sex with these guys. So she used to have sex with the pastors, and the pastors are married, and the young girls also used to have sex with the, with the … with the women of the pastors … and then they used to be given hooves, you know hooves, cow hooves, and I think this thing has the thing of retarding your brain or something, I didn't remember … So she really lived a very hard life. And they were locked up in the, like a cemetery. (Interview with Miriam, Nairobi 2012)

Another eerie element mentioned by Miriam was the drinking of blood brought in from Nigeria, which was mixed with wine and served at the Lord's Table.[26] Eventually, after running into an old friend from university, Sarah was convinced that she should run away. Having escaped to Nairobi, she was forced to change her name and live under a false identity. The story's veracity is secondary to its demonstration of real concerns regarding the gravity that it portrays regarding engagement with religious forms that are widely deemed as suspicious.

Less dramatic, yet in some respects similar, was the story of Charles, a Kisumu family man in his late thirties, who told us of an old friend named Mike. Mike was said to have been conned by his pastor at Redeemed Church, who convinced him to donate a large plot from his countryside home to the church. Charles explained that, for Mike's family, the most disturbing aspect of that decision was that his stepmother was buried there.[27] The pastor, it appeared, had "lied to Mike that he is going to put that plot into the church, but then he went and put that plot in his own name." A year after registering the plot under his name, Mike found out, to his dismay, that the pastor had sold the plot, and Mike decided to take the buyer to court. "Mike spent much of his money, the money that he gained from selling plots," Charles said, "battling for that piece of plot that he had given unto the pastor, so Mike ended up with no money."

Such widely circulated stories have clear ramifications for religious mobility. The story of Miriam's university friend Sarah ends with her becoming a changed person and losing all faith in churches. According to Miriam, as a result of her traumatic experiences, today Sarah "just lives; she goes through life like that [without religion], she can't go to church, she can't pray, she doesn't know what to believe in." Similarly, Charles's story about Mike ended with religious mobility, because "after

[Mike's] frustration [with the pastor], he left the church, and I understand he went back to [the] Catholic [Church], and he is now living somewhere in Uganda across the border." Both Miriam and Charles drew from these stories lessons for their own religious "dos and don'ts." Charles – an unaffiliated Christian – concluded that "after listening to Mike's story with the reverend, there are so many stories with reverends that I have heard, that make me get scared being involved with so many churches at the same time, you see? So that's why I said I am not so sure which church I can follow."

Often related to scandals – but not necessarily – are instances of church schism. By that we refer to the precariousness of religious institutions, especially with regard to small independent denominations, which are highly prone to splintering, most commonly due to leadership wrangles between charismatic leaders. Moreover, small denominations often suffer from instability due to lack of funds, insufficient support base, and inefficient management, which may lead to their eventual collapse.[28] Demonstrating how leadership wrangles and church collapses due to inadequate foundations are linked to religious mobility, let us consider the story told by Simon, a lay Pentecostal in his thirties from Kisumu. Recounting how he ended up in his present church, he first explained the circumstances in his previous two churches:

> We had mismanagement of the church fund, so some members who were in the [church] committee they start fighting with the leader of the church. By that time he was a bishop. So they decided to split. When they split, that bishop went, now he is in Kilifi, Eastern [Province], and the other members made their [own] church. So when that bishop left, he left me with some members, few members, and he told me that I will be acting as a pastor first, before he arranges for the next move. (Interview with Simon, Kisumu 2014)

Having had no prior experience in church leadership, Simon felt unable to keep the few remaining congregants under him. Moreover, he soon discovered that maintaining a church is expensive and impossible to do without generous congregational contributions:

> When he [the bishop] decided to move, he left me, he left me, it was about three members that he left me with, so we had to pay the rent of the church, [as well as] other payments, you see. If a member had a problem, you are a leader, you have to deal with that. At such time, those members start moving to other churches, so I remained, I remained alone. (Interview with Simon, Kisumu 2014)

A few months after the schism, Simon gave up, and on the symbolic date of January first, he closed down the church and joined another – this time as a lay person. Simon's story tells us about the impact of institutional instability on individual butinage: first, we observed the mobility of leaders and congregants at his church following the splinter; second, we observed the gradual trickling out of members from the church that Simon tried to maintain after the split; and last, we observed Simon's own mobility due to his eventual decision to abandon his unviable church and join another.

In this section, we discussed the question of religious schisms, sects, and scandals. We suggested that they can be understood as related to an atmosphere of disrupted trust and that together they draw an image of a precarious religious landscape.[29] In many cases, they go hand in hand, as schism may result from disillusionment with the conduct of a religious leader; from suspicion over non-normative, sect-like practices; or from leadership wrangles that went sour to the point that congregants lost faith in their leader. We further observed how such experiences influence religious butinage. Practitioners are either pushed out by a splintering or collapsing church, or choose to leave following institutional disillusionment.

On a more general level, we suggest that the precariousness of the religious landscape, where new independent churches and their leaders may be here today and gone tomorrow, intensifies a sense of dissociation between individual religious identity and the organizations followed. It appears that the central definer of religious identity in urban Kenya today is not so much the religious institutions to which the practitioner belongs, but the personal manifestation of religious devotion and the personal relation to God, as displayed most prominently in the division into born-again and non–born-again Christians. Independent of the religious institution as a key religious definer, and in light of the changing face of an unstable religious landscape, the religious practitioner is free to chart their own religious itinerary – keeping in mind the risks of certain socially unacceptable sects and the social expectations to keep to the territory of normative Christianity.

Conclusion

In the early 2000s, the Nairobi Urban Integration Research Project collected questionnaire data on over 1,500 respondents in the city of Nairobi. Out of this total, 457 (nearly 30 percent) claimed to have changed their religious denomination at least once since birth (Wafula 2003; Bocquier et al. 2009). While our findings in this chapter fit well with such data, we dwelled on a number of features easily overlooked in statistical analysis by discussing the structure of often-minute forms of mobility, such as the distinction between membership and visits, and the popularity of return mobility. To offer a fuller picture of the socioreligious ethos in Christian Kenya, we also discussed key features of the religious landscape itself, including the explosion of new religious forms and the prevalence of schisms, scandals, and sects.

The Kenyan case confronts us with an interesting tension. On the one hand, this religious landscape is replete with discourse advocating the legitimacy of religious mobility through ideas of "freedom of worship" and "following God's call" wherever it may lead. On the other hand, it also tends to sanction practitioners' practice outside the legitimate sphere of mainstream Christianity. Some indication of how this tension is maintained was provided through the hierarchical distinction between membership and visits, which compartmentalizes some instances of religion practice as belonging and other instances as exploration. Another part of the answer to the apparent tension between freedom and confinement can be drawn from the notion of territories, which we will return to in chapter 7. In exercising their religious freedom, Kenyans largely keep to a particular territory that we may call legitimate Christianity. Beyond that territory, and in line with the concern over institutional trust mentioned earlier, Kenyans fear not only corrupt leaders but also cult-like tendencies involving religious traditions posing as legitimate, but actually drawing their powers from the spiritual "dark side." Indeed, while Kenyan Christians may be fascinated with religious forms located outside this territory or at its edge, they tend to be wary of crossing over and actually engaging with them. Clearly, such a reading should not ignore the significant disagreements between Christian denominations themselves and the obvious differences in personal variations and preferences. Yet, by and large, when asked to draw up an imaginary map of the territory of their potential religious engagements, our interviewees presented it in inclusive normative Christian terms, suggesting that they would be willing to engage themselves – at least as visitors – with a wide range of denominations as long as they qualify as "genuine" or "legitimate" Christian churches.

At the same time, the Kenyan preoccupation with truthfulness and trust versus hypocrisy highlights core questions with regard to the tension between confession and practice, and draws attention to the performative side of religion. In this respect, there is much to learn from the field of anthropology, in which social performance is recognized through a host of religious and other social rituals. This outlook has even led the prominent scholar of rituals, Victor Turner (1982), to liken the work of the ethnographer to that of the ethno-dramaturge. Beyond the study of faraway cultures and rituals, performance is embedded in everyday social practices. According to Goffman (1959), social life is organized largely through inference regarding reported events that take place beyond an individual's immediate sphere of perception. This absence of direct knowledge allows people significant leeway in developing and perfecting their images and roles so as to elicit particular social responses. As we have discussed throughout this book, conversion narratives, testimonies, and statements of religious conviction all involve a declarative aspect of social performance, which may be tainted by implicit pressure on the narrator to conform to normative paradigms and to proselytize others. Performativity in religion becomes especially noteworthy when we recognize that religious identity may not be reified as stable and fixed, but is associated with an ongoing project of locating identity within the social matrix (Day 2011).

The Kenyan case demonstrates how the language of performance is especially intuitive when speaking about Pentecostals and charismatics, who are prone to professing and enacting their religion publicly (see, for example, Gez 2018; Gez and Droz 2015) and whose millenarian goals of evangelizing and reenchanting a secularized world seek to imbue everyday action, from a handshake to picking up a phone call. Moreover, belief in the spiritual potency of words leads many Pentecostals and charismatics to endorse what is sometimes referred to as "naming and claiming": making declarative statements about desired outcomes in order to attract them into their life or acting as if these are already within reach. Beyond these everyday practices, Pentecostalism also involves straightforward staged spectacles animated by religious specialists, ranging from Sunday services to open air "crusades" to televised shows. While such staged performances may be presented as spontaneous and adhering to direct pneumatological inspiration, they tend to follow more or less fixed scripts (Droz 2000a, 2000b). Pursuing this line of inquiry can shed new light on personal – both social and psychological – tensions and raise new questions regarding the coexistence of the declarative and the practiced registers of religious identity.

5 Mobility Intertwined: Migration, Kinship, and Education in Ghana

In this chapter, we discuss how complex patterns of geographic mobility serve as an underlying structure for religious mobility in Ghana and how mobility along geographic, familial, and educational lines may go hand in hand with changes in religious practices. Over the last two decades, scholars have increasingly addressed the role of religion in the context of migration and mobility. Geographic relocation, international migration, change of residence within a country or even within an immediate neighborhood – in other words, changing a person's living conditions – has a bearing on their religious practices and belongings. Scholars have commonly observed how, to quote Afe Adogame, "religion is largely at the pivot of immigrants' sense of individual and collective identities, and immigrant communities serve as focal points for religious and social networks" (Adogame 2003, 24). Scholarship in migratory – mostly Western – contexts discusses how religion becomes a key social institution, which offers an enclave of familiarity and empowerment where tensions between integration and group distinctiveness and cohesion are worked out.[1]

To adopt a schematic and somewhat simplistic perspective, it appears that two avenues for religious engagement are open to the migrant.[2] The first involves persisting in their former practices and affiliations, using them to form a safe haven of familiarity and stability in the face of changing circumstances. Such religious continuity can be taken to prove the transnationalization of religion, which is closely associated with the age of globalization whose hallmark is the circulation of individuals and ideas around the globe. The second entails adapting to the new setting by assuming an alternative religious affiliation. As we have seen with regard to rural-urban mobility in Kenya, geographic mobility challenges the smooth continuity of religious practices: just as some individuals may assert their faith in the face of new cultural settings, others might be inspired to rethink their religious practices and even to jettison their old religious affiliation in favor of a new one (Chen 2005). Such religious mobility may be encouraged by a feeling of liberation from former social constraints and by the intent to uncover their "authentic" self in the migratory context (Griffith 1997). It may also act as a coping strategy, a means for integration, or simply a response to newly encountered temptations. At times, such religious butinage is prompted by pragmatic considerations or mere necessity, as when moving to an area where their former denomination is not practiced. For some, geographic mobility can provide an opportunity to "take a breather" or abandon their religious involvement altogether (Bibby 1997). In the context of global migration, our exchanges with practicing Christians who have been living abroad for long periods of time show that living in a less religious setting, or in a setting where their own religion becomes a minority, strains their faith and may result in a religious crisis.

In fact, we believe that both options – geographic migration as resulting in withdrawal into "identity asylums" or as facilitating linear "religious transits" from one well-defined site to another – fail to exhaust the complex reorientations of identity that occur in the new setting. More often than not, the migratory moment is not finite, but proves to be only one moment within a wider pattern of circular or return migration (Newbold 2001; Duany 2002; Droz 2002a, 2016). In the previous chapter on Kenya, where rural and urban lives are strongly interwoven (Droz 1999), we saw how it is common to maintain a rich yet geographically well-demarcated religious identity. Thus, some people may consider themselves members of their family's traditional religious denomination whenever they stay in their rural home. When in the city, however, they might keep a different affiliation and set of practices. Interestingly, such identity compartmentalization is widely accepted.

Despite evidence to the contrary, religious mobility within migratory contexts is frequently portrayed in terms of unidirectional movements, an image strengthened by a common depiction of the migrant as disempowered and passive, led by push and pull factors such as political hazards (for example, armed conflicts and violence "at home") and geoeconomic considerations (for example, attractive employment conditions in the host setting). In fact, far from being the "victim" of external forces, the migrant can also be an active agent, taking responsibility by shaping their own life trajectory (Monnier and Droz 2004). While mobility trajectories may take place within a single religious worldview, the possibility of coming into contact with similar religious systems allows the migrant to actively engage with and negotiate between the familiar and the new, infusing a worldview with novel, borrowed, and adjusted content.

Research in Ghana was conducted in 2014 by Rey, who had already studied the transnational Ghanaian diaspora during her doctoral work in Switzerland (2007–10) and in Ghana (2010). She later extended her fieldwork to the Ghanaian diaspora in Canada (Toronto, 2013–14) and narrowed down her focus to religious mobility. In 2014, she returned to Accra to expand her study. Most of the interview examples presented here derive from this latter field research period, where Rey drew on previously established contacts from religious – mostly Pentecostal-charismatic – networks using the snowball method. At the same time, she expanded her research to new religious territories and visited other Christian denominations as well as mosques. In order to limit biases caused by the choice of religious entry points, she also identified some of her interviewees in public places, including markets, streets, and public transportation.

Religious Pluralism in Ghana

Long before the Abrahamic religions made their way to the coast and the northern part of what is now Ghana, the ancient Gold Coast had been home to a wide repertoire of religious traditions. The plurality of spiritual entities in Akan and other West African cosmogonies were the outcome of encounters with, and incorporation of, "foreign" traditions over the course of history, in which human migrations, trade, conflicts, and wars all played a role. This process continued during and after colonial times. The emergence of the figure of Mami Wata – a "water spirit" whose multiple traits are often associated with wealth – offers an excellent example of the emergence of a new, syncretistic entity, with local variations and a plurality of discursive, ritualistic, and artistic expressions, along the Guinea Gulf (Drewal 2008; Jewsiewicki 2003) and, eventually, the Ghanaian diaspora (Rey 2013a). Indeed, the process of invention, appropriation, and re-signification of spiritual entities and their associated practices is at the heart of the creative "vitality of paganism" (Mary 1998).

The gradual penetration of Islam and Christianity into the region since the fifteenth century meant not only the dissemination of new religious systems but also the arrival of new power configurations and cultural technologies, such as books. One major expression of this new power, to take a Foucauldian perspective (Foucault 1984), was the definition of new religious boundaries and principles of differentiation based on the idea of "faith," alongside their concomitant practices. Christian and Muslim institutions, which rely on the idea of exclusivism in religious affiliation, practices, and beliefs as well as clear universal categories of "religion" (Horton 1971), spread through the construction of churches, mosques, mission dispensaries, and schools (Graham 1971; Skinner 2013). This expansion led to a sharper differentiation between religious identities, with consequences ranging from the destruction of indigenous shrines to peaceful cohabitation and cross-fertilization between religious practices. In the nineteenth-century Ashanti Kingdom, for example, "Muslims lived under the hospitality of infidel kings, who generally were praised by Muslims for their benevolence toward the believers" (Levtzion and Pouwels 2000, 3). The Ashanti King (*Asantehene*) Osei Tutu Kwame recognized both traditional and Muslim remedies and healing rituals (Owusu-Ansah 2000). Ghana's contemporary medical pluralism (Krause 2006) seems to be rooted in that particular political history. At the same time, traditional Ashanti authorities also perceived external ideologies advocated by European missionaries and orthodox Muslims as a threat to the internal peace of Ashanti society, which strongly relied on indigenous religious mediation (Müller 2013).

Nowadays, Ghana is a country with significant religious pluralism, which has continued to diversify over recent decades. For example, in his book *The Lies That Bind*, Ghanaian-American thinker Kwame Anthony Appiah (2018, 66) describes traditional Ashanti ancestral worship as "taken by most people – Asante Catholic bishops and imams included! – to be perfectly consistent with having other confessional allegiances, with being Muslim or Christian." While northern Ghana is considered to be predominantly Muslim and southern Ghana predominantly Christian, a long history of migration and proselytism has created a complex religious tapestry. Besides Islam, Christianity, and indigenous ritual systems, other religious traditions – such as Buddhism and Hinduism (Wuaku 2009) – have also gained presence, albeit a more modest and less visible one, contributing to religious cross-fertilization. But even within the country's three principle religious traditions, Ghana has experienced great religious diversification associated with new developments within these religions themselves: most notably, the expansion of Pentecostal-charismatic movements and reformist Islam throughout the twentieth and twenty-first centuries (Kaba 2000; Larbi 2001). In the case of the former, the pluralization of the religious field is further enhanced by schismatic tendencies nurtured by institutional competition and the hope for social mobility through church planting (Rey 2019). In southern Ghana, ever since the 1990s we have witnessed a resurgence of indigenous ritual practices, which often go unnoticed in official statistics (Müller 2013).

On the public and political level, religious pluralism is supported by councils and institutions, such as the Ghana Conference of Religions for Peace. On the level of individual practitioners, religious boundaries can be overcome through conversion, intermarriage, or an interplay of religious practices (for example, Islamic or Christian and indigenous ritual practices). Thus, writing on Christianity in Ghana, Elizabeth Graveling recognizes this tendency for mobility by assessing that "very few people attend only one denomination of church throughout their life; most switch at least three times" (Graveling 2010, 207). And yet, peaceful religious coexistence is not always guaranteed, and tensions between religious groups do sometimes emerge. Within both Christian and Muslim conservative circles, a change in religious affiliation can have dramatic consequences, even resulting in becoming distanced from family. Beyond the psychological distress that such estrangement entails, it often has a bearing on access to material resources. Notably, in Ghana as in other places, the Pentecostal injunction to "break with the past" (Meyer 1998) often implies severing ties with extended family, which, due to the "pagan" nature of kinship-related indigenous rituals, is seen as a point of entry for demonic influences.[3] Traditionalists have been responding to the breaking of customary religious rituals by members of other religious groups with sanctions and protests, which at times escalate into outright conflict (Van Dijk 2001).

Religious Trajectories: Intertwined Kinship, Migration, and Educational Strategies

Prior to studying religious mobility in Ghana, Rey's (2013b, 2018) ethnography of African migrants in Switzerland highlighted the strong appeal of charismatic diasporic churches. For many participants in African-led church services, migration from Africa to Europe coincided with a change in religious affiliation. People who had been Presbyterians, Catholics, Adventists, or Methodists in Ghana turned to charismatic or Pentecostal groups upon arrival to Switzerland. This move was often preceded by a period of active butinage within the new country, involving both visits and temporary engagement with multiple churches. Such intense mobility, however, tended to attenuate over time, ending with an affiliation with a single church that most fitted the migrant's preferences, even though occasional visits to other churches were never completely abandoned. Rey further noted that most migrants paid little attention to the question of their own religious mobility. For most of them, changing affiliations was not an issue per se and was not conceived in dramatic terms. Rather, it was simply a response to the new social context and an alternative to integrating into a local "white" church belonging with their original denomination (see Fancello and Mary 2010). Social, cultural, and linguistic barriers, as well as networking opportunities, proved to be much more significant factors in migrants' religious trajectories than institutional continuity or prior familiarity with formal church doctrine. These findings support the premise that migration and religious mobility often go hand in hand.

In Ghana, too, geographic mobility is very commonly intertwined with religious mobility. There, geographic mobility (for example, from a village to the city) often implies other types of mobility, such as mobility within kinship systems or educational mobility. Mobility within kinship systems includes any change in an individual's household unit, for instance, due to marriage and work opportunities, as well as any circulation within a multisited kinship structure. In the Kenyan context, Droz and Sottas (1997) observed that the multisited nature of family structures supports mobility strategies both at the individual and collective levels, opening opportunities for accessing various resources. In Ghana, multisited kinship structures are also common and open new perspectives for family members, in particular for the youth. Educational mobility similarly constitutes a frequent motivation for geographic mobility – within or outside family household networks – at an age when individuals are particularly prone to religious conversion and change in religious affiliation. Religious mobility thus appears to be embedded in a broader set of mobility patterns involving geographical, kinship, and educational dimensions, as we will present throughout the following case studies.

Anita: From the Village to the City

Anita's parents live in Ghana's Upper East Region, where she grew up as a Muslim. As the daughter of a pious *hajji*,[4] back in the village her religious education and identity were confined to Islam. Anita never set foot in a church until she first visited her family in Accra as a high school student. While in the city, she accepted an invitation from her sister's friend to visit her charismatic church. There, Anita says, she was "touched by the message," and once she returned to her parents' home, she refused to recite the Islamic prayers. Worried, her parents questioned her, but she refused to explain the motivation for her decision. After finishing high school, in 2012, she moved to Accra, where she lived with her maternal aunt and studied business and marketing. She converted to Christianity at the same charismatic church she visited several months earlier and became a full member. She received her Christian name, and her sister and aunt, both of whom have also converted to Christianity, recognized her by her new name, "Anita." Her parents, however, continue to use her Muslim name, "Amina," as she did not reveal her conversion to them. According to Anita, her parents would not tolerate her choice and, should they discover her conversion, would stop funding her studies in Accra, putting her in a precarious situation. She noted that, compared to other families around her, her parents – especially her father – are less tolerant toward conversion to other religions. While some families in the Upper East Region accommodate members of different religions without conflict, Anita attributes her father's intolerance to his strong attachment to Islam, his piety, and his status as a *hajji*. Yet, she suggested that she would reveal her new religion to her parents once she completed her studies and no longer depended on them financially.

Anita's strategy for coping with her diachronic religious mobility while preserving kinship relationships and ensuring her parents' financial support relies on a concealment strategy, where each religious affiliation is mobilized in a geographically distinct context. In the north, she is still perceived as a Muslim, albeit non-practicing; in the south, she evolves within her new identity as a charismatic Christian. Her case is not exceptional, though strategies for coping with such a situation vary. As conversion to Christianity often occurs among Ghanaian Muslims moving to study in larger cities like Accra, their families may react in different ways. As we were later told by a leader at the Assemblies of God in Ghana, in some cases, the church would take over and sponsor students who were disowned by their families due to conversion to Christianity. In other cases, church leaders would pragmatically advise the students to be cautious about announcing their conversion to relatives, proposing instead to wait for the right moment. Anita' story shows how geographic mobility may facilitate religious change, especially in social settings that impose strict institutional religious loyalty, while regarding diachronic religious mobility – certainty into a completely different, Christian, territory – as transgressive.

More broadly, Anita's trajectory is illustrative of a broader trend, which contributed to the continuous growth of Pentecostal and charismatic Christianity in Ghana over the last decades: migration from rural regions to large urban environments (Fancello 2006). In cities, these churches, whose size and organizational structures range from small "prayer cells" to megachurches, offer a tightly knit social environment that recreates a sense of community and even family, as exemplified by support to dispossessed students: a particularly meaningful experience for migrants who feel disoriented in the new urban setting.

George: Moving along Kinship and Educational Lines

George is a retired minister at a large Ghanaian Pentecostal denomination. We first met at the launching event of his denomination's new mission program. In our successive meetings, George recounted his twenty-odd years of experience as a church program manager, overseeing evangelization throughout the country, including in the countryside. While his church's modes of operation developed over time through new evangelization techniques, George argued that the general attitude toward other religious groups and practitioners has remained essentially unchanged since he entered the congregation. In a religiously diverse country like Ghana, many religious practitioners share the idea that they should avoid aggressive proselytization. George explained that his preachers are very careful about not insulting other religions when they go on a mission (for example, in villages), and they do not criticize "fetish priests" and their "idols" directly. "Jesus came for fetish priests, too," he said. Yet, he admitted that some Pentecostal or charismatic preachers "lack wisdom" and criticize idols and indigenous ritual practices, which inevitably creates tensions between born-again preachers and followers of traditional religions.

George's own acceptance of Pentecostalism, back in the late 1960s during his high school days near Accra, was itself the result of mission activities, which have brought him to renounce his Muslim faith. And yet, George was not born a Muslim but was brought up Christian in a family of mixed religious traditions. His father was a Fanti traditional chief in the Central Region. As part of his duty, he participated in religious ceremonies whenever needed, be they Christian or Islamic, and performed all the traditional rituals associated with his status. Like other chiefs in Ghana, he was closer to customary rituals than to any monotheistic faith; yet, he did not perceive them as religious. After his death, he had a traditional funeral, without any church involvement. George's mother, by contrast, was a Methodist. Although she did not go to church on a regular basis, George attended church services with her from time to time. Things changed when George moved to his maternal uncle's household in the Central Region to attend middle school. His uncle and cousins were all members of the Muslim Ahmadi community. When George's uncle asked him to convert to Islam, George accepted and, as long as he remained in his uncle's home, performed all the Islamic prayers and duties. After graduating from middle school, George left the Central Region to live in the Greater Accra region, where he attended high school. There, he met born-again Christians, converted, and became a member of the Pentecostal church where he would eventually minister.

As in Anita's case, the intertwining of geographic and religious mobility is obvious in George's trajectory. However, George's case is even more striking due to his mobility between households within the same kinship structure as well as his educational mobility, both of which have induced a diachronic butinage. George's decision to convert to a new religion when integrating into a new household might be considered in terms of respect toward his hosts within the nexus of family hierarchies and multisited kinship systems. Indeed, beyond George's case, we observed such a pattern of temporary religious mobility on several occasions. The young and mobile family member would adopt the religious practices of their elder and more senior host, with such temporary conversions making household routine more harmonious by having all household members follow a single religious code of conduct. Such were also our observations in Kenya.

In addition, we note how George's diachronic religious mobility is also linked to his educational trajectory. At each step of his formal studies, he shifted to another religion. His case points to the intersectionality of geographic, educational, and religious mobility. In the Kenyan context, Droz (1999; Droz et al. 2019) showed how geographic mobility and aspirations for socioeconomic advancement, together with religious mobility, are drawn upon in the context of individual quests for self-accomplishment. In George's trajectory, too, the three dimensions have intertwined, following his schooling trajectory. His educational projects required him to change geographic location, and the resulting shifts between households stimulated religious mobility.

Due to the historical intertwinement of specific religious practices with Ghana's formal educational system, religious mobility can also be related to adaptive educational strategies. George's conversion to Pentecostalism in the late 1960s happened at the dawn of a historical decade, when the Pentecostal-charismatic movement in Ghana was about to strike roots in university campuses and beyond (Gifford 2004a; Van Dijk 2001). Since then, major Pentecostal churches have continued to be active in (higher) education. In recent years, Ghanaian Pentecostal denominations (for example, the Assemblies of God) launched their own university programs, teaching "secular" subjects such as information technology (IT) and business administration. Thus, the intertwining of conversion to Pentecostalism and educational trajectories relates to the broader context of a changing educational landscape and new proselytizing strategies.

The analogy between kinship and religious belonging, which is a common trope used by many religious groups (Sharma 2012; Bonsu and Belk 2010), also carries implications for how education and religious mobility are interlaced. By using a kinship terminology ("brothers" and "sisters"), some religious groups may imitate the pattern of mobility within kinship structures. The church thus assumes the role of a "surrogate family," with its own parental hierarchy, obligations, and redistributive system, creating a sense of familiarity that may facilitate religious mobility toward charismatic churches. This pattern is strengthened by scholarship schemes, which churches sometimes offer to selected members. Thus, they assume the educational funding function that is usually associated with family. Such surrogate kinship may ease shifts from one religious system to another. In the same way that mobility within multi-sited families may result in religious mobility toward the host's religious practice, so might educational mobility intertwine with religious mobility. We observed such a pattern in a Pentecostal university offering "secular" bachelor's programs (for example, in business and engineering) in Kofuridua,[5] where Muslim students regularly participated in Christian prayers, at least for the duration of their studies at the Pentecostal campus.

Unlike Anita, George's successive conversions did not cause major troubles for his family relationships. Tolerance toward religious mobility is common in Ghanaian families and is sometimes explained in terms of preexisting religious diversity within the family. One interviewee, a leader of an Ahmadi community, elaborated on the movement's teaching whereby there should be no coercion in religious matters, which, according to him, explains why Ahmadi families often show a high degree of religious pluralism. Similarly, a young ambulance driver from Kumasi described how each of his siblings had been baptized in a different church. He had chosen to become Catholic, like his parents, but his four sisters decided to be baptized in four different churches: the eldest in the Church of Pentecost; the second in the Methodist Church; the third in the Presbyterian Church; and the youngest, who recently turned eighteen and was thereby granted religious autonomy by the family, was recently baptized in a charismatic church. The family's parents have been accommodating, believing that religious affiliation is a choice that must be made by the children themselves. To illustrate what was for him self-evident, the young driver said: "If you like fufu,[6] you cannot force your child to like and eat fufu." This quotation illustrates how some families are reluctant to intervene in their members' religious decisions and impose their religious identities as a kinship obligation. Such a view is further supported by popular wisdom about the obvious character of the existence of God, which is explicit in the Akan proverb "*obi nkyere akwadaa Nyame*" ("nobody can teach a child about God"). While the belief in God is perceived as self-evident, the fufu metaphor highlights the relative tolerance toward diverse religious affiliations within the same family – as if it were a question of personal culinary taste – as accommodating the practice of butinage.

Abraham and Grace: When Religion and Kinship Overlap

The family's attitude toward religious mobility may also depend on the type of religious affiliation taken up by its members and the position that they occupy within a religious institution. Some religious contexts – like the Catholic or Ahmadi communities in Ghana – seem more porous than others and serve as a lenient basis for diachronic mobility. Other institutions conceive religious mobility as more transgressive and tend to enforce severe sanctions on their members who cross boundaries, sometimes to the effect of jeopardizing an entire kinship system. Such a strict stance is evident in the case of Abraham and Grace, two committed members of Jehovah's Witnesses.

Abraham's father converted to Jehovah's Witnesses in order to marry Abraham's mother, who became a member in her youth, following her parents' conversion. As Jehovah's Witnesses only allow marriage within their own community, the couple and their four children – Abraham has three sisters – joined the community in Accra. Grace, by contrast, came from a Catholic family in the Volta Region, where she grew up and lived until moving to the capital. When Abraham and Grace first met, she worked as a secretary at a foreign embassy, while he was employed in an export company in the city of Tema, right outside Accra. At that time, he was seeking to extricate himself from his family's grasp and was therefore living at his employer's home. He met Grace in the street, and they began to meet regularly and soon fell in love. When Grace got pregnant, they announced it to her family, who suggested they should marry. Abraham, however, knew that his parents would not accept the marriage, both because sexual intercourse before marriage is forbidden among Jehovah's Witnesses and because Grace was a Catholic. Indeed, his parents informed the church leaders, who then summoned Abraham to clarify his situation. He confessed to his actions and consequently lost his position as a ministering servant within the church.

Even though Abraham's parents reproved his marriage with a Catholic woman, he and Grace still decided to get married. Despite Jehovah's Witnesses' view that marriage should be carried out either in the church or in a traditional way, Grace and Abraham did both. They first got married in Grace's village, close to the town of Hohoe, according to Ewe customs, and then got married at the Catholic Church. Nobody from Abraham's immediate family attended the wedding, which they opposed on religious grounds. Abraham's best man thus symbolically filled the role of his family, inviting some of his own family members as a substitute. Yet, Abraham felt an urge to restore relations with his family, and only Grace's conversion to Jehovah's Witnesses, after their marriage, succeeded in partly relieving the tensions with Abraham's family. The couple integrated into the community, and Grace became a very active church member, while Abraham was allowed to pray with the congregation again. Abraham improved his relationship with his parents, although he felt that his father was still upset with him, suggesting that their relationship has changed forever. Abraham argues that it is "normal" that his family was absent from his wedding, because he had committed a sin and had to pay for it. Grace's conversion also had an impact on her own family, as it resulted in religious mobility among some of her family members. For example, Grace's younger sister had been living in Accra and was hosted in the couple's house. During her stay, she became a committed Jehovah's Witness, to the delight of her hosts. Yet, since her return to the Volta Region, she did not visit Jehovah's Witnesses again and instead went back to the Catholic Church – to which most of her family members were affiliated.

Abraham's departure from Jehovah's Witnesses had been forced on him due to his religious transgression. And yet, his role in the story was not entirely passive, and his actions show how individual religious practitioners may at times risk defying church rules. Indeed, even in contexts where institutional norms strictly prohibit religious mobility or intimate relationships with nonbelievers, people might not comply, but seek to balance their various commitments, roles, and interests. In the final analysis, transgression and rupture are sometimes perceived as the "right" thing to do, as they allow one to pragmatically balance conflicting commitments in a given situation (Daswani 2013; Lambek 2010). Unlike Anita, Abraham and Grace enjoyed financial autonomy, which significantly lowered their degree of dependency on their families and allowed them to temporarily sever ties with them. Nevertheless, in order to restore their relationships with Abraham's family, Grace had to convert to Abraham's faith and become a committed member of Jehovah's Witnesses. Religious mobility helped the couple resolve a crucial dilemma: Abraham's Catholic wedding and Grace's subsequent conversion to the Jehovah's Witnesses allowed them to find a way through this complex situation, despite incompatible family expectations and religious obligations.

In a neighboring West African context, Katrin Langewiesche (2003) analyzed religious boundaries in Burkina Faso. She observed that these boundaries have a strong discursive nature and tend to be much more porous in practice than in theory. While both individual practitioners and religious institutions emphasize the role of fixed and bounded religious identities, these boundaries are crossed more often than these discourses suggest. Other authors referred to similar practices in other West African countries, such as the "religious shoppers" in Nigeria (Janson 2016) and, to a lesser extent, the occasional socially or practically motivated mobile practitioner in Mali (Soares 2016). These observations are also relevant to our case study in Accra. And yet, the institutional factor remains important, as not all religious groups offer a similar degree of tolerance toward religious mobility. Rupture in social relationships, including kinship ties, is one of the most common patterns exhibited by strict religious institutions in sanctioning departing members.

One reason why religious mobility may have a transgressive character from an institutional point of view lies in the conflict between different normative practices and prohibitions across religious institutions. In hindsight, the most problematic element for Abraham with regard to his own religious trajectory was linked to the fact that he had to take communion at his Catholic wedding. According to him, because the wedding was his own, he had no choice but to take communion, despite Jehovah's Witnesses' teachings that only certain God-chosen people, who remain virgin their entire life, may take communion and, even then, would do so only once a year. Those who know they are not among these chosen people and yet transgress this prohibition will draw a curse upon themselves. This teaching has brought about significant worries for Abraham, and he still prays to be forgiven for his transgressions. He is still struggling to deal with the gap between these two normative systems of practice that he has engaged in throughout his religious trajectory.

Additional Practices: Logics and Economies of Religious Mobility

Besides diachronic trajectories, religious mobility may also unfold through multiple concurrent practices within the same temporal frame, which we call synchronic mobility. Like in Kenya, Ghanaian religious practitioners tend to maintain a single main affiliation – their primary one, which we shall later term a "pivot" – while potentially incorporating secondary practices. We propose that these additional practices may be embedded in specific "economies" that carry implications for how religious mobility is enacted.

As in Kenya and Brazil, visiting other people's church is part of the social fabric of Christians in Accra, a practice that contributes to the consolidation of social ties among neighbors, friends, and relatives. Accepting such an invitation is a matter of courtesy, as is its reciprocal nature. At the same time, such invitations are highly ambiguous because, by inviting acquaintances to their congregation, church members show their institutional loyalty and commitment to "gaining new souls" in the form of new members. Still, church visits vary between denominations and congregations, with some stricter congregations showing reluctance to let their members wander elsewhere, even temporarily (Gez and Droz 2017). Besides responding to such occasional invitations, all our interviewees in Ghana admitted attending religious services outside their own community on specific occasions as part of their social obligations to take part in rites of passages such as weddings or funerals.

Anita, George, Abraham, and Grace all visit other religious communities on particular occasions. While Anita would go to Catholic services or to charismatic churches upon invitation, Abraham and Grace would not visit acquaintances' churches, as they stringently adhere to their church's exclusivist stance. During important social rituals such as funerals or weddings, they would attend ceremonies held by other religious communities, but will avoid active participation. For example, Abraham would not take communion if attending a funeral organized by his wife's Catholic family. By taking a back seat during such events, Abraham is not taking his cue only from Jehovah's Witnesses' exclusivist stance, but also from their teachings whereby, unlike the wider Ghanaian custom, funerals should not be celebrated in an extravagant fashion. For his part, George would also attend ceremonies related to various traditions within his multireligious family. He explained, moreover, that, due to his formal function in his Pentecostal church, he sometimes has to represent his congregation in religious events outside the church, mainly in other Pentecostal functions.

Mobility among religious and political leaders is also common in Ghana and highlights how the fragile balance between clearly delineated religious identities and the porousness of religious practices is a central component of the exercise of power in the country. The president of Ghana at the time we conducted our research, John Dramani Mahama (2012–17), hails from a multifaith family consisting of both Muslims and Christians, a fact that he often emphasized. Raised in the Presbyterian Church, he became a member of the Assemblies of God when he married his Pentecostal wife, who belongs to another ethnic group. With his roots in a religiously mixed family from northern Ghana and currently living in the southern capital as a member of the Assemblies of God, the president's trajectory supposedly embodied the socioreligious ethos of the Ghanaian nation, united across heterogeneous cultures, regions, and religions. The quest for unity across religious boundaries also remains the main objective of such institutions as the National Peace Council, which brings together religious representatives and leaders from Christian, Muslim, and traditional organizations. In moments of national transition, such as after the death of President John Atta Mills in 2012 and the elections that ensued later that year, this council implores the nation to maintain peace.

When it comes to accommodating public life, religious authorities enter various compromises, which sometimes go against their own institutional directives. One example is the funeral of the Ahmadi Amir of Ghana, Abdul Wahab Adam, who died in June 2014. While the Ahmadi religious directive clearly states that the burial should immediately follow the person's death and remain modest, the Ahmadi organization in Ghana decided to concede exceptions to that rule. As the Amir was an important state official, the community leaders decided to organize a formal funeral and to delay the burial in order to give political and religious dignitaries time to arrive. This decision, which met with criticism within the Ahmadi community, illustrates how compromises are reached in order to accommodate the conflicting expectations of multiple religious and social groups, as well as the requirements associated with community representation in a diverse country such as Ghana.

Besides social logic and institutional strategies, synchronic religious mobility may also involve practical logic oriented toward the achievement of specific goals or the resolution of concrete life challenges. These may include overcoming misfortunes and seeking healing and fertility, achieving financial and social prosperity, or seeking protection or justice. While this kind of religious mobility may eventually engender new religious affiliations (Droz 2002b), it often unfolds synchronically and without impacting the person's official religious identity. Indeed, for many people, such practically motivated mobility, consisting of "consultations" with people of great spiritual power, is seen as separate from questions of religious affiliation.

A good illustration of such mobility is offered by the case of Mehdi, a Sunni Muslim born in Accra, whose parents immigrated from Benin. Every Friday, Mehdi goes to the mosque for prayer, and he insists that he is a practicing Muslim, showing the mark on his forehead (*zebiba*) as proof of his piety. Nevertheless, whenever Mehdi wants to address a specific problem, he turns to a Christian pastor. Mehdi explained that he first tried to address his problems through Islamic prayer, but as no positive change occurred, he visited a pastor for help, which, in his experience, turned out to be more effective. Since then, he has been going to the mosque on Friday and to the church on weekdays (see Janson 2016). Despite these frequent visits to churches and even though he considers Christian prayers to be more effective, Mehdi claims that he has no intention of converting to Christianity. While Mehdi never consulted a local *juju* (fetish) priest about his problems, he would not rule out visiting one, for example, when accompanying a friend. In the months leading to our interview, he has been going to a church run by a female pastor from the northern part of Accra, whom he has been visiting with his sister who was worried about her pregnancy. The pastor prayed for her and, sure enough, Mehdi's sister gave birth to a healthy baby. When we interviewed him, Mehdi and his sister were intending to go back to the pastor and show her the baby so that she can pray for all of them. At times, Mehdi frequents another Christian pastor who would pray for his prosperity. His hope is that, one day, he could open his own business and achieve economic success.

This type of pragmatic religious mobility is supported by an "economy of blessings" (Rey 2015), which, in Ghana and beyond, underlies the religious landscape of Pentecostal prosperity theology (Heuser 2015). This economy involves an exchange between God and the religious practitioner, which is often mediated and regulated by religious specialists and institutions. Prayer, tithe, trust, intimacy, patience, as well as material goods are all central to this economy of blessings. To illustrate how this economy engenders religious mobility, we can consider the case of Kofi, a single young Catholic man, whose main dream has been to start a family. And yet, before marrying, Kofi said he would "need to do certain things," that is, ensure his economic success. He disapproves of Ghanaians who start a family at a very young age, as he believes that their children are doomed to economic deprivation. Kofi explained that he would first need to establish himself financially, because he wants his children to go to school. In order to achieve this objective, he ambitiously runs several businesses in parallel, and he expects that his prospective wife will be just as entrepreneurial. Having arrived in Accra from the Ashanti Region some ten years before our encounter, following in the footsteps of his maternal uncle's son, Kofi studied and worked for four years in a pharmacy until he received authorization to open his own drugstore. Yet, lacking the necessary funds, he turned to odd jobs in the hope of saving enough money to open his own pharmacy in a few years.

One of Kofi's various occupations has been as a taxi driver, and it is through that job that he met the pastor of the charismatic church he now attends on specific weekdays. He usually goes there on Wednesday or Friday evenings, when the church offers all-night prayers. Once, that pastor forgot his mobile phone in the car Kofi was renting. Even though selling the pastor's lost mobile phone could have been lucrative, Kofi decided to give it back. The pastor, touched by the young man's integrity, asked what he could give him in return. Kofi asked the pastor to pray for him every day. The pastor agreed and advised Kofi to remain virtuous and honest in the future. After that encounter, Kofi regularly returned to the pastor's charismatic church, until one day, the pastor offered him an old car, which he now uses for his work.[7] Owning a car allows Kofi to save up money and to come ever closer to his goal of opening a pharmacy. As a short-term goal, he would like to buy a *tro-tro* (Ghanaian "coach" or transport vehicle) for intercity transport or a second car that he could rent out to another driver. Attending Catholic Mass every Sunday did not keep Kofi from visiting the pastor's charismatic church and offering generous financial contributions there, sometimes as high as 200 or 300 cedis.[8] The pastor has become a trusted figure in Kofi's life, and Kofi regularly confides in him. For example, whenever Kofi has to travel outside Accra, he asks the pastor for spiritual guidance. Kofi believes in the pastor's spiritual powers, including his "gift of knowledge," and attentively follows his practical recommendations, which could range from caution in drinking certain types of filtered water to abstaining from certain journeys.

Kofi's relationship with the charismatic pastor involves the exchange of prayers, trust, and advice, as well as money and other material goods. It is representative of exchange practices that rely on a larger "economy of blessings," where God appears as the dispenser of wealth and other blessings. Yet, despite the importance of this religious involvement for his daily life and future projects, Kofi would not want to leave the Catholic Church, where he was baptized at the age of fourteen. His Sunday church attendance remains almost exclusively limited to his main affiliation with the Catholic Church. Like Mehdi, Kofi's synchronic religious mobility and multiple practices are temporally demarcated, with clear differentiation between his main affiliation and his additional weekdays practices.

Conclusion

Research on religion in Africa has had a tendency to explore Islam and Christianity along separate lines and to treat them as two distinct groups (Janson and Meyer 2016). Even in places where there is a long history of coexistence, such as Ghana, religious traditions, practices, and practitioners have rarely been analyzed as belonging to a "shared field of religious practices" (Dilger and Schulz 2013, 372). And yet, by analyzing the dynamism of individual religious practice, we observe that circulation across religious boundaries, including between Christian and Islamic territories, is common in the Ghanaian capital, as in neighboring Nigeria (Janson 2016). Thus, one important feature highlighted by the Ghanaian case study is that religious territories visited by religious practitioners might not be confined to a specific religion (for example, Christian denominations). As rightly stated by Larkin (2016, 634), "the emphasis on difference [between religions] is that it makes it difficult to analyze this more thickly constituted religious and secular environment and to understand quotidian entanglements of everyday encounter."

Therefore, we invite researchers to devote more attention to religious circulation across separate religious territories. On the institutional level, we can identify symbolic "bridges" (Birman 1996) between different religious spaces, which allow practitioners to overcome the often-transgressive nature of crossing religious boundaries. These bridges reduce the weight of institutional reluctance – or prohibition – regarding religious mobility by offering counter-discourses and counter-symbols. In Ghana, such bridges may, for example, include indigenous symbols, such as the *adinkra* symbols among the Ashantis,[9] which carry particular religious meanings while being largely understood and shared by Ashantis across different religious groups. Such symbols are often painted, carved, and attached to houses, shops, and cars, and are part and parcel of the visual urban landscape. They may refer to "God" (for example, *Gye Nyame*[10]) without betraying a sectarian association with a stated religious group. These bridges may also rely on the borrowing of forms from other religions, such as the Pentecostalization of other Christian community practices or Islamic prayer (Obadare 2016). In Ghana, we were also told how some techniques were borrowed not only from other Christian denominations but also from other so-called world religions. Without downplaying the significance of historical differences between religions and their traditions (Peel 2015), we argue that long-standing entanglements and transmission of ideas facilitate mobility across institutional boundaries otherwise thought of as impassable.

While some bridges are part of the religious landscape, others imply widely shared ideas among Ghanaians, such as the belief that God is similar everywhere and that one can worship him through every religion. These unifying themes are common and are conveyed by popular musicians and other artists who lament the enmity between institutionalized religions. Such stances shed light on a comment shared by Mehdi, which carries a strong critique of the institutional prohibition of religious mobility: "Both pastors and imams hide the truth: there is only one God, to whom you can pray in different places." In contrast to such inclusive statements, distinct religious territories are elaborated through the various institutional stances toward members' propensity for religious mobility, which vary from a high degree of tolerance to strict prohibition, including sanctions against those straying from exclusive institutional loyalty. Even when subjected to such institutional prohibitions and even when risking their affiliation or kinship relationships, practitioners may still maintain their mobile behavior. In some cases, in order to avoid negative repercussions, religious mobility might be concealed. This sharp contrast between institutional prohibitions and de facto practice exposes the limitations of the authority of the religious elites. Indeed, addressing religious institutions alone does not do justice to the complex patterns underlying religious mobility in Ghana – hence the importance of reaching a conceptualization of religious mobility that would capture practice in the making and contribute to our critical reading of formal institutional prescriptions.

6 Religion and Mobility in Switzerland: A Most Private Affair

In Switzerland, our work focused on two cities, Geneva and Fribourg. The cradle of Calvinism, also known as "Protestant Rome," the francophone city of Geneva is today characterized by multiculturalism and great social diversity – a fact that can be explained by its hosting of multiple international organization and its many migrant workers and experts. By contrast, Fribourg is a bilingual (German/French) city located on one of Switzerland's several linguistic frontiers and is recognized as a significant site of the Catholic Counter-Reformation. The capital of a predominantly rural canton, the city of Fribourg is a bridge between francophone and germanophone Switzerland. Despite its significant Christian heritage, nowadays religious practice in Switzerland is highly diverse. Already in 1992, Roland Campiche and his colleagues (Campiche et al. 1992) noted that, in Switzerland, faith is offered "à la carte" (Hervieu-Léger 1999; Schlegel 1995). In Switzerland, it is said that "each one makes their own religious tour: a little bit of Hinduism, a big portion of Christianity, a pinch of Islam and Judaism, and a glassful of Buddhism" (Cuénod 1992; our translation). Similar findings are reported by the Swiss Centre intercantonal d'information sur les croyances:

> In this age of individualization and subjectification, sociologists notice that individuals in the West feel less and less concerned with doctrines, moral prescriptions, and worldviews that the historical churches present as universally valid sets of values. On the religious level, it means that each person who so wishes, whether Christian in their own eyes or not, may find a belief or a set thereof that is to their liking. This development toward the provision of religious forms "à la carte," although often described negatively – by referring to the loss and depreciation of points of reference, to the "bricolage" to which individuals lend themselves, and to the weight of carrying full responsibility for their choices – nevertheless constitutes one of the

dominant traits of contemporary spiritual expression. (Centre intercantonal d'information sur les croyances 2004, 1; our translation)

In many respects, these features are not unique to Switzerland and, indeed, have parallels in other Western European countries such as France, whose religious landscape is increasingly marked by "individualization, globalization, relativization and pragmatism" (Lambert 1994), or Belgium, where scholars speak of "composite religions" in which "it is no longer possible to draw a clear line between Catholic and non-Catholic, and more so, between religious and non-religious" (Dobbelaere and Voyé 1992, 227).

A useful source of information in this respect is a large-scale study conducted by Jörg Stoltz and his team from the University of Lausanne (Stolz et al. 2015). Their research presents us with rich data, both quantitative (1,200 questionnaires) as well as interview-based (70 interviews from across Switzerland). From this study, we learn that the Swiss may be divided into four general categories: (1) institutionalists – conceived from a Christian perspective, this category mainly refers to devout Catholics and Protestants, as well as Evangelists and some Pentecostalists; (2) distanced – religious members who largely belong to a denomination, but are not regular practitioners; (3) seculars – who have left all denominational ties and may even strongly oppose them; (4) alternatives – who construct their religion à la carte, borrowing from different religious traditions (Abrahamic religions, Eastern spirituality, New Age practices, and so forth). This broad distinction is further divided into finer subcategories, offering a comprehensive understanding of religious leanings in Switzerland circa 2010.[1] The authors compare these results with those of the two studies conducted by Campiche and his colleagues (Campiche et al. 2004, 1992) and note a trending shift toward "secularism," alongside the increasing appeal of the "alternative" category, including consultations with shamans and fortune tellers as well as visits to alternative therapists, neuro-linguistic programming (NLP) specialists, and acupuncturists.[2] Even though religious mobility is not at the center of their concerns, we find the classification offered by Stolz and his team – together with their general insights – to be useful, and we echo their four categories in the structure of this chapter.

Interviews in Switzerland were conducted primarily by Rey and Soares; the two remaining team members joined in for some interviews and helped with data analysis. At the same time, fieldwork in Switzerland benefited from firsthand familiarity by the entire research team, as all of us had been living in the country for at least several years at the time of the research. Two of us (Droz and Rey) were born in Switzerland

and have lived there most of our lives, while three of us (Droz, Rey, and Soares) had already conducted other research projects in Switzerland, including in Geneva. Initial interviews were conducted using a snowball method based on personal contacts, but later interviews relied on a random method, when Rey identified her interlocutors in public places around Geneva: in parks, street corners, shops, or near the lake and across several neighborhoods (Les Eaux-Vives, Carouge).

Uneasiness with Religion: "Institutionalists" versus "Seculars"

Rebecca is a Kenyan Pentecostal whom we met and interviewed in Switzerland, where she came for a several-month religious training course. Between discussions on her devout practices and obligations back in Kenya, she shared her impressions from a recent educational visit to a local parish and revisited her astonishment at the sight of the empty church:

> We went for a parish visit this weekend, from Friday to Sunday, and I was surprised that people don't go to church. Only old people go to church, like the church we went to. So to me that is very different. That is strange in Africa and especially in Kenya. (Interview with Rebecca, Geneva 2012)

Rebecca's astonishment is well understood. As a strict Pentecostal, she came to Switzerland with practices and a worldview that would only resonate with the small minority of Swiss whom Stolz and his team have termed "institutionalists" – that is, "model" religious practitioners. In our research in Switzerland, we came across several of them, such as Daniel, a member of the Evangelical Church of Brothers. Daniel emphasized the importance of institutional affiliation, which he contrasted with the concept of faith and personal relations to God, and he indeed kept his practices within the exclusive sphere of his conservative church. A similar example involved Nicola and Ruth, a married couple in their mid-twenties, who, coming from a diverse Christian background, have made a joint decision to become dedicated Evangelicals.

These examples are, we suggest, exceptions that prove the rule. The vast majority of Swiss do not maintain such strict affiliations and regimented practices. As we have seen in the previous chapters, in Kenya, Brazil, and Ghana, secularism is widely perceived in negative terms. In some cases, non-practitioners are stigmatized as depraved hedonists or even as Satanists who have entered into some wicked covenant with the "dark side." In Switzerland, however, the opposite is true: institutionalized religion in its traditional forms is often perceived negatively. Those who "too often" visit the cathedrals, the mosques, or the synagogues – for the critique does not limit itself to Christianity – are suspected of following an ideology blindly and unquestionably, and therefore perhaps dangerously. The idea of adhering to a dogma without applying a critical view and without adapting it to a local context and to personal leanings is thus regarded pejoratively. For example, Marie, a young woman of about twenty, expressed her rejection of "*prêt-à-croire*" (predetermined, "ready-to-believe" recipe) religion and its supposed contempt for individual perspectives:

> Within these [Christian] teachings [of my youth], we, first of all, got to know Jesus's whole life. What I do not like is that they force us, that we must think the same way as them, and when we are young we just follow. Now, I tell myself, I don't like this way of doing things, saying that, "Well, we have to do things like this." But I think that, at the end of the day, all religions, they all have their codes: "If you believe in this, you must think and do like that." I think that in all religions it's the same like that. They all have ways of getting us to gradually do the things that they want us to. (Interview with Marie, Geneva 2013; our translation)

This aversion to dogmas is often linked to the privileging of personal experience over formal religious precepts, as suggested by Michel:

> In my own experience, over the years, I met people who were a-religious in the institutional sense of the term, but who were, in my view, good people nonetheless. They help others and are kind, friendly. But within a religious context, I met the opposite. My parents, for example, whom I criticize … And I told myself: "What do these people do that they haven't ever asked themselves questions, never found any blemish in their practices, in the way they do things?" You see? For me, religiousness is associated with not having this perspective, not questioning things. Anyway, me, I had put it all aside. I kind of rejected religion. (Interview with Michel, Geneva 2013; our translation)

This rejection of institutionalized religion may sometimes manifest as early as childhood or adolescence. While the family context of some of our interlocutors showed support for children's free choice on religious matters, others presented a more constraining environment, leading rebelling youth to develop resistance strategies. In Michel's case, the religious ritual itself had become a mockery: "At the time when I had my [Catholic] confirmation, I was already anti-papal, anti-church. When we were supposed to say 'I believe,' that profession of faith, I remember that, at my confirmation, when there were words that I did not like, I did not say anything. I just pretended."

The notion that religiosity is somehow associated with conservative values that may be seen as problematic to the average liberal Swiss was not overlooked by Stolz and his team, who characterized the ethos of each of the four categories previously outlined. They proposed that "institutionalists" tend to consider religious beliefs as important, view homosexuality as an error, and believe that men should provide for their families, while women should take care of the children. The difference in views between this group and the three others is striking, even troubling (Stolz et al. 2015, 133). However, we also see how this stance, which – to avoid a harsher term – can be classified as conservative, corresponds to the age curve (142). Less than 15 percent of those between eighteen and twenty years of age consider homosexuality an error, while more than 40 percent of those over the age of seventy agree with that statement. We can therefore anticipate a rapid transformation of social values in the years to come with regard to pre-marital sex, traditional division of gender roles, and so on. It was unsurprising, unfortunately, that among those belonging to the "institutional" type, more than 20 percent have negative perceptions of Islam, and 17 percent are averse to atheism (181).

Moreover, in our interviews we found that, without the question ever being raised directly, many interlocutors expressed disdain toward religion once it becomes a justification for violent acts. This finding, again, confirms the work of Stolz and his team, who suggested that "85 percent of the people questioned either completely or partially agreed with the affirmation that 'when you see what is happening in the world today, religions encourage war more than they encourage peace'" (Stolz et al. 2015, 179; our translation). Indeed, several of our interlocutors explained their mistrust in such "*prêt-à-croire*" views by pointing to global geopolitical circumstances, speaking of "wars of religion" either past or present and, in short, stressing their aversion toward religious fundamentalism of any sort. This rejection of strict dogmas was often accompanied by a validation of personal experiences:

> All that which is extreme, those fundamentalists, be they Catholic or Muslim, I find that absurd and horrible, and I would oppose this kind of thing. But, by contrast, if these are people who practice and who are tolerant toward others, it does not disturb me in the least ... But the moment that they are completely driven to convince others, me I wouldn't let myself be convinced. (Interview with Raymond, Fribourg 2013; our translation)
>
> When I started to better understand that which I have been taught [in my religious upbringing], that which they told us to do, and I would listen

> to the news, and I realized that religion is a source of conflict in the world, and that is a shame, because religion is personal ... That was the beginning of me taking a step back. I think that, generally speaking, religion is not a healthy thing. (Interview with Marie, Geneva 2013; our translation)

Such views fit the local *zeitgeist* in more ways than one, not only with regard to liberal values and the emphasis on personal autonomy and scientific or economic materialism, but also with regard to perspectives on current affairs, which associate religion – and Islam in particular – with extremism and violence. Acts of terrorism committed by jihadists, allegedly in the name of religion, disturb and tarnish religion's already questionable reputation, especially when conducted on European soil. For example, on January 8, 2015, the day after the massacre committed in the offices of the satirical magazine *Charlie Hebdo* in Paris, a French comedian said the following on Radio France Inter: "In the absence of personal intervention by God himself, I think that there are two possible hypotheses: either He really doesn't care, or He definitely does not exist. Personally, the macabre raid by these three sinister creatures makes me automatically lean toward the latter hypothesis" (our translation). The comedian presented her critique of the vision of a personal and transcendent monotheistic God, which only increases confusion in the face of suffering on both the personal and collective levels, all the more so considering that this grief stems from allegedly religious ideology. Her words strike a chord with the sentiments of many in Switzerland and across Western Europe, who feel nauseated at the sight of religio-political manifestations of extremism around the world.

But even as the discourse on religion and violence revolves around current affairs, French, Swiss, and other Western Europeans might also draw their concerns from another historical source, namely the bloody trail of religious wars within Europe, especially following the Reformation. In Switzerland, where the nineteenth-century civil war still revolved around the conflict between Catholic and Protestant cantons, the religious divide appears to be diminishing rapidly. And yet, the specter of religious wars might still inform opinions about the place of religious authority in Switzerland. Today, the social silence imposed on matters of belief lends itself to associating religion with constraints and violence. It is marked by a categorical refusal of "*prêt-à-croire*" creeds and the symbolic violence that, in the eyes of many, religions continue to exert.

Thus, in Switzerland, the common association of religion with extremism makes butinage, hybridization, and intermixing of various religious and spiritual traditions appear all the more appealing, as they can be considered proud manifestations of anti-fundamentalism. This, for instance, is the opinion of Fernand, who received a Catholic education and married a Muslim woman:

> Mixing is good, religious mixing included. I live with my wife for fifteen years now and it is great to have two different faiths because we get to share many things. I learned so many things with her – it's really good! That is why I keep my distance from all that stuff that can get extreme – Catholic, Muslim, or any other – because the more you combine things together, the less communitarian you become ... That can get dangerous, when we decide that other human beings are inferior because they do not have the same religion or whatever. So it can get dangerous. And this is why I don't like joining these big movements and participating in these actions, because they can be negative when you refuse to see anything but that. I try to stay open to anything, but I also try to stay – even when I meet religious people – I try not to have prejudices about them, in the same way that I would not have prejudice against someone who says "death to God!" or whatever. I try to be open to everyone. (Interview with Fernand, Geneva 2013; our translation)

This avoidance of dogmatism and celebration of differences reminds us that, in this highly mixed Swiss environment, the four categories identified by Stolz and his team can seldom be found as unadulterated ideal types. In reality, the average Swiss is given to combinations of practices and ideology. A telling example, in this respect, is that of Noémie, a nurse in her fifties, whose nuanced story shows the blurring of the dividing line between "institutionalist"' and "distanced" types. On the face of it, Noémie would appear to fit into the straightforward "institutionalist" category, as she identifies herself as Catholic and has been part of a Catholic community since childhood. Noémie's father was a sacristan in the countryside, and she recalls how the parish environment was central to her personal development back in a world that revolved "around the local bar, church, and school":

> Toward the age of twenty, I stopped, I simply stopped. I was asking myself a lot of questions, I was thinking a lot. And then, in my nursing school there was a small church, and at times of difficulty, I found it necessary to go there and pray. It was a small Catholic church, a little chapel, and I used to go there a lot to pray by myself. It did me a lot of good to be there alone and to reconnect to my faith. (Interview with Noémie, Fribourg 2013; our translation)

Despite personalizing her faith, Noémie maintained ties with her church. After getting married, she kept her spiritual search within Christianity, while at the same time thinking about the multiplicity of other religions that she could have involved herself with:

> [My husband] and I, we were searching together. Because [he] traveled extensively, and having met a lot of religions – Islam, Hinduism – and having stayed open to this religious plurality, that got us asking many questions about the Catholic Church: "Is our church the best?" And so we went to Taizé in France, they have an ecumenical church there, and there we found the answer to our question ... We do not hold the truth; the truth is inside the heart. (Interview with Noémie, Fribourg 2013; our translation)

The encounter with the ecumenical group in Taizé prompted Noémie to assume some religious individualism and to dissociate the religious institution (the Catholic Church) from any monopoly over the truth. Still, Noémie's current religious practices largely fall within the parameters of the Catholic Church, and she does not consider butinage to be desirable behavior. Noémie and her husband have thus maintained their clear attachment to the Catholic confession and made sure that their children will be educated accordingly:

> The children's celebrations, baptism, first communion, preparations to all these, these celebrations nurture our family, our relations with our friends, and the relations between us as a couple. If I had to start again, I would have done it the same way ... We have the feeling of being nurtured, and at the same time we are able to stay critical toward our institutional church. Me, as a nurse ... that church has caused many injuries ... I think about Africa, about the question of sexuality. We have a critical stance. (Interview with Noémie, Fribourg 2013; our translation)

This critical stance toward institutionalized religion is coupled with a degree of agnosticism when it comes to Christian dogmas:

> I do not know if I believe in what lies beyond. I do think that the good things that we do will not be lost. Will there be a resurrection or not? We are told about this, but me I am not sure. And it is all the same to me, it doesn't really matter. And still, I continue going to Mass, and I am active in my church. I am a florist there, I like it a lot. (Interview with Noémie, Fribourg 2013; our translation)

In certain respects, Noémie's profile corresponds to a form of religious belonging detached from dogmas – a distant believer according to Stoltz's categories, whose engagement with institutionalized religion is characterized by critique. At the same time, and despite their disagreements with the church, Noémie and her husband remain anchored within their single church, which remains central to their community life, rites, and values. Her story shows how the rejection of "*prêt-à-croire*" creeds and dogmatism does not spare even those who comfortably identify themselves with traditional Swiss religions, such as Catholic and mainstream Protestant denominations.

Between Embrace and Suspicion: "Distanced" Practitioners

In light of the discomfort with institutionalized religion, we may ask what it means in Switzerland's widely secular society to engage with religion. Many of our interlocutors might not be classifiable as "secular" – that is, according to Stolz and his team's four categories, as anti-religious. However, more subtly, they place themselves in a primarily a-religious and nonbelieving position. Religious experience and practice are in no way central to their lives, and they do not show particular curiosity toward religious teachings and experiences. Some even find the very question of belief to be strange and somehow far from their world of reference. This group, which corresponds to Stolz's idea of the "distanced," is important to recognize in light of the potential bias of the interview setting: by putting the spotlight on religion and practice over the course of the conversation, a deceptive image might emerge that appears as if religion were a regularly considered topic for all interviewees. However, as Stolz and his team suggest, "for the 'distanced,' religion and spirituality are not in any way important" (Stolz et al. 2015, 88; our translation).

> I think I am a nonbeliever ... I don't think I need all this in order to reassure myself. Me, I don't need it, but others do. Those who believe need something that would bring them together, they need some founding myth or something else that would make them feel part of a community. You know, when I was little I used to have these games of faith, playing with spirits. But that was just for a bit of a laugh, nothing more. (Interview with Stéphanie, Geneva 2013; our translation)

But while religion appears to be less central for the average Swiss as a marker of identity or values than it is for the average Kenyan, for example, it might still draw attention from a more intellectual angle, be it historical, political, or philosophical. In such instances, we see how religious heritage tends to be reinterpreted in light of a less enchanted, more rational vision. Sergio, for example, reconsidered his Catholic education by adopting a new vision, one more compatible with his training as a medical doctor:

> Increasingly, I began to regard what they had taught us about religion as metaphors, rather than as stories that are true in and of themselves. The resurrection, for example: rather than suggesting that someone has died and became alive again, it can actually be seen as a concept compatible with a rational vision of the world. Or, say, the fact that … for example, desacralize something a bit rather than thinking that, for example, Jesus was here and he did this in that manner on that particular day. We can think that Jesus was simply someone who had a new vision of the world and who succeeded in introducing a new way of thinking. (Interview with Sergio, Geneva 2013; our translation)

In this sense, we see how religion often undergoes abstraction, being presented in terms of personal conduct, values, or the pursuit of the common good. Melinda, for example, spoke of her religious education in terms of values, such as sharing and helping one another, rather than in terms of dogmas and obligations. While today she does not practice any religion, she still feels that she has retained some values from her religious upbringing, which in turn she incorporated into her social and political engagement. Similarly, Zoe received a religious education that she associates primarily with values. Muslim by confession, she says that she used to practice as a child, but without it ever becoming an obligation. During Ramadan, her parents encouraged her to donate money: "We used to do a tour of orphanages … in order to feel what it does … to give out a little of our income."

Several of our interlocutors did not grow up in a religious universe from which they would eventually distance themselves. Such was the case of Pierre, a Genevese in his fifties, who grew up in an environment distant from all things religious. What used to be the exception only several generations ago has increasingly become the norm: many of today's Swiss adults were not brought up in a religious environment. Pierre admitted that he does not know whether his parents believed in anything religious and said that he, at any rate, was never on the receiving end of religious education: "We are originally Protestants, but we never practiced. My parents were not practitioners. They were barely believers, I don't know, but they didn't practice anyway. At the time, I never went to church. And I still do not practice today." Pierre does not reject religion outright, but he suggested that, for him, religion is, first of all, synonymous with ethics, openness, and coming to terms with mistakes: "I am 'old school,'

I like things that are simple. Behaving well, in the best way possible, that is religion. If we make mistakes, we need to accept them, talk about them. We often think that we are right about all sorts of things. Religion is to remain open." Pierre also did not rule out metaphysical hypotheses and admitted that he does believe in something beyond, though he cannot fully define it: "I have the impression that there is something beyond it all, but I don't know what it is. But for this, I don't need to go to church or anywhere else. For me it's like that, I just feel it a bit ... it's something that is felt but not necessarily put into words." Without any religious socialization either in childhood or later in life, Pierre feels no need for religious practice, and yet he does not deny a certain mystery to life that is alluded to through the language of religion and spirituality.

The way that Sergio, Pierre, Melinda, and Zoe each (re)interpreted their religious heritage – or absence thereof – through the lens of a critical intellectual or moral reading begins to illustrate an important point, namely, the heterogeneity of the group of "distanced" practitioners. This heterogeneity stems from the group's relative detachment from institutional dogmas, on the one hand, and from sweeping anti-religious sentiments – which can be equally dogmatic – on the other. While distanced practitioners might not practice their religion in the traditional sense of the word, they may still engage with it in creative ways, recognizing and drawing some benefits from it. In some cases, distanced practitioners – much like the group of "alternatives" discussed later – might identify themselves as "spiritual" rather than "religious," as in the case of our interviewee Marie, who rejected having a religion but admitted to "some spirituality."

Contrasted with those who appreciate the abstract value of religion without engaging in actual practice are those who maintain some religious practices while rejecting religious institutions in and of themselves. Our research showed how practices that are qualified as typically religious, such as prayers, can sometimes be performed independently of theological convictions regarding a divine recipient. Sergio, for example, claimed to have no faith in the traditional sense of the term, but he did disclose his practice of prayer:

> Reciting the classic prayers, such as Our Father or Ave Maria ... for example, when certain ideas take over us ... or when some worry overwhelms us so that we can no longer advance ... Isn't it true that, in such moments, taking a moment to regain your senses, saying a prayer, it can help. It gives a certain focus to the spirit. And then, there is also thankfulness, in moments of hardship, by being thankful – there, too, I pray. (Interview with Sergio, Geneva 2015; our translation)

Sergio's words demonstrate how prayer is an open technique whose foundations are acquired in childhood through primary socialization. Similarly, Samantha, of Jewish origin, admitted praying regularly, without being sure whether she believes in the existence of the god she addresses:

> When I made this choice [of coming back to practicing Judaism], I had faith. I prayed quite regularly, a little more than today, almost by superstition. Yeah, I pray that all will go well for those that I love. And this, I do it all the time, these little Jewish prayers in Hebrew. When I go to bed I may do them a little quicker, but when there is something major at stake I would [pray longer and] make explicit requests. Still, if you ask me whether there is a god or not, I would say that I have no idea. (Interview with Samantha, Geneva 2013; our translation)

In some cases, such distancing from a birth religion emerges rather late in life, possibly as a result of personal crises and tragedies, such as the sudden death of a loved one, as the following interviewee shared:

> In fact, I still have some faith, but much of it is already lost. And the reason why is very simple. My parents and my big sister, who were all very religious, God has taken all of them away, all three, and all by the same illness. The most religious of people, God's most faithful servants, they all left. And ever since, I have taken my distance, because I cannot understand why. I have always been told that God sends people down to this earth to do good, and within my family there was no one who could do more good than them. And now they are all gone. I found this unjust and I rebelled. And so, I now have very little faith left. (Interview with Fernand, Geneva 2013; our translation)

We noticed such experiences of distancing as a result of mourning in a number of cases, such as that of Alexandre, who used to be a practicing Catholic together with his wife, but ever since her death found himself unable to practice. His wife's illness and slow decline, her suffering, and the coldness of the medical institution have prompted him to join the association Exit[3] so as to spare his children and grandchildren the suffering that he underwent in accompanying his wife. In the course of his wife's funeral arrangements, his interaction with the Catholic vicar was tarnished by a discussion over economic costs. In the interview, he spoke of his religious practices as a thing of the past.

Again and again, among interviewees of all age groups, we noted that mourning constituted an important factor in the erosion – and only seldom, intensification – of institutionalized religious identities (Campiche et al. 1992). Raymond, for example, who estimates to "have had a religious education of the kind that you can barely find nowadays," explained that "at the time, in the 1950s, we obviously had to go to Mass every Sunday and to the Vespers, or we would have been badly regarded by the priest and the teacher." Throughout the years, Raymond kept to his Christian faith, but separation from his partner in the 1990s led him to reduce the frequency of his church visits. Years later, the tragic accidental loss of one of his children continued eroding his religious practice:

> It is true that today I practice very little ... I have had a great calamity a year and a half ago. My son died in a mountain accident. And when I saw him on his deathbed, I told myself: "No, it is finished. His body is here, and there is nothing after this life." And then, I can't say why exactly, I had this kind of revelation, and I told myself: "It is not possible that there is anything after this, otherwise things would not happen like that, and we would have some information about it, had there been something after this life – but to this day, nobody came back from the dead to tell us." And then, I remembered the words of my father – it was very recent, less than two years ago – and I told myself: "He was right, there is nothing after this, there is only this one chapter, on this earth." And, well, this is where I currently stand. (Interview with Raymond, Fribourg 2013; our translation)

Such questions of theodicy and divine grace have often been raised. When finding no answer in the face of misfortune, our interviewees often revolted against God and against religion more broadly. Emilie, an octogenarian, told us the heartbreaking story of how her young husband, a medical doctor, died of acute encephalitis when their son was only two months old: "That experience made me fall out with God, with Jesus. I revolted ... I could no longer speak about it, it was horrific, I could not talk about religion or anything. I became a rebel, I put it all to fire and the sword. I lost my loved one, the father of my son. Do you understand?"

Eastern Religions, Animism, and New Age: "Alternatives"

Among Stolz and his team's four categories, we find what they call "alternatives." According to the researchers, this large group, which is gauged at more than a third of the Swiss population (Stolz et al. 2015, 78), brings together multiple religious or therapeutic practices that are predominantly inspired by Eastern religions and philosophies, as well as by the New Age movement. The appeal of such traditions, we learn, is fairly recent and has emerged "in the course of the 1970s" (233; our translation) as part of a rise of alternative spiritual traditions, especially in the West.

To discuss this category, we first have to clarify the use of the term "spirituality." The term has been in common use at least since the mid-nineteenth century, representing various forms of engagement with "the beyond" (Kale 2004). Its early use was closely associated with the notion of religion, and it is only in the mid-to-late twentieth century that it has asserted itself as an independant category, distinct from – sometimes opposed to – religion (Sheldrake 1992; Wulff 1991). One strong impetus for the entrenchment of this distinction has been the experiences of the American baby boom generation, many of whom have drifted out of organized religion, adopting multiple and fluid religious – in the broad sense of the term – inspirations, focused on personal experience and an individual quest for meaning (Roof 1993). Contemporary spirituality has come to be associated with a strong sense of personal religious latitude, linked to the erosion of traditional life-regulating religious authority and wider social structures. By putting the individual and their subjectivity, aims, and quest for ultimate meaning at the center, spirituality is often seen as opposing the popular Durkheimian reading of religion in pure social terms. Indeed, the popularity of this notion of spirituality seems to be in line with what Graham Ward, following Charles Taylor, called the "post-Durkheimian" era of religion, which is marked by "hyper-individualism, self-help as self-grooming, custom-made eclecticism that proffer a pop transcendence and pamper to the need for 'good vibrations'" (Ward 2006, 185). Moreover, contemporary spirituality informs us of the diversification of the religious landscape, within which practitioners may pick and choose elements – Hervieu-Léger's "religion à la carte" – from a wide variety of sources in ways that give them meaning or make personal sense. Such selectivity can be read in line with the postmodern tendency to be critical of master narratives and non-negotiable ultimacies in general and of religious ideologies in particular (Schneiders 2003).

So far, we have kept the term "spirituality" in check, as the religion/spirituality distinction, which Western observers have come to see as "a key conflict at the heart of modern religion" (Vincett and Woodhead 2009, 320), has been largely absent in our three case studies in the Global South. This observation may not be completely unexpected: after all, the very distinction between religion and spirituality answers to a particular fragmentation of the totality of human experience into distinct social fields,[4] which answers to a particularly Western "deinstitutionalization" of religion (Hunter 1983) as related to a particular climate of individual autonomy, thirst for personal meaning, intergenerational cultural gaps, and protests. While scholars such as Kenneth Pargament (1999) suggest that personal spirituality is an integral part of virtually all religious forms, our multisited research casts doubt on this assertion, at least as far as the common use of the term is concerned.

Another reason why we find the religion/spirituality distinction to be of limited appeal has to do with terminological elusiveness. Allie B. Scott (1997), for example, identified nine distinct readings of how the terminologies of religion and spirituality have come to be understood, demonstrating a lack of scholarly consensus (Zinnbauer, Pargament, and Scott 1999). Similarly, Hans Stifoss-Hanssen (2009) argues that connotations associated with the two terms may vary from one culture to another, raising doubts as to whether their uniform employment is at all possible. Such lack of agreement may impair communication and complicate the prospect for arriving at generalized conclusions (Zinnbauer et al. 1997). The distinction is particularly challenging because, in its common Western use, a spiritual person may or may not also engage in concrete practices that we might call religious. Indeed, the term "spirituality" lends itself to abstract realms of contemplation, existential meaning-making, and often-vague intuitions regarding the ineffable. People may consider themselves spiritual even if nothing about their actual lives translates these sentiments into collective, or even fully individualized, practice.

Despite these challenges, today, especially in the Global North, a terminological dichotomy between the two terms is widely assumed by both lay people and scholars. It is this assumption of a meaningful distinction between the two categories that allowed scholars to recognize instances of people who are "spiritual but not religious" and "religious but not spiritual" (Zinnbauer et al. 1997), and even to suggest that such independence of terms "has become a standard part of many papers on spirituality" (Pargament 1999, 6). Even so, and though they are often presented in opposition, there are significant overlaps between religion and spirituality, a fact recognized by religious professionals (Hyman and Handal 2006), as well as by lay individuals (Schlehofer, Omoto, and Adelman 2008; Marler and Hadaway 2002; Adler 2005; Zinnbauer et al. 1997). So much do the terms have in common that some scholars suggest they should be hyphenated as "religion-spirituality" (Zinnbauer et al. 1997).[5]

In our research in Switzerland, we noticed that, indeed, the use of the term "spirituality" tends to be associated with a rejection of (some aspects of) institutionalized religion. Our Swiss interviewees often referred to their sense of spirituality as a way of insisting that, while they may not be practicing a religion, their worldview is also not fully materialistic. As they dissociate themselves from institutional theologies, and especially from the heritage of mainstream Abrahamic theological traditions, the term "spirituality" becomes a useful marker for their often-vague recognition of some sense of transcendence. As Melinda, a Swiss spiritual seeker of Jewish descent, typically explained:

> Integrating this idea that "the good" does not really exist, "the bad" does not really exist, this really requires deconstructing some principles that are put forth within my original religion, Judaism. That religion is full of prohibitions and rules that, when practiced fully, bring to my mind a kind of fascism and reduction of self. It's a reduction of personal identity, even though for me, at the end of the day, the religious feeling or the desire for spirituality is really about an expansion beyond the body, an expansion of the spirit that is necessarily accompanied by a deconstruction of principles. (Interview with Melinda, Geneva 2013; our translation)

For those Swiss who claim spirituality, eroding attachments to the family's historical religious heritage make religion a land of experimentation, subject to (changing) personal taste and curiosity. Such experimentation often manifests itself in intellectual and ethnographic encounters rather than deep engagements and full institutional adherence. In the same way that Stolz and his team recognize that those within the "distanced" category might still be attracted to alternative religiosity, so does the distanced position of some of our interviewees not rule out the possibility of attending religious rituals and raising questions without actually identifying themselves with an institution through conviction, conversion, and membership. In the case of Stéphanie, for example, the absence of religious attachment and objects of belief does not translate into complete rejection of each and every manifestation of religion. Like others, she demonstrated openness and curiosity, especially with regard to Buddhist spirituality and Shamanism:

> I went with a friend who was doing sacred Shaman dances. It got me thinking! ... [My friend] did that in different places as part of her training in personal development – she traveled with her group in Peru, in South Africa, and once they had an event in Geneva, and they invited some people including me. And then, this got me thinking, because I didn't understand it. And I also wondered what state of awareness these people were in. A friend told me: "It requires being highly present even as you are focused on yourself." At the end of the day, I think that there are things that you cannot explain, you can only live them. These questions will remain open. (Interview with Stéphanie, Geneva 2013; our translation)

We thus noted how religious mobility in Switzerland shows a great attraction toward worldviews (Geertz 2002) associated with Eastern religions, and in particular with Buddhism and Hinduism. In many cases, the Eastern traditions in question appear to already be "processed" for consumption by Western publics (for example so-called Western Buddhism, Coleman 2001) and are combined with a dash of New Age and Shamanic teachings. Contrary to Eastern spirituality, practices, and worldviews, which are the alternative of choice for many of our interlocutors of Christian background, Islam seems to evoke genuine repulsion. On the rise in Switzerland today, Islam is widely perceived as a religion of dogmas and literalism, which leaves little room for individual autonomy. While Eastern practices are associated with flexibility and inclusiveness, and are seen as preoccupied with the individual and their personal growth, Islam is perceived as something of a caricature of strict institutionalized religion, one that rejects individual autonomy in the service of rigid principles that must be followed to the letter. In this respect as well, our findings are in line with those of Stolz's team, who suggest that "contrary to Buddhism, which is identified through positive stereotypes, Islam is stereotypically perceived as the incarnation of the negative religion" (Stolz et al. 2015, 186, our translation). Islam is perceived as inciting violence, mistreating women, and exploiting people's gullibility and the wealth of the countries where it is widely practiced. Needless to say, these common Swiss perceptions of Islam – mediated, to an extent, by negative media images, a particular reading of global geopolitics, and possibly xenophobic and Islamophobic sentiments – are highly simplistic and generalizing. While they may attest to many people's fears and prejudices, some interviewees merely expressed less interest in Islam than in other religious traditions.

> Islam does not interest me much, and then, whenever I move in that direction, these people they, they don't attract me. They don't sell their religion very well, I find. And my yoga teachers, the Indians that I meet, they are more peaceful, more … I get more feeling with these people. And then, their religion [Islam] does not interest me much. (Interview with Yannick, Geneva 2013; our translation)

Contrary to views on Islam, the attraction toward Eastern spirituality seems to affect people of different backgrounds and generations. As an example, we can think of Emilie, who was born in the 1940s to a Protestant father and a Catholic mother and was given a strict education at a religious school. Later in life, however, she became critical of her strict religious upbringing, embracing, for example, Darwinian ideas. Her attraction to Oriental spirituality – and to Buddhism in particular – while founded on deep appreciation and supported by firsthand experiences from traveling to the East, never translated into actual practice. She explained:

> I love Buddhism ... I have really been attracted by it. I love the Dalai Lama, I love Buddhist ideas. Because they are tolerant – tolerance, compassion, loving one another. I like Buddhists a lot. When I went to Cambodia, to Vietnam, we visited a lot of temples, it was really most interesting, very captivating. And then there is this beauty, all these colors. They have exceptional spirituality, but that's another thing. (Interview with Emilie, Geneva 2013; our translation)

Besides attraction to Oriental spirituality, several "alternative" interlocutors are interested in religions – ritualized or not – that revolve around connection with nature, as demonstrated by the work of Jean Chamel (2018). Michel, for example, suggested that "me, if I had to believe in anything at all, I would doubtlessly prefer to associate myself with these [animist] beliefs than with those that say, 'God descended to the earth.'" Although declaring himself an atheist, Michel admits to being fascinated by practices that he identifies with nature worship and the natural order of things. These range from Shamanism, through practicing *le secret*,[6] to self-mortification practices:

> I would be more attracted by animist cultures. Me, I am convinced that we are part of nature, of the earth, and you see how things are in balance and everything is interrelated. The bees cannot see things that we can see! So definitely, there must be things that are hidden from us as well. There are these waves, you know? Plants emit these electromagnetic fields and, according to their field, they can grow immensely, and then you can really see results. Some people can talk to plants – I don't think that they do that using words – and they do amazing stuff. The size of the vegetables, the production, it all depends on these interactions. These people usually have a different relation to nature – much more respectful, more thoughtful. (Interview with Michel, Geneva 2013; our translation)

The link with nature refers to a certain approach to the body and to health, which is perhaps why Stolz and his team have included within the category of "alternatives" not only Eastern religions but also schools of alternative medicine often linked to New Age teachings. It seems important to distinguish pragmatic healing-seeking techniques from those that locate therapy within a given religious universe. Indeed, in the course of many interviews, the discussion of the religious ended up touching on the domain of health, understood in holistic, rather than biomedical, terms. Some of our interviewees made this therapeutic connection explicit, as in the case of Didier, who spoke of a "religion of health":

> It was a way to somehow distance myself from this Catholic and Protestant culture. I wanted to experiment with something different, and also with the spiritual. So I ended up, among other things, in courses on natural therapy, where you might find a link ... between energetic work and all that, so it's more than just religiousness. The best of these natural therapies, to my experience at the time, came from Buddhism. It is like a religion of health. (Interview with Didier, Geneva 2015; our translation)

Didier's emphasis on well-being resonates with the words of several other interviewees, for whom the religious dimension manifests itself through serviceable techniques, without any moral or faith elements attached. Yannick, for example, likened his yoga practice to dancing: a corporeal approach, with therapeutic overtones, which can extend into trance-like states, offering a sense of "liberation" and calm that is also familiar to him from sports and singing. While he would sometimes borrow Eastern religious references to describe his experience of the "divine" within his yoga practice, he is not interested in dogmas, institutions, morality, or cosmogonies. He is not even interested in yoga groups as a community and a locus of identification and belonging, but rather presents his practice in terms of a bodily and spiritual technique, pure and simple: "What is my religion? Me, I would tell you that I don't have a religion as such, a religion that you can name. But I would then add and say that I am a '*bobo*' [that is, bohemian bourgeoisie], that I ... I like salsa, I do yoga from time to time, and I love playing the guitar and singing, you see."

Similar ideas were presented by Stéphanie, who, like Yannick, has been practicing yoga, but does not consider it a religious practice:

> I had the opportunity of doing some yoga meditation training and I suddenly got sucked into another religion. But what I was looking for there, it wasn't the religious aspect, but rather the idea of being centered within myself – hence the yoga. It goes without saying that I was a little bit into Buddhism, but without really getting into it. I think that was something that I really appreciated. (Interview with Stéphanie, Geneva 2015; our translation)

Such an emphasis on the usefulness of technique dissociates practices from "worldviews" as formulated by Geertz (1973). Such disassociation is further manifest in the common separation between the variables of belief and institutional affiliation, in line with Grace Davie's (1990) idea – based on findings from the United Kingdom – of "believing without belonging." Still, most of our interviewees did not express clear atheistic convictions and may be classified as "agnostics," pleading ignorance on spiritual matters. Their practices are not dependent on integration into a similar-minded community group, and it might be that the absence of such belonging is part of what makes it so difficult for them to talk about their religiosity, adding an apologetic overtone to the discussion. The idea of praying without either believing or belonging offers, perhaps, a way of integrating their religious heritage – as we saw earlier, Judaism in Samantha's case and Catholicism in Sergio's case – into Swiss secular life.

Moreover, as practice becomes dissociated from formal institutional beliefs, we may wonder about its classification as indeed religious. From an admittedly dualistic – and in this sense, Christian-Cartesian – perspective, which considers religion as preoccupied with the "beyond" and the "sacred," we suggest that practices such as yoga or alternative healing techniques may be practiced with the intention of attaining physical well-being or spiritual transformation but that only in the latter case could they be regarded as "religious." For those interviewees who associated religious practice with physical health, this material preoccupation may offer a rationale that allows them to bypass uncomfortable questions involving faith and dogmas and keep practices as (physical) wellness techniques. For example, *le secret*, which has been enjoying large media attention in the western part of Switzerland in recent years, was often evoked by our interviewees toward the end of the interview, ostensibly in order to propose a connection between these alternative practices – or techniques – and the religious. While it is true that the reciters of *le secret* make use of arcane prayers inspired by a Catholic liturgy, the appeal that these healers enjoy falls within a pragmatic approach to health that is dissociated from dogmatic prerequisites, institutional affiliation, and personal commitment. Still, *le secret* does represent, for many of our interlocutors, the effectiveness of some mysterious, invisible powers, classifiable under "religious." As Michel told us, "I do draw, however, a distinction between different religious beliefs. It's strange, in fact, because you see the practice of those 'bone setters.' You don't really know what's going on there, but I really do believe in it! In this sense, then, I am not really an atheist, I guess."

And then, should the practice of yoga, or even dance, sports, or singing, which Yannick and Stéphanie have mentioned, be regarded as religious? This question has long been debated and was already evoked in the first part of the book, where we referred to McGuire's (2008, 7–8) example of the spiritually minded gardener and our similar example involving Zara, the Swiss pianist. Such personal imbuing of whatever practices with spiritual content raises a fundamental question regarding the confinement of the religious to consensual practices limited to certain spaces and moments. There is, perhaps, an irony of sorts in that, in Western Europe, the birthplace of the category of religion, the frontiers of the religious seem so porous and confused that they may render that very concept and its derivatives inadequate when confronted with the actual experiences of the majority of the population.

Lastly, it is interesting to compare the intuitive use of the term "spirituality" by Swiss interviewees such as Melinda to its virtual absence from discourse in our three other case studies. This stark difference seems to support the idea whereby appeal to spirituality as a conceptual framework goes hand in hand with the erosion of institutionalized religion, which is most strongly felt in the Swiss case. For many scholars, the growing appeal of the notion of spirituality is indeed regarded as a harbinger of decline in formal religious affiliation (Marler and Hadaway 2002; Schneiders 2003; Vincett and Woodhead 2009). At the same time, some scholars wonder whether interest in spirituality is indeed a novel phenomenon (Stark, Hamberg, and Miller 2005; Lippy 1994). Aware of the baggage that words carry and their wider semantic connotations, we caution against any simplistic-dichotomist view of religion as portrayed in terms of power structures and hierarchies, or of spirituality as tied to a "heartfelt" quest for the transcendent (Turner et al. 1995; Pargament 1997). Such a value-laden interpretation is often fed by (mainly Western) anti-institutional sentiments that serve those who reject religious institutions outright and should be recognized for its prejudice (Vincett and Woodhead 2009).[7] If nothing else, those very elements that make religion seem unappealing to Western spiritual seekers (for example, dogmatism, rigidity, institutional hierarchy) also fuel the development of social capital and a sense of stable social identity.

Butinage in Action

So far, we have discussed different tendencies within religious practice in Switzerland, echoing Stolz and his team's four categories of Swiss religious practitioners. But would we find, within Switzerland, such committed butineurs as those that Soares (2009) identifies in the Brazilian city of Joinville? That is to say, would we find people who add and extend their religious practices following the model offered by Riobaldo, who wished to "drink water from any river" because "it all calms me down, allays my worries" (Rosa 1963, 10–11)? On the face of it, such a profile would not fit that of the typical Genevese, but it does appear at times, such as in the case of Yannick, who states: "I gather from the left, the right, whatever I can, with whatever I have at my disposal," and echoes the trajectories of such interviewees as Melinda, Blaise, or Sonia – whom we shall explore in this section.

Melinda is a school teacher who was born into a Jewish family. She recalls her mother instructing her about such festivals as Hanukkah and Passover. As a young adolescent, she celebrated her bat mitzvah. However, while she does intend to transfer her religious heritage to her children one day, she would like to pass it on in the form of a cultural heritage, rather than as a complete system of religious precepts. In her personal life, Melinda's most significant affinity is to Buddhism and Kashmir Shaivism, which she had learned and practiced alongside Judaism. She also has a soft spot for Taoism, which inspires some of her critique of her birth religion. She is above all concerned with her spiritual quest, which freely draws on various traditions. Among her various religious influences, she has practiced and taught yoga, finding inspiration in the teachings of Tibetan masters. But her religious trajectory was not limited to Eastern religions. After meeting a missionary friend in the Netherlands, Melinda had a vision of Jesus who spoke to her:

> I was in bed and I saw Jesus all surrounded by a rainbow halo, and he told me, he spoke to my heart, and he said: "I love you, I love you, I love you. I protect you, I am here for you, do not be afraid of life, et cetera.' And for several days, I was reinvigorated, fully assured by this vision of unconditional love ... That is a rather strange experience to have, I may say, and it has opened me up a lot. Because all of a sudden I was confronted, on a sensory and visual level, with something I did not believe in. And this kind of thing actually happened to me a number of times. (Interview with Melinda, Geneva 2013; our translation)

That experience prompted Melinda to keep her religious horizons open, contrary to the exclusivity prescribed by the "institutionalist" monotheistic believer model. Pursuing her personal religious trajectory, she also experimented with Shamanism, which affected her greatly and led her to understand that she can be "touched by something" within just about any religious tradition.

Blaise can be considered as another example of a highly mobile butineur. He was born in Lausanne and had no formal religious education. His parents, of African origin, had their own religious faith but did not impart it to their children. Blaise occasionally went to church, following invitations by acquaintances to join their Evangelical group, but as he found the group too sectarian and their codes too strict, he lost interest. In Geneva, he shared a house with a Calvinist pastor for some time and visited his church. He once went to the synagogue to accompany a Jewish friend, and went two or three times to a mosque with Muslim friends. The previous year, he joined a friend in practicing Ramadan and had a positive recollection of the dedication that it required. He said that he thinks he will observe Ramadan once again the following year.

We thus see that highly mobile Swiss butineurs are characterized, like their Brazilian counterparts, by openness, curiosity, and autonomy vis-à-vis institutional constraints and boundaries. Swiss butineurs are nevertheless much more explicit than their Brazilian counterparts in their critique of institutional religion and in associating their mobile behavior with dissatisfaction with institutional prescriptions. Sonia, for example, came from a Protestant family. Her two parents were practicing, her father was a member of the parish council, and she used to attend Sunday school. But while she seldom talked about religion with her parents, the family's affiliation was self-evident. Now a mother herself, Sonia does not see the need to identify herself with any particular religion, despite her rather intense religious activities: "I cannot identify myself with any single religion. I have put together a mixture that fits me. It is something between personal development, spirituality, a bit of Buddhism, things like that. I am interested in Islam, and currently I am actually attending an African Evangelical church."

While Sonia keeps her distance from certain demands made by Evangelical pastors or imams, she has gradually forged her own religious practice within highly heterogeneous contexts, influenced by her social bonds and her marital trajectory. At the age of twenty-five, following a period of psychological hardship, she came into contact with what she termed "personal development." She read Buddhist books and opened herself to their teachings without necessarily translating that into regular practice; she underwent various therapies, attended events, and gravitated toward a world that she associates with spiritual practice. She married for the first time "in church, but quoting the Quran" with a Moroccan man, and she observed Ramadan with him several times. She says that she had done that as "experimentation" and in order to support her husband in his own practice, but she never converted to Islam. Some of her husband's co-religionists pointed out that a non-Muslim should not observe Ramadan, to which she responded: "If you can prove to me that a god has said that it is wrong to support one's husband, then for me it is better not to believe in that god. For me, that is not a problem. I found this interesting really, the feeling of unity with many people who fast at the same time. You feel this spiritual communion."

Sonia's second marriage, with an Ivorian man, led her to regularly visit an Evangelical African church cofounded by her sister-in-law. She liked the songs, which convincingly communicated people's religious convictions, but she deplored the moralistic tone of the sermons:

> I have a lot of difficulty with this judgmental attitude that if you do this then that would happen to you ... I don't like it so much. Because for me, actually, what I feel the most is love. And I think that, after that, there are many different ways of making this connection and practicing a religion, but I do find it hard when people want to impose their faith ... [and say] that if you do not do this, then you will burn in hell. They sow fear within us ... Asking questions cannot be a frightening act – it leads us to either embrace our beliefs, or to change them. (Interview with Sonia, Geneva 2013; our translation)

The position adopted by Sonia clearly transcends institutional dogmas and teachings, even though she does take part in groups where religious exclusivism is advocated. Her observation of Ramadan and her visit to the Evangelical church show her rejection of the idea of complete and exclusive membership at a single religious tradition. Her interest in Eastern religions and New Age practices shows how diverse some practitioners are in combining their Abrahamic religious heritage with other monotheistic strands as well as with alternative practices.

Such diverse trajectories as those of Melinda, Blaise, and Sonia – all of which correspond to what we shall refer to in the next chapter as polyfloral butinage – bring together multidimensional and changing, often disorganized and even contradictory, practices that assert themselves as a departure from the expectations and demands that religious institutions impose on believers. In terms of motivation for their mobility, our Swiss interviewees put the emphasis primarily on spiritual attraction, quest for personal meaning, and simple curiosity. To a lesser extent, they also emphasized a social logic, which manifests in invitations by friends and family members to special life-cycle occasions such as church weddings and funerals, and in cases of intermarriage. Interestingly, of our four case studies, our Swiss interviewees were the least likely to emphasize practical and material considerations. While in Kenya and Ghana in particular, the prominence of practical concerns often extended as far as the financial costs of commuting to church, it seems that, in affluent Switzerland, material considerations were much less discussed. The only aspect where our Swiss interviewees showed preoccupation with practical concerns was in the context of a quest for personal health, as discussed in the previous section.

Between Religious Heritage and Religion as a Taboo

Despite all that has been said about the erosion of birth religions and affiliations, the Swiss still tend to maintain religious heritages, most notably through rites of passage (Van Gennep 1909). Notwithstanding diverse ages and backgrounds, nearly all of our interlocutors recalled some religious socialization from their childhood, though it had not always played a formative role for them. This socialization often involved religious rituals, such as baptism among Christians:

> I have first gone through baptism, but then, I was a baby. My mother did it very early, and we had a priest. I have once seen it in a photo, and I think I must have had holy water poured on my forehead and that was all. Afterwards, actually, I was supposed to start catechism, at my primary school, up to age ten or eleven. I was supposed to do two years of catechism in order to have my confirmation, because I was already baptized, so I could have my confirmation. But I did not do it in the end, because, I don't know why, I stopped along the way and my mother did not force me to continue, even though I was getting along well with the person who was teaching the catechism. (Interview with Didier, Geneva 2013; our translation)

Beyond this early religious socialization, our interlocutors have all – with no exception – demonstrated some religious mobility. Even though their points of departure have been different in terms of family and religious upbringing, when examined through the prism of life stages, their personal religious trajectories shared a common tendency of gradual distancing from institutional religion throughout their adolescence or early adulthood. While Stolz and his team suggest that older people in Switzerland tend to be more practicing in the institutional sense (Stolz et al. 2015), it is not fully clear whether we can identify a trend of return to religion later in life or whether these older practitioners represent a bygone time when religious institutions enjoyed wider social adherence.

The idea that an erosion – or reinvigoration – of practice is tangible along a person's life path, or even across generations, is a hypothesis that may be examined by considering personal and intergenerational perspectives. The intergenerational succession between grandparents, parents, and children often betrays a palpable shift, even rupture, with regard to religious beliefs and practices. This shift is demonstrated by Yannick's familial trajectory. His grandparents, who originally came from the countryside, were highly attached to Catholicism and assiduously attended Sunday Mass. His parents distanced themselves and no longer practiced Catholicism, except – in the case of his mother – for family festivals and Christmas Eve. His father, at the same time, was attracted by what Yannick calls New Age, reading books such as *The Alchemist, The Celestine Prophecy,* and *Conversations with God,* while practicing massage and experimenting with the healing powers of magnets. As an adolescent, Yannick found that conversations on spiritual matters were necessary in order to get through to his father: "The only way of having something of an intimate and close relationship with my father, reaching him, was by getting into his New Age stuff, to talk to him about energies, chakras, all of that." Yannick studied philosophy in secondary school and then turned to economics and social sciences in university, an education that helped him contextualize his father's beliefs and assess them by applying the scrutiny of Platonian philosophy and critical thinking. He adopted a rationalist stance regarding religion and distanced himself from it without turning his back on all practices. He dedicatedly practices yoga, which he discovered through his father, but he sees it as a technique that allows one to "feel good inside one's body" rather than as a clear-cut religious practice. Moreover, he deplores the excessive ritualization and rigidity of certain practices.

From an intergenerational perspective, Yannick's trajectory tells us of a movement that began within institutionalized religion, which was devoutly practiced by the grandparents, continued through partial distancing from that tradition by his mother and the adoption of alternative religiosity by his father, and was concluded, for now, with Yannick's distanced attitude toward religion in the name of rationalism. This example offers an illustration of the process of detachment or the "slide toward secularism," which Stolz and his team identified (Stolz et al. 2015, 224–8). At the same time, this example offers no indication that what we are witnessing is necessarily the demise of religion in Switzerland. As we suggested, Yannick himself does engage in some practices of his own, even though his interpretation of them is insistently unreligious. Moreover, in line with the religious repertoire approach presented in the next part of the book, we may propose a counter-perspective that emphasizes the richness of Yannick's religious family heritage – with Catholicism on one side and various New Age practices on the other – as a pool of potential practices. This wealth is, in a sense, a privilege that was not readily available to the older generations in Yannick's family, and Yannick and his future progeny will choose whether or not to draw on it. These observations bring to mind the work of Voas and Crockett (2005) based on data gathered in the United Kingdom. According to the two scholars, the decline in religious practice, belief, and affiliation is of a generational nature. Their findings propose that, among religious parents, only half of that religiosity is transmitted to the children, while among non-religious parents, the absence of religion almost always perpetuates itself in the children's generation.

While many of our interlocutors were brought up in a family setting where religion played only a minor role, generational differences may mean that religious attachments may skip a generation. Marie, for example, suggested that "I do not have a religion, or any degree of belief, or of practice." Despite these clear words, Marie maintains great affection for a ceramic angel, which was given to her by her grandmother and to which she would turn in times of need:

> Even today, when I am worried about something, I kiss the angel and I put it down. I could never throw it away. In fact, it is extremely important to me because it also represents my grandmother. It is the same with all those little things that we do – we do not necessarily believe in them, but we do them all the same, because we cannot do otherwise. Are these superstitions? (Interview with Marie, Geneva 2013; our translation)

The ceramic angel brings to Marie's mind her grandmother's religiosity, as she was the only person in the family with whom she had prayed when she was a child. Despite being a nonbeliever and a non-practitioner, Marie's daily life integrates some small gestures that evoke her grandmother's religious universe, permitting her to recall their special bond. Her practice-without-belief emphasizes the power of rituals, whose significance is independent – at least somewhat – from the belief that is purported to generate it. Marie's embrace of the ceramic angel points to religious objects and practice as vehicles through which people express not only belonging and conviction but also more abstract sentiments such as longing and nostalgia. The turn by many interviewees to abstract concepts suggests that, even as explicit doctrines lose their appeal, people still see religious traditions as charged with potent and meaningful symbolic value, such as a connection with departed loved ones that is not easily matched outside a religious worldview.

For many interviewees, religious practice involves identification with a certain family member. The person concerned is often a father or a mother, and we noted that such identification is often formed between family members of the same gender (father-son, mother-daughter). In other cases, identification skips a generation, and it is the grandfather or the grandmother who serves as the model or symbol of religious identity.[8] It should be said that such identification and influence are not only reserved for the resurgence of practice. Raymond provides the reverse example. He received traditional religious education and was still practicing when his children were young, but later in life was influenced by his father's atheism and became an atheist himself, believing, as he put it, "neither in God nor in the Devil."

In the absence of a unanimous belief system shared across the previous generation(s), our Swiss interviewees were in a position to choose their familial religious identification. In traditions that value material objects, such as Catholicism, transmission of religious objects such as the one handed to Marie by her grandmother may serve as a point of intergenerational transmission, even as the original designation of the object might undergo reinterpretation. Thus, Sergio keeps a statue of Padre Pio that was given to him by his mother, a bottle of blessed water, and blessed salt. And even though he contests the protective virtues his mother attributed to these objects, he still keeps them within reach: "I am critical, but I still keep this bottle of water because it is a gift from my mother. So the bottle is here and it does nobody any harm. I will not drink the water, because, well, the water has been in this bottle for many years already." Engagement with such sacred objects can thus be interpreted both in sentimental terms of carrying intergenerational significance and in terms of the object's perceived spiritual potency. While the carriers of such religious objects may themselves be thoroughly secularized, their respect and even jealously toward the steadfast faith of the older generation may be read as a variation on the notion of "vicarious religion" (Davie 2007).

Importantly, the Swiss personalization of religious experiences is not limited to breaks from family religious heritage; rather, it is a mirror of a general attitude toward the role of religion in society. While in Brazil, Kenya, and Ghana, people are largely willing, even keen and enthusiastic, to express their religious persuasion and practices publicly, in Switzerland, it is only dedicated mainstream practitioners – whom Stolz and his team call "institutionalists" – who publicly present their religious convictions. Even then, all but some Evangelicals and Pentecostals may only do so in private: "I can discuss it with you, but only with you," some interlocutors said before asking out loud whether they should get their ideas in order before they would be ready to be recorded. Personal, discreet, even a taboo, religion in Geneva and Fribourg appears to be a topic seldom discussed in public. This reality is not always easy, and several practitioners have lamented – almost in a whisper – the lack of companions with whom to discuss their religious questions. "I never shared my beliefs, not even with my family," one of our interviewees said.

Several of our interlocutors indicated that even using the first-person pronoun to talk about religion ("my beliefs," "my practices," "my convictions," or "my doubts") may appear transgressive to their surroundings. For example, Michel said: "I have made a considerable effort to make it here and talk [about religion]. Within my family, these days, nobody knows what others think and nobody talks about it. In fact, I think that here, in Geneva, religion is not well perceived." Melissa spoke along similar lines:

> [To talk about religion] is not at all appropriate. There's no place for that. I find that this is something that unfortunately must remain intimate and discreet ... That's too bad! It's a shame but there really is a certain closeness with regard to it, and then, there is such Manichaeism within our society. It seems that we are caught between this frantic capitalist rhythm, and our place within the society and in general. Oh no, there is simply no room for that [religion]. (Interview with Melinda, Geneva 2013; our translation)

The interview setting lends itself to articulating, in a coherent and relatively systematic manner, ideas and practices that may otherwise be unexamined. To say this much is simply to recognize the uncommon reflexivity inherent in the interview itself. In this respect, we may recall how interviewees in our other case studies also admitted that they seldom had the opportunity to put forth and reflect on their beliefs in public in such a distanced and nonjudgmental manner. Still, the motivations for this reticence vary between Switzerland and, for example, Kenya. While in Kenya discussions on religious mobility are limited by normative expectations (avoidance of showing too many theological doubts; strict adherence to religious forms publicly deemed as legitimate), in Switzerland it is the very topic of religion that appears to be something of a taboo.

Paradoxically, this taboo is often particularly pronounced within the family sphere, even as the family has traditionally represented the first locus of religious socialization. Thus, Marie affirmed that she never spoke about religion with her parents, to such an extent that she is unfamiliar with their views and beliefs. A similar experience was described by Noémie, who admitted that she knows neither the practices nor the beliefs of her adult children:

> My children, I don't know exactly [whether they are practicing a religion]. I kind of let them be ... I do not think [that they practice a religion], but I don't really know. If there is a Mass, they will go to Mass, they would even take communion. But I do not think that they are practitioners. I don't know. In fact, it's up to them. I should not ask whether they practice or not ... It's a bit of a taboo. Well, not a taboo, maybe a kind of respect. Respecting their choices, their own way of life and its development. Our own beliefs are not those of our children. The world today is not what it was in our days. One needs to try and respect that. (Interview with Noémie, Fribourg 2013; our translation)

Considering such taboos, it is all the more surprising to note that, at the end of the day, many rites of passage in Switzerland such as marriages, funerals, and, of course, baptisms are still often celebrated within religious settings. Attending such an event despite not being a practitioner in this or any other denomination appears to be the norm rather than the exception in Switzerland, and it is easily justified in the name of social ties with the people concerned. As such, attendance at such rituals can be fully detached from any spiritual endorsement or conviction – something that would be less clear-cut in Ghana, for example. Indeed, this participation consolidates social ties without necessitating any doctrinal adherence. Stéphanie said: "When there is a ceremony, such as a marriage or a burial, I go to the church, and it doesn't matter which tradition it is – Catholic, Protestant, or something else. I do not go there to attend the Mass – but only to be with the people."

Illustrating this notion that the social logic is given precedence over confessional divisions, we may consider the trajectory recounted by our interviewee Zoe. Having received, as a young girl, what she described as a non-constraining Muslim religious education, she expressed her wish to transmit its values to her children. While she does not observe either prayers or Ramadan, neither she nor her children eat pork, a choice that she considers a religious practice. To protect her children from the evil eye, she hung Quranic verses at the entrance to their room. Her husband, whom she married according to Muslim tradition, is a non-practicing Protestant. Still, out of solidarity with his wife, he also abstains from eating pork. While she suggests that it is harder to call herself a Muslim believer and practitioner in the current political climate, her husband's family has always shown respect toward her convictions. When friends hold religious rites of passage such as a wedding, a funeral, or even a Jewish bar mitzvah, Zoe is in attendance. She is somewhat interested in Buddhism, which she admires for its tolerance, but she never actually pursued this interest further. Additionally, she is surrounded by "atheists, agnostics, practicing Jews, and Catholics, people of all kinds. And they do not necessarily talk about it [their religion]. In moments of hardship, they say that it does them well to go and light an alter candle or go and pray, but nothing more." Zoe is the one in charge of the religious education of her children, who have been assigned a godfather and a godmother in line with Christian tradition, without having been baptized. Her daughter's godparent – a family friend – is a practicing Buddhist.

Zoe's case, which is representative of many others that we collected, underlines how preexisting social ties largely constitute the raison d'être of a person's religious visits. Strong kinship and social ties, even circumstantial relationships as those created while traveling, create bonds that form the basis for such secondary practices. Despite the religious superficiality that may be associated with such visits, it is worth noting how social relations trump religious content itself. The actual destination of religious visits is of lesser importance than the sustaining of social relations.

Another example in which we can see the direct link between religious mobility and social bonds is provided by the case of Caroline, who is in her mid-twenties. Caroline received her religious education in an Evangelical church. Her grandfather – whom she loved dearly – was directly responsible for her religious instruction, which she qualified as "Calvinist" and "austere." As a child, Caroline regularly served at the Mass in a nearby Catholic Church, where she was accompanying her best friend:

> This friend of mine, we grew up together, and anyway she has always been my best friend. And her parents were very engaged in the [Catholic] Church, and we were serving at the Mass, because I was with her ... Well, we only had to ring the bells at the time of the Eucharist. Sometimes I hid a bit, because following what was done or said, the congregation had to answer back. And me, I never knew what I should answer back, I just thought it was cute. But it wasn't anything official, it was simply because we were children. (Interview with Caroline, Geneva 2013; our translation)

Today an affiliated Calvinist, Caroline is engaged in her parish council. She prays and reads the Bible daily. Interestingly, despite the centrality of the parish community in her religious life, Caroline is a representative of the view that religion is a highly personal affair:

> Religion is important for me, but that's actually very personal. I do not see myself as a religious person in the sense in which I understand the concept of religion. ... Because, for me, it does not concern anyone else ... As far as I am concerned, I do not support the idea that religion should be used toward someone else. I only consider religion with regard to myself. I would never use religion to judge someone else ... I don't like religion being used for social pressure, to discriminate people. (Interview with Caroline, Geneva 2013; our translation)

Caroline's formal church role does not prevent her from expanding her religious experiences outside Christianity. On several occasions, she visited a mosque "to accompany friends" and also visited synagogues when the occasion presented itself. Interested in the Middle East, Caroline studies Arabic and learns about Islam. When we met, she had recently returned from an educational field trip, in the course of which she attended a Catholic Mass. Discussing her religious exposures, she emphasized the occasions that presented themselves to her while traveling and meeting people of different persuasions:

> Once, when I was traveling together with a language school, there was a majority of Muslims there. So they tried to observe the evening prayer, a general prayer. And one of the teachers was also a muezzin, who called us to the prayer, and I was very touched by these calls to prayer. And that was sometimes taking place outside, in nature, and sometimes it was inside a mosque ... And I guess I prayed there too, in my own way. And nobody looked at us strangely there, so it was really very inclusive. (Interview with Caroline, Geneva 2013; our translation)

Caroline's association of religious encounters and travels strikes a chord with the experiences of several of our interlocutors, such as the earlier-mentioned Emilie and her exposure to Buddhism through her travel to Cambodia and Vietnam. This idea of the centrality of geographic travel takes on additional meaning if considered from the perspective of the many Swiss residents whose origins are in other countries, as their religious practices tend to diverge greatly from those of their parents, who remained in the country of origin. Thus, for example, Zaid declares himself an atheist, bluntly adding that "the three monotheistic religions, that's the dumbest bullshit that man has created." Instead, he considers the prophets as great writers and the Quran as a literary and poetic work: "These are great writers, great poets, and their poetry, in the Quran everything is poetic, it penetrates the hearts and the spirits." Still, whenever he goes to Morocco to visit his family there, he respects local religious prohibitions, avoids eating pork and expressing his personal views on religion. Another interviewee, Diego, presented a similar approach. Originally from Sardinia, he only goes to church for the main festivals. But when visiting Sardinia, he intensifies his religious practices, which he sometimes combines with visits to cemeteries, a practice that draws him closer to his family and his origin. The same tendency is found in the case of Martina, also Italian by origin, who only attends religious services when she is back in Italy. The notion that geographic return is intertwined with changing the degree of involvement and set of religious practices is in line with our discussions in the chapters on Kenya and Ghana. As we have discussed there, visits to the family homestead often involve participation in a different set of religious practices, which demonstrate religion's social significance in reconnecting the migrant to their place of origin.

In conclusion, it is common for the Swiss to cross confessional lines for an occasional practice or for visiting an event within another religious tradition. We also saw how common it is to form some personalized practices, a fact that challenges researchers. However, many Swiss publicly regard religion as a kind of a taboo, and the question of religious belonging – at whichever level (practice, dogmas, institutional membership, cosmogony, ethics) – is considered a private affair. Restraint and discretion are the rule when it comes to intimate matters of spiritual convictions, and in extreme cases even loved ones might not be aware of what a person believes in and practices.

Conclusion

Our Swiss fieldwork confronted us with fundamental questions. Among them were questions regarding the distinction between religion and spirituality (and the absence thereof), the meaning of religious affiliation within a predominantly secular society, and the subtleties of highly personalized forms of religious practice. No wonder then, that in conducting our interviews in Switzerland, a significant segment of the interview was often dedicated to trying to unravel what we mean exactly by religion. Interviews started by discussing the interviewee's religious socialization, following religious biographies and current practices, to which institutionalized religious forms served as points of reference. While approaching the exchange from such a consensual perspective should have made the terms of discussion easy to follow, as the conversation advanced both interviewee and interviewer were faced with increasingly complex questions. As most interviewees expressed their distaste and rejection of (some elements of) institutionalized religion, a question was raised regarding "substitutions": Has anything emerged in lieu of these criticized formal religions, so often associated with childhood? As interviews were not fully structured, this basic question took various directions. Some interviewees chose to touch on physical practices from their daily lives, such as those related to body-soul well-being, or personalized practices that they apologetically referred to as "superstition." More commonly, however, interviewees brought us into their world of ideas: inspirational readings, existential hypotheses, personal ethics, cosmogonic representations and philosophies, and at times also faith-based convictions in line with institutional dogmas. Could these varied elements, which differ greatly from one person to the next and represent highly personal beliefs, be taken as superseding the role of institutionalized religion?

Indeed, the religious mobility of the Swiss practitioner contains its own particularities, which ought to be taken into account when considering the manifestations of religious butinage. A key characteristic of religion in Switzerland, which we also observed in Ghana, is the frequent refusal to automatically transmit religious belonging in the name of the perpetuation of tradition and identity: "I am not going to baptize my children, as my parents have done with me; my children will need to choose their own religious path for themselves." For most Kenyans, by contrast, the idea of carefully avoiding the imposition of a tradition on their children would seem illogical and problematic, as religion is accepted as a key contributor to the moral education of the child and a safeguard against unruly behavior. Failing to impart this foundation would be regarded as betraying parental duties and may even trigger rumors attributing the family's motivation to ungodly spiritual alliances. In those settings, the rejection of what has been called "*prêt-à-croire*" religion would appear perfectly out of place. As we suggest, even as this Swiss distaste for religious transmission is influenced by a tradition that emphasizes individual autonomy, we propose that it also relies heavily on negative views of institutionalized religion in general.

Thus, the Swiss case study, more than the previous ones, questions the very category of religion, which seems to be transformed out of its original conception, according to Durkheim, as a bond between an institutionalized community, beliefs or dogmas, and ritualized practices. Despite significant internal diversity, we can suggest that contemporary Swiss ways of engaging with religion depart from this conception, which nonetheless remains familiar to our interlocutors, who intuitively divide themselves according to traditional religious categories – Christianity, Buddhism, Islam, and other faiths. However, the socioreligious ethos and actual practices render these categories largely muddled. A person may pray without believing, observe Ramadan without being a Muslim, become part of a religious community without adhering to it institutionally, participate in the religious rituals of others (who might not believe in them either), become fascinated by faraway religious universes that they will never be part of, or privilege ethics over dogma. Institutionalized religions seem to continue playing a role in the construction of identities; in coping with personal crises, above all health-related ones; in joining a personal trajectory to a collective social or cultural belonging; and in the consolidation of social ties. All this happens through borrowing, through to-ing and fro-ing, through hedging and experimenting. Without necessarily praising the practice of religious butinage, nearly all of our Swiss interviewees seemed to suggest that, in the field of religion, "excessive" immobility may turn into a dangerous affair, associated with close-mindedness, bigotry, and intolerance.

PART III

Beyond the Metaphor

7 Between Bees and Flowers

In the previous part of the book, we examined four, predominantly Christian case studies spread across three continents. In all four, we identified meaningful patterns of religious mobility that are especially common and recognizable. For example, in Brazil's Joinville, we noted that butinage tends to be practiced unapologetically and with great diversity, and gives ample consideration to neighborly ties; in Christian urban Kenya, widespread concern with religious misconduct and questions of trust means that religious mobility tends to be cautious and to keep to a mainstream Christian territory; in Ghana, religious mobility is widely associated with social and educational ascension as well as with geographic mobility and kinship; and lastly, in Switzerland, widespread distaste for institutionalized religion means that the religious "buffet" is mainly approached from an individual spiritual perspective, with little commitment to the institution and its social components. Of course, such local generalizations should be qualified on a case-by-case basis. It goes without saying that not all Joinvillians are enthusiastically mobile; not all Nairobians have a sense of institutional religious membership; not all residents of Accra acknowledge religious reaffiliation among youth with a tolerant mindset; and not all Genevese engage in a spiritual search while shying away from formal religious affiliation. Indeed, the careful reader would have noticed that none of these themes is unique to any single case. The acted-upon assertion of individual latitude for religious mobility in the face of institutional prescriptions and social expectations; the compartmentalization of multiple practices; the challenges of trust and mistrust; the intertwinement of motivations for mobility – all these themes emerge and reemerge across all case studies. Our multisited ethnography was thus used to search out key trends that, in some case studies, would have otherwise been overlooked.

In exploring our case studies, we were continuously led by the triangular relationship, discussed in the first part of the book, between religious-institutional scripts, social norms, and individual agency. The case studies, we have seen, offer a diverse range of articulations of this triangular relationship. In some cases, notably in Brazil, we observed a greater emphasis on social norms, in particular through the emphasis on *voisinage* or neighborliness, while in Ghana, kinship is of central importance. In Kenya, on the whole, we have seen greater concern with formal institutional scripts and prohibitions, while our Swiss interviewees in turn tended to assert personal free choice. To be clear, the three perspectives are strongly related, and it is hardly within our interest to draw a clear line between them. When a Joinvillian visits a friend's church, are they abiding by social norms or exerting personal agency? When a Ghanaian Pentecostal warns against traditional churches, is it because they have fully internalized institutional rules? These perspectives, we have seen, are fundamentally intertwined and difficult, sometimes impossible, to isolate.

In this chapter, we take a step forward in linking our case studies and extracting generalized insights from their comparison. We begin to typologize religious butinage based on a continuum of intensities and to observe its dynamic patterns. Importantly, recognizing that butineurs are not always free flowing and inclusive, we discuss in this chapter the notion of territories, to which we have already alluded several times throughout the second part of this work. By territories, we refer to privileged environments and ranges to which groups and individuals may limit their religious mobility. We then discuss the problem of identifying motivations for religious mobility, which has emerged several times throughout our case studies. We argue that this issue is far from straightforward and that it raises many theoretical and methodological challenges. As it is difficult to disentangle any single motivation from the wider context at play in moments of religious change, and while it may be tempting to read the dynamism of religious repertoires[1] through the prism of a simple gain-seeking strategy, we suggest that a more holistic approach should be pursued. We thus introduce the notion of "the three logics." The notion of logics allows us to simply point out the effects of the reoriented positionality of the mobile practitioner on social, material, and other personal factors, while avoiding simplifications of multifactored causality and the suspicion of siding with reductionist instrumentalization.

In bringing together and translating our broad body of material into a set of applicable principles, we cannot avoid returning, once again, to an age-old question: What is religion all about and, in particular, should it be read through the prism of its social, practical, or spiritual value? Fittingly for our project, the word "religion" has been a subject of etymological controversy dating back to antiquity (Rey 1998). Since the works of Lactantius and Tertullian, Christian authors have associated the Latin word "*religio*" with the verb *religare* (rebind). For them, this word alluded to the essential Christian notion of a binding relationship between man and the divine. And yet, another etymology was proposed by Cicero and supported by the great orator's stature: *religio* as derived from *relegere* (to recollect). This second derivation sees religion as emphasizing careful attention and repetition. Understood thus, the word refers to practice, to the minute and vigilant application of rules pertaining to rituals and ceremonies. We thereby note two schools of interpretation concerning the very concept of religion, each of which is supported not only by linguistics but also by empirical – historical and observational – evidence.

While, of course, etymology can be a misleading muse, this double meaning of the word "religion" resonates with our four case studies, which brought up aspects of *religare* in the sense of social and spiritual binding and *relegere* in the sense of repeated and careful practice. We have seen this duality in practice. A practitioner inviting friends and family to their denomination, for example, demonstrates religion's binding ties (*religare*) – not only with God, but also with acquaintances and wider social networks (the Brazilian "neighborliness"). At the same time, the *relegere* etymology challenges us to go beyond a view of religion as binding – either horizontally or vertically (Tarot 1999) – and see its importance within practice itself, whether for the sake of comfort, peace of mind, or possibly a meditative disposition sought through "meticulous concern" and "restless fervor" (Rey 1998, 3161; our translation). Views on religion as a chain and a heritage, such as those suggested by Hervieu-Léger (2000), may bring together both readings: an abstract sense of binding with a given history and an imagined community, achieved through meticulous practice that may or may not be communal.

A Typology of Butineurs

As a first step, we propose a typology of religious butineurs, for which we extend our metaphoric apicultural language. We invite the reader to imagine a continuum: at one end, we find what we will call a "polyfloral" butineur – an avid, limitless peripatetic practitioner – and at the other end, we find the "monofloral" butineur – a model exclusive member of their church who never engages with another tradition. In between these two, we identify "monochrome" butineurs, whose range of practice is limited to one or several religious universes, such as Pentecostal or Afro-Brazilian. Following a Weberian approach, we put forth such a classification of ideal types as a heuristic tool to help us navigate through the blurriness of personal orientations. To be clear, the proposed ideal types are highly dynamic and refer to a given moment in time rather than to any essential characteristic of the person in question. A person may shift orientations over time, adopting an inclusive, dynamic territory of practice at a certain juncture only to opt for a narrower, delimited territory later in life.

Let us consider the first ideal type, that of the polyfloral butineur. Such a practitioner would be a devout butineur who, like João Guimarães Rosa's previously mentioned Riobaldo, "drinks water from any river." In the Brazilian chapter, we observed multiple instances of such polyfloral butinage in Joinville (Soares 2009). In the other case studies, such tendencies were more moderate and discreet. In Kenya, for example, while such mobility is present, it is certainly not the rule. Taking its moral-theological justification from the common maxim "We all believe in the same God," it seems to be especially common among the youth, who would mainly keep to the Christian territory (Gez 2018). For example, Kelly, a university student of about twenty years of age living in Nairobi, has already been to multiple religious services, which she explains in terms of innate curiosity and spiritual openness. Originally from a mixed Catholic/Adventist family background, Kelly attended church twice a week as a child – both on Saturday and on Sunday. When her mother died, she went back to her rural home, where she stayed with her grandmother who draws on the family's traditional African religion. In school, she learned about Islam from her Muslim boyfriend. Beyond that, she has been fascinated by stories about spiritual matters and mysteries such as communication with the afterlife, witchcraft, and demons. For several months, she attended a yoga course at a Hindu temple in Nairobi, and all the while she was influenced by her brother, an adamant atheist who mocks people's religious convictions. According to Kelly, what matters most is for a person to simply follow a religious path that makes sense to them. When we asked her about her religious affiliation, she responded that she sees herself simply as a Christian and added: "I cannot say anything specific because, all these different denominations, we are all worshiping one God ... I don't want to say, like I'm Catholic, I'm Protestant. You know if, if need be and you ask me, I will tell you, but I am a Christian, that's bottom line, yeah." In line with her diverse religious exposures and going beyond a Christian-only territory, Kelly added later in the discussion that "religion is just, it's the same thing, it's one and the same thing, only that people use different words to describe it and maybe they add a few more practices." Among the general Kenyan public, however, fully indiscriminate polyfloral butinage tends to be regarded critically. A believer is expected to have at least some grounding in one privileged tradition, the absence of which may lead to accusations of lack of commitment or ulterior motives.

In Geneva, too, we find polyfloral butineurs, who prefer multiple and diverse practices over exclusive membership. These practitioners develop their own range of practice in the face of institutional distaste for butinage, manifesting an autonomy that is accompanied by an often-critical view of religious institutions themselves. In some cases, mobility is thus explained in terms of discontent with institutional injunctions and control. We recall, for example, our earlier discussion of the case of Sonia, who came from a practicing Protestant Swiss family but has been traveling far and wide with her own practices, often under the influence of the men in her life. Having been married to both a Muslim and an Evangelical Christian, she had the opportunity to experiment with both these religious forms, while at the same time she also engaged with and found inspiration in New Age spirituality and Buddhism. By contrast, a minority of Swiss, whom we've already encountered under Stolz's category of "institutionalists," limit their butinage to narrow territories and might even shun mobility altogether.

We thus see that religious butinage consists of varying degrees of dynamism. Some practitioners may adopt a strictly sedentary religious lifestyle either temporarily or permanently, making up our second ideal type, the monofloral butineur. Among our interviewees who have described their religious identity as fully and loyally subscribing to the demands of their single religious membership, we noted – unexpectedly – a high percentage of clergy and religious specialists. These monofloral butineurs fully "endorse" the formal theological-liturgical prescriptions of their religious institutions and are the unwavering believers imagined by Abrahamic religious traditions who have shaped the classical scholarly conception of what makes a practitioner. One example of this kind of monofloral category was mentioned in our chapter on Switzerland as a minority within Stolz's four-type classification of the Swiss religious landscape:

> Most people interviewed [who are active members of established churches] clearly refuse to leave their church, often announcing this refusal even as they vehemently criticize their church. Some have only little faith, or even none whatsoever, and some have not been to their church in a long time. Their reasons for staying are multiple. In most cases, church affiliation is to them an unquestionable part of their tradition. (Stolz et al. 2015, 157; our translation)

The idea of monofloral butineurs might appear counterintuitive: why insist on the inclusion of sedentary practitioners within a mobile conceptual framework? However, framing non-mobile practitioners as a subset of butinage is an extension of our commitment to the reversal of normativity: the conceptual marginalization of sedentarism is an extension of our privilege of mobility and critique of fully exclusive religious adherence. It is certainly possible that; at a certain point in time, the practitioner may disengage with mobility, but such sedentarism is approached with a pinch of salt – a reminder that it may be partial, temporary, or both. The monofloral butineur is, after all, an ideal type – one that might not fully take form – and serves as an invitation for scholars to consider additional, subtle layers of practice. Indeed, considering the pressures and rewards that often motivate the presentation of such a loyalist discourse as well as our mapping of de facto lived religion, the monofloral category can be read as an expression of our skepticism and our recognition that self-ascription can be deployed rhetorically in the service of projecting institutional piety. In this way, to speak of monofloral butinage as the counterpoint to polyfloral is to establish a continuum between the two ends, and through it, emphasize dynamism. This notion follows from our focus on the fluidity of practice, as fluidity entails the very prospect of both dis- and re-engagement with mobility. Thus, by subsuming full-fledged religious loyalists – if we accept that those truly exist – into a dynamic framework, we draw attention to how sedentarism forever maintains its potential for changeability, subtle though it may be.

It is between the two ends of monofloral and polyfloral that most religious practitioners live out their religious identity, operating within what we would call a monochrome mobility – that is to say, mobility within a well-recognized institutional range or "family" of traditions. In thinking about what makes a unified religious field, we may draw on the breakdown of relevant religious forms in the image of a genealogical tree or an archipelago that divides into religious traditions, denominations, and possibly even specific branches.[2] Thus, for example, we may consider, conservatively and expectedly, that two Pentecostal denominations of a similar orientation should be placed alongside one another, with the Pentecostal-only practitioner being classified as a monochrome butineur. Presbyterianism, for example, would be imagined as being further away, and Islam – with its own myriad traditions and denominations – is further still, across the ocean, as it were. As we have shown in the chapter on Joinville, this mobility pattern presented itself as particularly common in our Brazilian case study. A Pentecostal practitioner at the Assemblies of God, for instance, may gladly take part in services at other popular Pentecostal churches (for example, God Is Love, International Church of the Foursquare Gospel), but would be hesitant about attending a Catholic Mass or visiting a Candomblé *terreiro*, where they would be expected to make a sacrifice to one of the Afro-Brazilian spirits. A Catholic may agree to take part in Christian-ecumenical services, but is less likely to venture out as far as praying at a mosque. In short, this kind of butineur travels within a given territory. To stick to the spatial image, they may travel off to nearby countries, but would avoid the kind of transoceanic voyage that leads to a *terra nova*.

Having mentioned Brazil, we have seen examples of this kind of monochrome butinage in our three other case studies as well. In Kenya, where Christians are accustomed to visiting religious services in churches other than their own, we spoke to Katia, a Pentecostal teacher in the Kibera slum, who told us: "Yeah, I go to other churches when I'm invited to go and minister, I go to churches. Sometimes I just go to a church for a change, see the way they worship, you know, just for a change." In the same breath, Katia specified that her visits are limited to Pentecostal churches of the same ilk as her own. In non-Pentecostal churches, she suggested: "I will not be blessed. I think I just have that mentality ... I need the fiery ministry. I want the humility that comes from the heart that is provided by the Holy Spirit. [In other churches,] I will not be blessed, my brother." Religious territories organize themselves in accordance with specific institutional universes and familiar theologies and the images associated therewith. The same trend was found in Ghana, where charismatic religious leaders invite each other to preach. Such invitations establish a system of mutual recognition that is fundamental to the construction of charismatic authority within specific religious territories (Rey 2014, 2013a). But invitations are also at the heart of the religious mobility of lay practitioners, who maintain social connections through practices of reciprocal invitation between churches. Friendships, neighborly ties, and kinship nourish a butinage that draws on the words "I invite you to my church."

In Switzerland, where religious boundaries appear least strict, such mobility within a single religious universe is equally widespread. In our chapter on Switzerland, we discussed the case of Noémie, who was brought up Catholic but engaged in religious mobility, mainly within Christianity. Recognizing the limits of butinage, she suggested that "it is interesting being curious and seeing what is being done [elsewhere]. But sometimes, going out to taste all religions, you are left without really knowing which one you are attached to ... This can create some kind of instability." Similarly, Stolz and his team affirmed that, among Swiss Evangelicals, there is a tendency to adopt a monochrome mobility pattern that keeps to the same Evangelical universe:

> Among Evangelicals, we note a substantial tendency to change communities ... Many Evangelicals are ready to change their religious community if it would offer them a way of living out their faith more fully, of better

> educating their children according to Christian principles, or if their life circumstances lend themselves to change. According to their perspective, the important question has less to do with the choice of the community and more with belonging to a community within which their own faith will be reinforced and deepened. (Stolz et al. 2015, 160; our translation)

Complicating the notion of monochrome butineurs, however, is the fact that classification can vary. Attentiveness to local classifications can affect how we may choose to define what constitutes a field of mobility for the monochrome butineur. For example, we may introduce charismatic and traditional Catholicism as two separate religious forms or do the same with regard to denominations within the Pentecostal universe, which after all, to borrow from Ludwig Wittgenstein, makes up "a wide variety of movements scattered throughout the world that can be described as having 'family resemblance'" (cited in Anderson 2010, 15). In Ghana, the reference to religious leaders as "men of God" and their complex system of networks and associations is more revealing of the religious territories than churches' formal titles and theological orientations (Rey 2014, 2019). Such differences in perspectives are exacerbated the more attentive we are to people's own subjective understanding of the religious landscape around them, as influenced by personal experiences as well as preferences and taste. Indeed, when we take such subjectivity of perspective into consideration, the top-down categorization of religious traditions as implied by the notion of monochrome butinage may well be insufficient. How, then, do we account for the actual range of legitimate religious mobility as individually composed and negotiated? For that we shall now turn to discuss the notion of religious territories.

Territories

In the previous section, we introduced three ideal types of butineurs: the polyfloral and the monofloral as two opposites and in between them the monochrome, which refers to mobility within a particular range or "family" of religious traditions. In this section, we take this idea forward by arguing that all three categories are subsets of countless personal variations that we call religious territory. In using this spatial terminology, we consciously draw on the myriad ways in which "religions offer *geographies*, cognitive maps of the earth" (Tweed 2006, 113; emphasis in the original). Religions, for example, cultivate conceptions of collective "us" and "them," notions of "homeland" and "exile," and ideas about the self and its limits and of circles of intimacy and their boundaries. Our notion of territory considers one particular aspect of such orientation and affinities, and may be defined as an individual's range of conceivable practice, thought of as legitimate and personally relevant, whether or not supported by actual practice (Gez and Droz 2019). Being an imagined, hypothetical construct, such a personalized "cartography" of the conceivable is open to change over time and is often context specific. Religious territories follow from discourse and, as such, complement actual practice, lending themselves to a set of questions along the discourse-action nexus.

How might such hypothetical "turfs" be organized? As we have seen earlier in the book, and especially in relation to Janet McIntosh's work presented in the section on syncretism (McIntosh 2009), the expectation for an individual's range of religious practices to come together and make up a consistent, coherent whole is wishful and most likely flawed. Unlike the notion of the monochrome butineur, people's actual religious interests, curiosities, and combinations may exceed a single religious realm or cosmology and, even when they don't, may not fall into neat institutional categories. Indeed, accounting for personal territories passes through the recognized personalization of the religious landscape. Such personalization should take into consideration common themes or practices that cut across different religious denominations – for example, possession, Holy Spirit, healing, prosperity, teachings – addressing the in-between states that imply religiousness in the making. Indeed, personalized religious territories can make any number of connections between religious forms, including unexpected ones. Here, Hervieu-Léger's notion of "converters" (*convertisseurs*) – reminiscent of Birman's (1996) notion of "bridges" – seems adequate. This notion refers to "the thematic or practical devices of transposing from one religious universe to another; acts which, in turn, facilitate the mobility of believers" (Hervieu-Léger 2001a, 2001b, 107; our translation). A practitioner may emphasize converters/bridges and similarities in a manner that would bring together seemingly incommensurable religious contradictions and allow them to dwell side by side.

The actual deciphering of territories raises another epistemological challenge. As practitioners do not have to commit themselves to coherent theology or practice – recall McIntosh's (2009) notion of polyontology – territories may be fluid, possibly rhetorical utterances that depend on context and on the audience – a religious self-portrayal that takes us back to Goffman's (1959) previously mentioned reminder concerning the centrality of reported speech and the formation of social images through inference. To minimize the challenge of rhetorical self-misrepresentation – for example through noncommittal, lip-service discourse of inclusion – our research tried to identify territories in concrete terms. To seize these hypothetical contours – changeable as they may be – we employed, in our interview guide, both positive and negative articulations. While the positive articulations were used to assemble the religious forms that interlocutors would see themselves attending, whether as a member or as a visitor, the negative articulations sought to identify religious forms that would be a priori excluded from practice: "Are there any religions that you would never practice, or denominations that you would never set foot in? Which ones, and why?" These questions can be best understood in line with observations regarding the role played by the demarcation of identity frontiers for self-definition (Cohen 1982; Swidler 2001a). As we have seen in the chapter on Kenya, such negative articulations are often mediated through stories, rumors, and high-profile scandals.[3] As we show in that chapter, outside the territory of normativity, "foreign" religious forms tend to be delegitimized and discouraged, and are widely cast as "funny."

Indeed, while we think of territories from an individual point of view, such constructions may echo social conceptions about legitimacy and normativity. Here we again return to our basic distinction between religious-institutional, social-normative, and individual perspectives: territories may be phrased in a unique manner, and may well not correspond to formal institutional divisions, but at the same time, they tend to maintain relations with collective norms. One striking example, in this regard, is the discursive difference that we observed in Kenya and Brazil concerning the inclusivity of religious territory: while our Joinvillian interviewees on the whole seemed to embrace an inclusive discourse open to multiple cosmologies, our Kenyan interviewees largely shied away from recognizing the appeal of non-Christian – or rather non-normative Christian – religious forms. This finding does not mean Kenyans do not engage with non-Christian forms – traditional healers, for one thing, are alive and well in Kenya. However, it seems to be indicative of the central role played by formal institutional religions in that country. This prominence has complex reasons, but it might in part be explained in terms of the high presence of missionaries in the country, both historically and through the Pentecostal and Evangelical movements in recent decades, and more broadly in terms of the role of Christianity in the making of the Kenyan state. While the role of Christianity in state-building is also found in Brazil, it is in tension with the social code of *voisinage* and its celebration of Brazil as a land of unabashed diversity.

The articulation of territories can thus serve not only as a representational counterpart to the listing of a practitioner's range of actual religious practice but also as a way to unpack wider questions about sociopolitical and institutional representations. Indeed, implied in the contours of religious territory is the normative idea that mobility outside the territory is ill advised but that, within the territory, mobility can enjoy significant acceptance. In this respect, territories can be read – somewhat rationalized – as modes of personal and collective legitimization. By extension, shifting discourse may be indicative of intended shifts in practice. Such discourse-practice comparison thus opens up a wide set of questions regarding the socioreligious logic that guides the practitioner along multiple temporalities, including questions regarding relations with past practices and territories' predicative power concerning future practice.

If territories are a representational field, how do we propose accounting for its stated counterpart, namely, the *actual* range of practice? In the next chapter, we shall return to this question through our introduction of the religious repertoires model.

From Motivation to Logic

We recognize the substantial complexity associated with the question of religious motivation, for which we find no easy answers. Over the years, the question of religious motivation – why do people practice, modify their practices, or desist from practice? – has attracted many scholarly debates. From the emphasis on ties with the sacred or the "numinous" (Otto 1923), through Durkheim's (1968) readings emphasizing the importance of social consolidation, up to contemporary utilitarian readings along the lines of the religious economy school (Finke and Stark 1992; Iannaccone 1991; Iannaccone, Finke, and Stark 1997), there have been multiple attempts and angles from which to tackle the question of religious motivation. But while the "why" is certainly not irrelevant to the issue of religious mobility, it is highly contentious – both methodologically and conceptually – and easily leads to a disparity between practitioners' own emic views on the intrinsic value of their practice and scholars' utilitarian, and often reductionist, etic explanations. Moreover, touching on the fundamental tension between actual experience, memory, and linguistic reconstruction, actors' narratives might be "tainted" by after the fact reconstructions of events (Stromberg 1993; Wuthnow 2011). Indeed, practitioners actively engage in the kind of narrative building that tends to recast both past and present engagements as culminating in their current conviction, while religious groups may exert implicit pressure on the narrator to conform to a "normative" conversion paradigm. In other words, the narrative of a life history – or a conversion career (Gooren 2014) – is actually a present-time reconstruction, possibly a "biographic illusion" (Bourdieu 1986).

Earlier in the book, we saw the inadequacies of identifying religious mobility – and conversion in particular – with an utter spiritual transformation. Instead, many scholars, especially those whose work focuses on the Global South, have come to identify the practical side of religious mobility, though often with some self-conscious discomfort. Thus, David Smilde (2007) tells us how, when he began his exploration of Evangelical conversions in Venezuela, he was surprised and ill at ease with the extent to which interviewees themselves emphasized practical considerations as a motivation for their religious mobility:

> I entered the field with the idea that religious conversion was undertaken for religious reasons, not for the nonreligious rewards resulting from belief and practice. Nevertheless, from my first days in the field it became clear that my respondents did not support this assumption … [T]ime and time again people unabashedly said they had converted because of the perceived economic, social, and personal gains … Of course, it is hardly news that people intentionally change aspects of their lives in order to address the challenges they face: they get married or divorced, return to or drop out of school, move or stay put, apologize or take stands. But adopting a set of *beliefs* in order to address the pressing challenges of everyday life is different. Can people really *decide* to believe in a religion because it is in their interest to do so? (Smilde 2007, 7; emphasis in the original)

As the title of Smilde's book, *Reason to Believe*, suggests, his reply to whether people may "choose to believe" is affirmative (see also Kirsch 2004). Smilde argues that, indeed – to some extent at least – people may choose to adopt certain sets of religious beliefs that they think would serve their striving to overcome life's hurdles. Smilde recounts personal challenges among the lower and lower-middle classes of Caracas, whose hardships echo those of our interviewees in Kenya, Brazil, or Ghana, such as violence, abuse of alcohol and drugs, and socioeconomic marginalization, alongside other features of volatility including high levels of corruption. From this perspective, religious mobility may appear like blunt pragmatism, the type articulated by Frans Wijsen in his research in East Africa when he suggested that "most Africans have a pragmatic worldview … They look for health and wealth and go where it is available at the lowest cost. They just cannot afford to invest in things that yield no return" (Wijsen 2007, 176).[4] Such pragmatic focus certainly has its appeal, especially in fragile living circumstances. In our own research, we encountered many examples to that effect. In Nairobi, for example, we met such interviewees as Isaac, a young singer who made a conscious decision to shift to gospel music in order to avoid "the things that can make you fail in life"; Daniel, who explained that he presents himself as a born-again Christian in order to invite wholesome interactions; and Jennifer, who presented her quest for salvation as a conscious "plan," set in order to escape the vices of her family and her unhappy upbringing. Further reminiscent of Smilde's Caracas converts to Evangelicalism, Isaac, Daniel, and Jennifer all chose to adopt and consolidate a born-again identity.

And yet, thinking of religion in purely pragmatic terms has clear drawbacks. Above all, and as Smilde himself acknowledges, such a reading has a sharp instrumentalist tone, whose "Achilles' heel" Smilde identifies in the form of reductionism. A perspective limited to the study of external gains, he argues, "contradicts the analytic existence of what it is trying to explain" (Smilde 2007, 48) by ignoring the intrinsic value of the social phenomenon studied or subordinating it to external ends. Recognizing rational choice while trying to overcome instrumentalist reductionism, Smilde adopts the term "imaginative rationality" to refer to the way in which social agents may adopt a new set of religious beliefs as a way of reimagining their lives and their position within the social landscape.

Smilde's engagement with the difficulty of addressing motivation is to be saluted. In many cases, scholars stay away from this thorny affair, either dropping it altogether or steering the discussion away from this shaky ground in search of a firmer foothold. The same goes for the question of sincerity of the intention behind conversion. The very question brings to mind the problematic distinction between intrinsic and extrinsic orientations as developed by Gordon Allport (1966; see also Allport and Ross 1967).[5] While the model has been widely influential (Donahue 1985, 400), the intrinsic/extrinsic binary has multiple shortcomings – regarding epistemology, moralism, and clear-cut simplicity – which, in our view, serve as a warning against such a line of analysis (Kirkpatrick and Hood 1990). The challenge of identifying motivations appears particularly daunting in the personalized world of contemporary "Sheilaism" (Bellah et al. 1985), where self-fashioned, one-person quilts of meaning may overtake participation in a collective sacred canopy (Berger 1967b).

In light of such challenges, many anthropologists focus less on the "why" and more on the "how" of religious mobility, and note that conversions may occur without a clearly articulated, well-calculated "reason" (see, for example, Premawardhana 2018). We can see this focus, for example, in Attiya Ahmad's (2017) treatment of conversion to Islam among female South Asian domestic workers in Kuwait. Like Smilde, Ahmad has two obvious contenders to account for these conversions: on the one hand, the conversion can be framed as a response to Kuwait's active *da'wah* or proselytism movement, while, on the other hand, it can be taken as associated with practical benefits such as accumulating symbolic capital in a foreign country. Instead, however, Ahmad explores a more subtle explanation, and understands her interlocutors' transformation in quotidian terms and as a process of shifting habits and sensibilities that emerge over time. Rather than considering conversion as transcending everyday interactions, Ahmad firmly grounds it therein: "These women's conversions index emergent forms of subjectivity, affinity, and organizing that do not constitute an exception to everyday life, but rather, that constitute important forms thereof, ones anthropology increasingly needs to contend with in our contemporary world" (194).

We recognize the need to go beyond an intrinsic-extrinsic dichotomy, as well as beyond the reductionism of a fully fledged utilitarian approach. According to Ter Haar (2011), religion consists of four tangible categories: ideas, practices, organizations, and experiences. While it is possible, in theory, to draw on one aspect of this package to the exclusion of the others, practicing a religious form implies a degree of absorption, which makes it difficult to dissociate one aspect of engagement from the wider whole. Our basic argument is therefore that, within the actual experience of religiosity, the question of motivation is, by and large, inextricably entangled. Of course, some forms of religious engagement are clearly associated with a particular gain – for example, attending a healing session or being the beneficiary of a religious charity – but even these may raise questions as to the clear-cut certainty with which motivations can be isolated.

Recognizing the entanglement of motivations and the epistemological difficulty in determining them, we nonetheless recognize the validity of the question at hand. Rather than simplifying or avoiding it, we tackle this challenge by speaking in terms of logics. This approach stems from our understanding that religious motivation is a fluid term that is difficult to pinpoint and, as such, requires us to adopt a comprehensive perspective. The term "logic" is, in our view, more suitable than "motivation" in an attempt to avoid simplistic illusions and clear-cut causal relations. Rather than suggesting that practitioners turn to a particular religious practice as calculated rational entities with the intention of maximizing benefits, we suggest that multiple, sometimes-conflicting logics coexist, are embedded within the actors' habitus, and are not always reducible to well delineated, premeditated motivations (Bourdieu 1980). Epistemologically, the focus on "logic" offers an advantage over "motivation": while motivation belongs to the inner world of considerations that, for the scholar at least, is largely inaccessible or at least highly mediated, the notion of logic lays a more modest claim. Unlike any single identification of motivation, the notion of logic recognizes the intertwinement of elements into a constellation of actions that have interrelated outcomes. In particular, we identify three perspectives or logics associated with religious identity and religious mobility – practical, social, and inclinational.[6] Let us quickly explain the three logics.

By "practical logic," we refer to ways in which religious participation is supportive of practical considerations. These may include, most commonly, financial and material incentives such as healing or direct assistance from a religious organization. Less direct practical considerations would include, for instance, the availability of activities such as a church-operated school for children. Another significant practical consideration that we have observed involves geographic proximity and simple convenience. In our research in Accra, for instance, we were struck – much like Smilde (2007) in Caracas – by the prominence of such pragmatism. Very often, we learned that religious mobility was associated with health concerns, hope for social mobility, and financial or educational success. One major feature of this practical logic in Accra was its propensity to transcend religious boundaries, even across so-called world religions, for instance when Muslim practitioners seek a weekly prayer-blessing from Pentecostal "anointed men of God."

By "social logic," we refer to the consolidation of social ties as well as the boosting of social image or prestige. Such logic corresponds to a Durkheimian perspective and is at the core of Soares's (2009) observations with regard to Brazil. Through the notion of "*voisinage*" (neighborliness), Soares suggested that the reproduction of social ties is at the heart of butinage. Similar observations were also made in Kenya (Gez and Droz 2017), as well as in Ghana and Switzerland.

By "inclinational logic," we refer to the significance of religious participation in personal terms, such as leisure, feeling of well-being, and/or personal taste, as well as spiritual fulfillment and nourishment. At times, a person may feel attached to a particular religious form without being able to put this attachment into words. Indeed, inclinational logic does not limit itself to spiritual connection in any "deep" sense; attraction based on entertainment value and pastime may also influence personal preference in a way that is irreducible to any of the other two logics. From a scholarly perspective, we propose that giving inclinational considerations their due place – taking all claims for attachment to a certain religious form seriously, including "just because" argumentations – can help us to steer clear of reductionist, externally imposed interpretations.

Indeed, one of the implications of the three logics approach is the avoidance of a straightforward association of religious mobility with clear-cut utility and personal gain–seeking. Rather, keeping the three logics in view at all times allows us to consider the negotiated trade-off – and possible tensions – between the three elements in an irreducible manner. Above all, this approach can help us consider the interplay between social expectations and personal gain: A person ignores social expectations at their own peril, as practical gains may be offset by social penalties such as the depreciation of social image. Such tension between logics, which may at times backfire, calls for a nuanced understanding of expectations by the dominant ethos (for example, avoiding "too much" mobility; limiting mobility to a certain religious territory; refraining from seeming "too zealous"). Understanding how the three logics actually interact, we can evoke the following example from the world of employment to illustrate the significance of manifesting the social value of commitment even in the face of seeming personal gain:

> People feel that a man ought not to change his job too often and that one who does is erratic and untrustworthy. Two months after taking a job a man is offered a job he regards as much superior but finds that he has, on the side, bet his reputation for trustworthiness on not moving again for a period of a year and regretfully turns the job down. His decision about the new job is constrained by his having moved two months prior and his knowledge that, however attractive the new job, the penalty in the form of a reputation for being erratic and unstable will be severe if he takes it. The existence of generalized cultural expectations about the behavior of responsible adult males has combined with his recent move to stake his personal reputation, nominally extraneous to the decision about the new job, on that decision. (Becker 1960, 36)

The tension presented by Becker would be recognizable to many of our interviewees. In the chapter on Kenya, we have already met Leonard, a Kenyan interviewee who was torn between the practical economic boost he was receiving at his Pentecostal church and the social pressure from his girlfriend, coupled with his own intrinsic sense of belonging, which were beckoning him to return to the Catholic Church in which he was brought up. But the negotiation of logics does not have to imply a contradiction between them, and could entail mutual reinforcement. Becoming born again may be interpreted as a personal spiritual project (inclinational logic), but is also recognized for its social significance (social logic; see, for example, Englund 2007), as well as a means for reorienting life for practical purposes (practical logic; see, for example, Smilde 2007).

In summary, the three logics uncover a complex system of give and take, which transcends any straightforward advantage-seeking equation and should be analyzed case by case. While we have found this approach to offer a useful analytical framework, we emphasize that it merely represents one possible heuristic toolkit. In reality, practitioners may not be so reflexive as they blur boundaries of motivational categories within their processes of religious reorientation.

Degrees of Practice and Their Complementarity

An important classification that the butinage perspective allows us to consider concerns the hierarchy between different degrees of multiple, concurrent practices. Early in the book, we discussed our critique of the notion of conversion – especially when it is portrayed through the dramatic, Pauline "road to Damascus" paradigm – as representing only a fraction of the actual dynamism of religious mobility. In exploring de facto practice in our four case studies, we encountered a variety of subtler forms of mobility and constellations of elements within religious identity. According to our approach, self-identification through a given religious collective noun is insufficient, in and of itself, for recognizing a person's actual commitments and practice – the Pope would identify himself as Catholic, but so might a baptized yet non-practicing Swiss. Indeed, comparing formal affiliation with de facto practice may reveal fascinating tensions. In line with the butinage perspective's emphasis on practice, we thus offer a typology of degrees of intensity of practice.

Mapping degrees of practice allows us to recognize individual practices both at a given point in time and over time. We can observe temporal fluctuations and consider interrelations between multiple practices. Observing concurrent practices, we propose a hierarchical ordering of the relations between them. In Kenya as well as Ghana, our interviewees intuitively distinguished their primary practice at their "home church," where they might feature on the formal membership list, from secondary practices and visits elsewhere (Gez 2018). The home church represents the sense of institutional belonging and may – but not necessarily – correspond to formal membership. By contrast, secondary practices vary greatly and may include anything from occasional visits to a neighbor's church, through butinage in some formal capacity (for example, attending as a guest preacher), to forms of passive consumption such as "zapping" between religious media channels. We note, in particular, cases of episodic religious visits, often made in response to an invitation from a friend or a family member. Motivation for such participation may vary, and practices might even take the form of a pastime. This view undermines the dominant "theological" perspective, which regards the religious as too serious to be interpreted "merely" as a spectacle attended for its entertainment value. One Kenyan interviewee, a Pentecostal called

Deborah, explained this dual system using the terms "membership" and "church visits," starting with the latter:

> Occasionally going to another church, [that is when] you go, fellowship with them, and then go back to your church. That is an occasional moving. But moving [completely is when] you are out, you go to another church, [and] you leave this one. Now that attachment is not there, you detach yourself … A visitor has no membership, he has gone to visit. You have gone maybe to fellowship once or a second time, there is no commitment. But [in] membership there is that commitment, maybe you take your tithe there, you fellowship each and every time, you get involved in the church programs. But [as] a visitor, I might be here today, [but] tomorrow I am in another church. (Interview with Deborah, Nairobi 2011)

Despite such simple-sounding discourse, assessing which is the home church and which is a locus of secondary practice is not always simple. If, indeed, we base our assessment on de facto practice and seek to marginalize theological concepts, we should cultivate a healthy skepticism toward such terms as "membership," which may hide more than they reveal. Within Christian tradition, the act of tithing is often a practice-based indicator of a practitioner's home church, as people would not normally divide their tithe but give it to the one church that they feel closest to and attend most regularly (Droz and Gez 2015). However, as discussed in the chapter on Kenya, such an indicator would marginalize non-Christian religious groups and, even within Christianity, may misrepresent those churches that put less emphasis on tithing.

To avoid such complications, we evoke a neutral image: the religious form practiced with the greatest intensity at any given time is termed the religious "pivot," and any additional, concurrent practices are regarded as "peripheral." The choice of the term "pivot" conveys the duality of changeability and stability; it is, according to the *Oxford Dictionary*, "the central point, pin, or shaft on which a mechanism turns or oscillates" and can also be applied to people and locations of central importance. In adopting this term, rather than a term such as "affiliation," we emphasize our distancing from institutional categories and our reliance on de facto experience. The pivot is the person's stable-yet-changeable center of practice, and it may or may not correspond to formal institutional membership. By contrast, the term "periphery" was chosen as it is defined in relation to this single, dominant practice, emphasizing their interrelatedness. As we will see later, this simple, dual distinction can be explained in line with the three logics and in terms of complementarity. The pivot serves as a vertical anchor of belonging, while peripheral practices offer horizontal paths of experimentation and dynamic expansion.

Implied here is the idea that the religious pivot is singular and privileged, while peripheral practices might be multiple. This general assertion is supported by our findings, as shown in the previous part of the book. As we have seen most clearly in Kenya and Ghana, our interviewees largely maintained a clear view of their singular institutional pivot, even as they occasionally expanded to include secondary practices, for example in response to invitations by friends. For these interviewees, secondary practices varied in number and intensity but were somehow controlled, as we consider in this section. The distinction between pivot and periphery was also common among many of our Brazilian interviewees, though not all, with some highly mobile ones showing no intuitive propensity toward forming hierarchies of belonging – supported by practice – between their multiple religious engagements. The case of our Swiss interviewees is different still, for many of them have not been highly practicing, at least not in terms of institutionalized religious forms. While they may have engaged in sporadic practices on occasion, these Swiss interviewees cannot be said to have a clear pivot around which additional, minor practices revolve. In Geneva and Freiburg, actual religious mobility seems to be accompanied by a weak degree of identification and adherence to formal religious ethos. Practice may be limited to rites of passage such as weddings and funerals, to moments of touristic exploration and intellectual curiosity, or to specific quests for exotic enrichment and entertainment, spiritual experience, or healing. All the while, however, practitioners seem to maintain an intellectual, ethical, and political distance. Their expectation from the religious forms with which they engage is soberly delimited – not a life-regulating totality but a selective adoption of elements of interest. We thus suggest that the single pivot/multiple peripheries model is applicable to many, but certainly not all, cases.

One way in which we can think about how relations between the pivot and peripheral practices can be conceptualized is through the introduction of the spatial image of two axes. The "vertical axis" makes up the principle religious anchor or pivot, a locus aimed at deepening familiarity and feelings of belonging within a single religious form. Practitioners become versed in the workings of their institution, developing important ties with the leadership and the congregation and immersing themselves in its teachings and practices over time. These characteristics contrast with the "horizontal axis" of secondary religious practices, which require little or no commitment and are therefore more flexible in their application. Unfettered by the history of institutional interaction and socialization, these secondary practices are sites of unattached, sometimes playful, exploration.

In terms of common social perception, both axes may be deemed virtuous in their own right. The pivot offers a locus of rootedness, seriousness, and belonging that is socially appreciated and rewarded by granting the practitioner an air of respectability. Peripheral practices are similarly upheld as virtuous in their own way, insofar as they emphasize religious solidarity and trust. For instance, we often noted how refusing to respond to invitations to visit other places of worship, thus foregoing opportunities to incorporate new peripheral practices, may risk classifying a practitioner as unfriendly and, in some cases, as a suspicious secularist or sect member. While interrelations between the two axes are – in most contexts – socially accepted, a practitioner may need to maintain a fine balance and hierarchy between them, in line with prevailing social norms. For example, in Kenya, a practitioner with multiple secondary practices and no single, stable pivot risks being denounced as a "church hopper." This borrowed term[7] refers to a person who too readily and too often shifts between religious forms without holding on to a clear center. The term evokes the secular – and, from a devout perspective, unflattering – connotations of "bar hopping" and "club hopping." The church hopper is widely regarded as religiously immature and unstable, and is looked upon with suspicion as a problematic individual who may have been forced to leave congregations due to poor moral standing or for having sown seeds of disunity.

The problem inherent in habitually changing pivot was captured by David, a Kenyan interviewee who – speaking in the presence of his wife – used an analogy to his marriage: "I have my wife here. Right now, we are with her, [but] next time if you come back, maybe you go back to your country and you come back, you find me I have another wife. I have chased her away, so I have another wife, [laughing] it won't look good, you see." Thinking in terms of this image of seemingly excessive mobility may help decipher the intriguing utterance of another Kenyan interviewee, Judy, who suggested that "it is fine going to maybe five churches, but it is too much going to twenty." Judy's claim can be understood as a warning to the effect that, while secondary practices are tolerated, shifting too much energy toward them can confuse their subsidiary status vis-à-vis the person's religious pivot. Another interviewee specified and proposed that, while church visits are not bad in and of themselves, they should be restricted to no more than once a month, lest they arouse confusion about the place of belonging.

Practitioners, we propose, often have an interest in maintaining this dual system, for it allows them to enjoy the complementary advantages of having two degrees of practice. While the full list of potential advantages is too vast and varied to present here, by way of illustration we use the notion of the three logics, which we discussed in the previous section, to hint at the usefulness of this dual, horizontal-vertical system. Speaking in general terms, the pivot of practice – the vertical axis – offers access to formal and informal "members only" advantages. In practical terms, the committed practitioner can rely on material aid, either formally through the church or informally through congregational ties. In Kenya, they may be allowed to hold a *harambee* (a "pulling together," in the form of a fundraiser) for a personal cause such as the payment of hospital bills. They would also be assisted in funeral arrangements for departed loved ones and may be invited to participate in a church-led money-saving group. In terms of social logic, the pivot can help the practitioner develop ties with fellow congregants, deepening their sense of belonging. By showing commitment, they may gain access to church leadership roles that are not available to the occasional visitor, thus gaining professional experience while cultivating social prestige and a feeling of self-worth. In terms of inclinational logic, interviewees testified to the spiritual benefits of institutional belonging, emphasizing the significance of trust in their pastor and the reassurance of theological consistency. The previously cited Deborah, for instance, emphasized the importance of "spiritual stability." She explained:

> I am in this church and this is what the church is teaching. Maybe there is a problem, maybe [it is] teaching for a whole month a topic and from there you move to the next topic, that one will be like, that growth is systematic. But, I mean, [if I go to] this church today, I go to another church tomorrow, [then in] the teachings, there is no flow. (Interview with Deborah, Nairobi 2011)

Joining the discussion, Deborah's friend Mary agreed that commitment to a single church supports systematic spiritual growth and added the idea of accountability: "You are accountable to someone. They know how you are doing. Maybe if you have a gift, a talent, someone can mentor you, you are accountable to someone, not like just you come, you go, no." Reserved for committed practitioners, such practical, social, and inclinational advantages are a point of appeal within religious institutions' attempts to draw in new followers – as well as to rein in existing ones.

Peripheral practices – the horizontal axis – hold different practical, social, and inclinational advantages. While the efficacy of the pivot is tied to the vertical axis of deepening ties, peripheral practices draw their efficacy from their horizontal spread and flexibility. Our interviewees often emphasized that specific religious forms and religious leaders are known for their distinctive qualities, such as their musical talents, inspirational sermons, or potent healing sessions. Exhibiting a flexible attitude toward engaging with multiple religious forms, practitioners may ideally draw on these specializations, which may be less compelling or simply unavailable in their home church. Practically, by associating themselves with a number of peripheral practices, practitioners are able to benefit from advantages unique to each religious form, such as in the case of the promise of miracles and the quest for healing. Socially, secondary practices can fulfill an important role in enlarging social horizons. Moreover, by joining family and friends in their places of worship and by complying with invitations, practitioners are able to consolidate existing ties, paying respect and emphasizing commonalities and brotherly love over denominational differences. Inclinationally as well, interviewees reported feeling inspired – though, at times, also confused – by occasional excursions beyond their religious pivot, enjoying the difference in emphasis compared to the form and content common at their home church. The two axes therefore have the potential of offering complementary advantages and benefits.

Among many of our interviewees, the double-axes distinction also manifested in their tentative range of prospective practice. As we suggested in our discussion on church visits in the chapter on Kenya, although most Kenyan interviewees said they would be willing to visit just about any church and sometimes even to step outside the territory of normative Christianity altogether, nearly all were only willing to consider becoming affiliated within a limited range of churches. Oftentimes, in discussing an unfamiliar religious form, interviewees told us they would like to attend it, but – they emphasized – only as visitors. The option of peripheral practices thus permits them to draw, in an explorative fashion, on those religious forms that are considered too remote to serve as official candidates for becoming a pivot without risking being labeled as "church hoppers." Insofar as the risk of undermining the primacy of the pivot is minimal and the hierarchy between pivot and periphery is maintained, practitioners can enjoy social legitimacy and various advantages through maintaining peripheral religious forms.

Conclusion

In this chapter, we further developed the religious butinage approach by exploring two basic assertions. First, we introduced distinctions between types of butineurs in given moments in their lives. These distinctions we examined through a basic typology of mobility orientations, which include monofloral, polyfloral, and monochrome butineurs. At one end of the continuum, we identified polyfloral practitioners who leave no stone unturned in their propensity toward diverse butinage, while at the other end, we found monofloral practitioners who appear to maintain affiliations with a single religious form. Second, we discussed the personalization of the religious landscape through its division into representational and concrete territories. We then argued that, within the practitioner's range of mobility, concurrent mobility practices are often organized hierarchically, revolving around a single religious form (pivot), that may or may not correspond to formal religious membership. Evoking the dual categories of pivot and periphery, we explored their interrelations and, taking into consideration that religious identity is a combination, we began considering religious identity as a "system" of intertwining and complementary elements. Using the image of horizontal and vertical axes, we considered this complementarity in terms of inclinational, social, and practical logics.

Two questions that emerge from this discussion await further study. First, we wonder what the impact of life moments is on the practitioner's mobile tendencies. The idea that certain moments in life tend to lend themselves to changes in intensity and range of mobility patterns is widely recognized, and as we mentioned in chapter 2, early scholarship on religious mobility – framed in terms of conversion – suggested that these moments are most likely to occur during middle and late adolescence. While the precise definition of this common age has been debated, over the years scholars have widely supported this assertion. Future research may wish to utilize the butinage metaphor in charting and identifying patterns of fluctuations in practice throughout the life cycle. Such research may also seek to consider common patterns of influence on religious mobility by rites of passage and dramatic life changes, such as divorce, illness, or drastic shifts in socioeconomic level. Second, and relatedly, a question remains regarding the interplay of mobility between people within a single social group, such as the domestic or family unit. Using the tools presented in this chapter, scholars may seek to map out the religious associations of individual members and set them within a larger, collective context. Such an approach may identify the phenomenon of religious mobility within a pattern of collective action or even strategy, especially when facing common transformations affecting all members such as changes of residence, changes in family status, a death in the family, or socioeconomic mobility. Thus, for instance, scholars may inquire how marriage affects religious mobility, recognizing the tension that we observed in Kenya and Ghana, whereby it is socially expected that the bride shift to her new husband's church even though women are often more practicing than men. Thus, approaching religious mobility from a collective perspective, scholars may gain new insights into marital shifts, for even as the wife yields and shifts to her husband's church, she may still keep ties to her old denomination and visit it on occasion, certainly when in the company of her blood relatives who continue to adhere to their original tradition.

In the next chapter, we build on these observations and, in particular, on the pivot-periphery distinction to propose a new model for religious identities that we call "religious repertoires." Maintaining the idea of religious identity as a constellation of elements, we respond to the challenge of return mobility by adding another component to the dual-axis model presented in this chapter, namely, the inactive religious domain. These three degrees of practice – pivot, periphery, and inactive – make use of the notion of "familiarity" as their organizing principle. By bringing all these factors together, we propose a comprehensive model to account for religious identity through close attention to the dynamic interplay between components.

8 From Religious Mobility to Dynamic Religious Identities

In the beginning of this book, we pointed to some core lacunas in the study of religious identities. In the course of this text, we offered to tackle these by introducing a terminological toolkit that includes such notions as butinage, territories, and the confluence of three perspectives (institutional, individual, and sociocultural) and three logics (practical, social, and inclinational). We explored how these concepts play out in particular settings, and combined empirical findings with the thickening of the theoretical perspective, examining the multiple and interrelated elements of religious identity. We have seen how people may engage with more than one religious tradition at a given time (synchronic butinage) and may re-engage with religious forms that were once dropped (return mobility). We also showed the tendency to uphold a hierarchy of practices, with some religious forms being practiced with greater devotion than others. But while all these ideas help to articulate the practitioner's range of practice, it does leave certain questions open: How is a new religious form subsumed and integrated into the practitioner's range of practice? What shall we make of multiple practices that feature different degrees of commitment and their interrelational dynamics? Does the practitioner's territory cover only present practice or does it also privilege former practices that have retained their appeal? We thus recognize the need for a model that would be both precise and flexible, both actor-based and aware of institutional structures and social norms.

Bringing together our various observations, we now move from offering our critique and our general toolkit to formulating a model that will encompass our various findings. We do so by once more evoking a spatial imagery, one with which to "map" and offer "cartographies" of the "landscapes" of individual religious identities: the "religious repertoire," first developed by Gez (2018, 2014). Despite the use of the term "model," we certainly do not intend to imply any finite and closed solution to the challenges of capturing complex religious identities. Rather, what we present should be regarded as a starting point, a conceptual experimentation, possibly an intended provocation. Just as we drew inspiration from our four case studies, additional research based on other observations may refine or even restructure this approach. Some paths for such future research are explored in the book's conclusion.

Central to this new model is our emphasis on the notion of the "familiar." As we have shown through our case studies, considerations related to social contact, trust, and mistrust are central to people's religious choice-making. The recognition of this centrality is in line with findings by other scholars, such as Englund (2007) who, in the context of Malawian Pentecostalism, proposed that religious associations may be better understood in terms of "trust" than "belief"; and Daswani (2015, 7), whose approach to studying the lives of Ghanaian Pentecostals was captured by one of his interviewees' questions, "How do I carry on with confidence?" While religion is often perceived as a sought-after island of institutional and interpersonal trust, in reality, religion's symbolic capital often risks erosion due to manipulations and "moral free riding" (Cullity 1995; Hull and Lipford 2010). Indeed, across our case studies, we noted systemic suspicion toward some religious denominations. In Kenya and Ghana, rumors about devil worshipers or ill-behaved pastors tarnish the church's image and the ideal of born-again piety (Gez and Droz 2015). In Brazil, too, there is a strong condemnation of Pentecostal cupidity and emphasis on monetary contributions inspired by the prosperity gospel and enacted through tithing and "seed planting." Many consider this appeal for money as, at best, betraying shameful greed for material wealth, if not as an institutionally sanctioned robbery and a "fleecing of the flock." While Kenya, Ghana, and Brazil present something of a battleground for the reputation of religion and Christianity in particular, in Switzerland, even before noting the erosion resulting from specific controversies, religious institutions are regarded as a priori suspicious and widely associated with intolerance, control, and brainwashing (Stolz et al. 2015, 179). Morally, the Swiss often regard religion as outdated – even dangerously so – pointing, for example, to Catholicism's campaign against abortion or contraceptives in some of the world's poorest countries or to its scandals involving pedophile priests.

Before we delve into the model, however, we wish to anticipate a critique that some careful readers may have as they read through this chapter with regard to the notion of familiarization, namely, the tension between this volume's point of departure as emphasizing fluidity and dynamism and the supposed reification of religious institutions as freestanding categories. To retain the language of butinage, and to think of religious institutions as the "flowers" between which practitioners travel, we may wonder to what extent such flowers constitute stable objects of study, as implied by the language of accumulated familiarization. After all, religions are social institutions, and social institutions, we have learned, are imagined communities – be they political, ethnic, or associative (Hobsbawm and Ranger 1983; Mudimbe 1988; Anderson 1983). By acknowledging the tangibility of churches and traditions, are we not, the argument goes, reifying what are no more than social conventions and sites of human encounter? After all, to use the metaphorical language of butinage, the religious landscape would have no flowers if there were no bees who would believe in them and sustain them. This much was noted by Durkheim long ago:

> The really religious beliefs are always common to a determined group, which makes a profession of adhering to them and of practicing the rites connected with them. They are not merely received individually by all members of this group; they are something belonging to the group, and they make its unity. The individuals which compose it feel themselves united to each other by the simple fact that they have a common faith. A society whose members are united by the fact that they think in the same way in regard to the sacred world and its relations with the profane world, and by the fact that they translate these common ideas into common practices, is what is called a Church. (Durkheim 1915, 59)

Another objection to such reification has to do with the supposed identification of a core, an unmoved essence, that is the heart of religious traditions. Are religious traditions not, in fact, subject to constant transformation over time and to the remaking of historical trajectories? Indeed, social categories are subject both to transformation over time as well as to individual interpretation and meaning-making, like in the case of the famous ship of Theseus, which continued to exist – or did it? – long after its planks and masts had all been replaced. Moreover, seeing as we emphasize the gap between dogma and practice, are we not marginalizing the diverse varieties of traditions as both enacted by formal agents of the faith and interpreted by individual practitioners depending on context? Scholars routinely debate definitions and genealogies of religious movements. How much more so, then, are such disagreements prevalent among lay practitioners, who may maintain personal and unique perspectives regarding the religious forms they practice, perspectives which may have formed through a combination of epistemes? We may think, for example, about the combined epistemological hold of traditional-animist, Christian-theological, and scientific thinking, all of which are considered valid candidates for truth claims (Ellis and Ter Haar 2004). To complicate matters further, the transmission of such epistemes is never complete, and people's own versions of understanding may rely on rumors, misinformation, and half-truths. It is indeed clear that, over time, religious forms change, both in the eyes of their individual followers as well as due to internal institutional processes.

This challenge can be extended even further, from religious institutions to the categories of communities and even individuals – after all, the mobile practitioner might have no single coherent center or essence but be a patchwork of potentially conflicted voices (Hermans and Kempen 1993; Keupp et al. 1999). As Heraclitus memorably said, you cannot step into the same river twice – a statement followed by his student Cratylus's reported statement whereby even once would be too many. This pushing of a theory of perpetual flux to what seems like its logical conclusion has been a subject of ridicule, which is one way of understanding Aristotle's presentation of Cratylus's application of his own philosophy: "he ended by thinking that one need not say anything, and only moved his finger."[1] Stopping short of saying nothing at all, we may wonder what stability of object is implied by both "Maria" and "Catholicism" in the phrase "Maria practices Catholicism." Indeed, we recognize Premawardhana's words whereby, "though there may be heuristic value in speaking of a Christian, or modern, ideology of the self, care must be taken not to ontologize ideologies" (Premawardhana 2015, 41). Aware of the risk of "ontologizing ideologies," in our work and in this chapter in particular, we recognize that, while the case can be made for both bees and flowers – or Maria and Catholicism – being fluid, nonessential categories, our approach stops short of letting distinct "things" dissipate into some blurry religious ecosystem. In taking this stance, we also acknowledge certain useful simplifications. After presenting the repertoires model, we will return to the question of methodological and epistemological challenges.

Familiarity and Familiarization

In the writings of Aristotle, we find – as is often found across the ancient Greek philosophical corpus – substantial preoccupation with the vexing question of change and mobility. Seeking to settle an already-old question, in which the solutions offered by pre-Socratic philosophers Heraclitus and Parmenides are often taken to represent two extreme ends, Aristotle's way forward involved an emphasis on the distinction between potentiality and actuality. Setting aside long-standing debates over the correct interpretation of Aristotle's sometimes-obscure wording for the purpose of the discussion that lies ahead in this section, it is enough to highlight two points – or rather, puzzles – raised by his distinction. First, Aristotle's ideas imply that potential traits may be unmanifested, or may manifest to varying degrees. In one section, for example, he suggests that the sleeping geometer is more distant from his actuality as a geometer than the waking one, who in turn is still far from actualization compared to when the geometer is actually theorizing.[2] Though not explicitly developed by Aristotle, such notions allow us to reasonably extrapolate an understanding of changing degrees of actualization as well as their possible inactivity or latency (Kosman 1969).[3] Second, Aristotle's understanding of the process of actualization raises questions related to gradation versus transformation: on the one hand, the fully grown oak tree has grown in incremental steps from a seed to a seedling and into its present form; and on the other hand, in its current form, it is fundamentally different from the seed. How and where do we draw the – somewhat arbitrary? – line between states of being and acknowledge that a new state has been attained or "mastered"?

Aristotle's own ideas on these questions are difficult to pin down and should be read in light of his fundamental commitment to a teleological framework, which goes along a different track than our present discussion on individual participation in religious markets. His thoughts, however, remain in the backdrop as timeless questions as we turn to discuss our notion of "familiarity," which makes up the foundation of the religious repertoires model presented in this chapter. The English term "familiarity" comes from the Latin root *familiaris*, which is related to the word "*familia*" or "family." The term's etymology thus conveys the interlacing of acquaintance with experience in an affective, socially meaningful way, which is irreducible to intellectual knowledge. With this in mind, we consider familiarity as the ostensible "domestication" – a term fittingly derived from *domus* or "home" – and mastering of new religious forms. Marking the acquisition of new forms through familiarization, we propose an imaginary border, which we term the "familiarity threshold." Inspired by the work of Erving Goffman (1967) and Robert Bellah (2011; see also Bellah and Tipton, 2006), we recognize the centrality of bodily presence in thorough – both affective and effective – religious engagement. Following Merlin Donald, Bellah and Tipton (2006, 7) suggest that mimetic – embodied and nonverbal – religious representations make up an important part of religious life. They join Randall Collins's (2004, 53–64) contention that, even as the modern world presents us with more and more ways of following social rituals through long-distance means of communication, these virtual observances cannot fully replace the experience of embodied presence. Moreover, acknowledging Wittgenstein's proposition that our experiences receive their coherence through social participation (see, for example, Bloor 2001), we posit that practices through which the familiarity threshold is crossed involve collectivity. Such collective participation is important in ensuring that what is being acquired by the individual practitioner conforms – at least to some extent – to institutional normativity.

Our notion of familiarity thresholds thus puts an emphasis on physical presence and immersion in shared religious rituals through actual practice. While local variations may well exist, we note that the quintessential moment of crossing a familiarity threshold is often associated with a first visit to a formal service at a new religious institution. This proposition explains why in Kenya, for example, "church visits" are considered extremely important both socially and spiritually, and are highly institutionalized and ritualized (Gez and Droz 2017). We suggest that it is through such embodied religious participation, which may follow a period of gradual familiarization, that the practitioner becomes absorbed and eventually versed in the spiritual, ritualistic, and social components unique to the religious form in question.

At the same time, we also acknowledge that practitioners may enjoy a minimal degree of familiarity with given religious forms simply by partaking in a given society and culture. Evoking Geertz's (1973) notion of culture as a symbolic system, we suggest that common symbols inform people in various subtle ways beyond direct practice. Through the idea of shared religious idioms, we accept that there can be some basic knowledge and rudimentary familiarity – including, conceivably, misconceptions and stigmas – concerning other religious forms. This basic familiarity may be informed by the public presence of religion or through interpersonal exchange, and can be the subject of personal inquiries by a curious practitioner who has not yet crossed – or has not yet dared to cross – a familiarity threshold. Such basic familiarity may also include ties with family traditions that the practitioner may not have been formally brought up in, but which nonetheless faintly register within their heritage. For example, in our fieldwork in urban Kenya, interlocutors sometimes said that they do not feel any need to actually practice a given religious form in order to get a basic sense of it. Merely by being immersed in that shared culture, they believe to have a certain understanding of it, as if by "cultural osmosis" – if we may use such a term. *Matatus* (public minibuses) dedicated to a particular church; gospel music in the supermarket and in the office; television screens in public institutions, even fitness clubs, set to weekday sermons; Christian ringtones; stylized jewelries; singing from a nearby church or a call to prayer from a mosque across the road – all these cultural aspects add up as forms of passive religious exposure and eventual orientation. Churches themselves tend to try to maximize visibility and emphasize evangelism, sometimes even by going door to door. Moreover, religion is a favored topic of conversation, and religious rumors and scandals are widely circulated, attracting much attention.

Linking this point with the discussion in the previous chapter about degrees of practice, we summarize four ways in which a religious form can be engaged with. A religious form may be unfamiliar, familiar but non-practiced, practiced and peripheral, or practiced and pivotal. Let us briefly review these four options. First, there are completely unfamiliar religious forms, which have never crossed the familiarity threshold through actual practice. Second, we identify religious forms that have been active in the past, but are presently not practiced. An important distinction is drawn here between the unfamiliar and the inactive. While both domains encompass unpracticed religious forms, the very fact of familiarization imbues inactive forms with pertinence and availability well beyond unfamiliar forms. As we shall show, inactive forms can later be reintroduced through return mobility. In other words, by traversing the familiarity threshold, a religious form remains at the disposal of the actor whether or not it is practiced at a given time. Third, entering the domain of active practices, we note peripheral religious forms, whose actual degree of engagement remains secondary compared to the actor's primary practice, the pivot. Religious forms situated in this category at a given time are often downplayed, as people tend to highlight the centrality of their primary practice.[4] Fourth, we identify the pivot, the actor's principal locus of religious practice. This most dominantly practiced religious form usually corresponds to the actor's religious self-identification.

The third and fourth degrees of practice – the periphery and the pivot, which we have already encountered in the previous chapter – thus comprise what we may term the domain of active religious practice. As we suggested in the previous chapter, while the active domain's spatial image of a single pivot surrounded by peripheral practices is widely applicable, it is not true for all cases. Indeed, while this arrangement dominated our two African case studies, active practice in Switzerland – and, to some extent, in Brazil – appears less likely to lend itself to this dual structure and is more likely to oscillate between multiple practices without a clear single anchor in the form of a pivot.

Religious Repertoires

Building on our original mission of seeking to map dynamic religious identities, we may now gather the various strands of our discussion and bind them together. Proceeding from the distinction between unfamiliar and familiar territories, we propose a model for mapping the practitioner's religious identity according to actual practice. Seeing religious identity as a pool of familiar religious forms, we suggest that newly familiarized religious forms are added to and accumulated in religious identity, while old ones may remain unpracticed but are nonetheless familiar. We introduce, therefore, the concept of religious repertoires, which accounts for religious identity as comprised of a given arrangement of a practitioner's familiar religious forms.[5]

The choice of the term "repertoire" (from the Latin *repertōrium*: storehouse, inventory, or catalogue) is most commonly associated with the performing arts, where it stands for the entire stock of works that an artistic ensemble or an individual, such as an actor or a musician, is familiar with and capable of performing. The term can also be used outside the artistic arena to allude to the host of skills, techniques, or devices at the disposal of an individual or a group. It therefore conveys not only the sense of acquired knowledge but also the potential for its reproduction, implying a certain readiness to "enact" or "perform" that knowledge either artistically or socially. In recent decades, the term "repertoire" has been gaining popularity among social scientists, who apply it to a wide range of areas.[6] Its spread is due, above all, to the work of Swidler (1986) in her classic article, "Culture in Action: Symbols and Strategies," and in her later work. Swidler's conceptualization of cultural repertoire and its creative application by scholars offers a non-deterministic, actor-based perspective, which stresses the potential for agency and action implied in cultural competences. This perspective allows us to consider not only those behavioral elements that are employed at a given time, but also those that are being excluded (Swidler 2001a, 24–5). Taking her cue from Geertz's (1973) notion of culture and from Bourdieu's (1980) notion of habitus, Swidler proposes that culture should be regarded as a "toolkit" or a "repertoire" of "habits, skills, and styles" (Swidler 1986, 273) available to the actor.[7] Swidler recognizes that people draw on different elements within a shared, yet vast, symbolic system that comprises their cultures and that this common idiom allows them to speak in a relatively unified tone. Within that broad range of reference and action, a person's unique habitus would favor tapping into and activating certain "pieces" – being Swidler's choice of terms for particular strands within the general cultural repertoire. Using such cultural references, practitioners set up their "strategies of action," a notion that Swidler insists should not be understood in terms suggesting a straightforward rational actor. In this sense, Swidler recognizes that culture offers a varied and polysemic vocabulary that can be employed in a range of possible actions.[8] The idea of cultural repertoires thus recognizes that culture is inherently diverse, at times self-contradictory, and therefore does not offer straightforward and coherent rules for governing action.

Swidler's work implies that, out of the collective cultural repertoire, individuals then draw and compose their own range of more or less stable competences and preferred practices. Inspired by Bourdieu's notion of the self-adjusting habitus, Swidler suggests that, although operating outside a person's habitual range is not impossible, it nonetheless requires "drastic and costly cultural retooling" (Swidler 1986, 277). As she explains, "people do not readily take advantage of new structural opportunities which would require them to abandon established ways of life. This is not because they cling to cultural values, but because they are reluctant to abandon familiar strategies of action for which they have the cultural equipment" (281). Like Bourdieu, Swidler acknowledges the old Latin adage, "*consuetudinis magna vis est*" ("the force of habit is great").

In this work, the term "repertoire" is used to emphasize the close link observed between social learning, the retention of this learning within an individual's mental repertoire, and the tendency to draw upon the elements comprising such repertoires. Swidler's observations are, in this respect, especially useful with regard to recognizing the lasting imprints and the tendency to "reenact" elements that have been "mastered." At the same time, however, there are also differences in how Swidler and we use the term. While Swidler is mainly interested in culture, our focus is on mapping individuals' unique religious makeup.[9] Thus, whereas the notion of cultural repertoire has mainly been used to explore discourses and discursive justifications (Silber 2003), our notion of religious repertoires refers to the composition of religious identities. Still, as individual religious repertoires are set within certain contexts and collective dispositions, the notion of collective cultural repertoires remains both relevant and revealing. Indeed, the term "territory," which we presented as referring to a person's prospective range of religious practice as influenced by personal inclinations and social ethos, may be considered an approximation of it. In urban Kenya, for example, we found that the territory of mainstream, normative Christianity – as constantly negotiated by public and personal debates – dominates views on legitimate practice and can thus be thought of as somewhat akin to a collective cultural (religious) repertoire.

Thinking in terms of individual religious repertoires invites us to recognize that, while a person may seek to narrate their religious identity as a coherent whole, it is likely to encompass multiple – possibly incongruent or even incommensurable – elements. Indeed, touching on the fundamental tension between actual experience, memory, and linguistic reconstruction, practitioners' narratives might be "tainted" by after the fact reconstructions of events, partially due to implicit pressure on the narrator by their religious group to conform to normative affiliation and conversion paradigms or to rational actor behavior.[10] Psychologically, our repertoire-based perspective goes hand in hand with a view of human personality as a patchwork of multiple and non-unitary "selves." These selves can be regarded as distinctive voices, whose ongoing internal dialogue produces personal identity (Hermans and Kempen 1993; Keupp et al. 1999). In this respect, the term "religious repertoires" might more adequately capture the changeability, dynamism, and internal diversity of individual religious makeups than the term "religious identity," which, if applied carelessly, might carry unfounded assumptions regarding internal coherence and "essence." By contrast, the actual structure of religious repertoires may vary from person to person and from setting to setting.

As mentioned, the organizing principle for the religious repertoires model is that of familiarity. The appeal of the familiar, which implies affective, family-like ties (*familia*), indicates a tendency to respond to acquired knowledge and competences, as suggested in the previous discussion of Swidler's notion of cultural repertoire, and may also find justification in the human tendency to form habits.[11] At the same time, we recognize that the way people would act upon their familiarity is far from predetermined, as evidenced by the very fact that religious repertoires are dynamic and potentially expanding. What we are suggesting, rather, is that the importance of familiarity with specific forms is akin to the way in which affective bonds with family or *familia* are extremely significant and retain a privileged place or imprint within a person's psyche. This importance is not swayed by complex, at times negative, sentiments toward the individual's *familia*. Similarly, the process of "domestication" of religious forms integrates them into religious identity and sets them apart from other, unfamiliar religious forms.

In Kenya, for example, while a minority of our interlocutors – mainly Pentecostal converts – rejected their former religious affiliations altogether, most of them defended the legitimacy of all religious forms within their repertoire, whether practiced or not at the time of our interview. Kenyan interviewees further told us that they do not engage in such and such religious forms because, being unfamiliar with their teachings and practices, they fear they might feel lost, or worse, unwittingly end up in league with devil worshipers or swindlers. Indeed, Kenyans' special relations with their familiar religious forms are all the more cherished considering the climate of mistrust toward unfamiliar religious forms and institutions, whose manifestations range from countless rumors about devil worshiping to frequent religious scandals involving sexual and monetary misconduct. Though the idea is complex and far from conclusive, it might be that the "homeliness" of familiarity tends to favor the maintaining of affective bonds, which in turn help explain people's tendency to renew ties with formerly practiced religious forms.

We thus propose that familiarity implies more than just keeping track of once-practiced religious forms. Rather, it is an organizing principle that can have significant ramifications for religious behavior. This proposal, of course, does not suggest that engagement with forms outside the repertoire is impossible – far from it. Indeed, without engagement with new religious forms, repertoires would remain invariant in size, which, as our research shows, is seldom the case. Conversely, it is also clear that some familiar forms are adamantly dropped and never recalled into active practice. We thus suggest that practitioners have a tendency to recognize the advantage associated with already-familiar religious forms and to utilize this familiarity as a privileged resource when reviewing their approach to religious practice.

Religious Identity in Context and Motion

The composite structure of religious repertoires allows us to draw a distinction between circular and return mobility. The notion of circular mobility follows an inclusivist logic, which allows for concurrent practices of several religious forms, and in itself offers a departure from most common conceptions of religious mobility. Approaches such as the conversion career (Richardson and Stewart 1977; Richardson 1978; Gooren 2010), which prides itself on offering a comprehensive perspective on religious mobility and its motivations, are limited to the presumption of diachronic, exclusive adherence to one religious form at any given time, ignoring the option of synchronic, concurrent practices. By contrast, the religious repertoires model allows for the synchronic presence of multiple religious forms within the domain of active practices, which, as suggested, is comprised of a single privileged religious form – a pivot – as well as additional, concurrently active, peripheral forms. The model's flexibility allows for personal variation and, while the presence of a single, privileged form or pivot is expected, the number of peripheral forms may range from none to several.

In some life moments or situations, people may engage in multiple peripheral practices in a way that questions the privilege of any single practice – which, indeed, has been the case for some of our interviewees in Switzerland but almost none of our interviewees in Ghana. Another way in which this basic distinction may be challenged has to do with the possible absence of secondary practices, typical of strict monofloral practitioners. While proposing that the basic model consists of a single pivot and multiple peripheral practices, we thus do not mean to suggest that these conditions must be satisfied in one particular way. Indeed, the more we expand our comparative frame of reference, the more we should recognize the possible existence of structural variants: periphery without a center, a center without periphery, or multiple centers. All these variants derive from the basic, widely intuitive two-axis principle discussed earlier: a single pivot/vertical axis representing belonging and commitment, and peripheral practices/horizontal axis representing exploration and inspiration.

Going further, the model also recognizes the possibility of return mobility. By and large, scholars have assumed religious mobility to be unidirectional, perhaps appealing to the assumption that, once a decision has been made to forsake a religious form, there is little reason to revert to it. With regard to his work on Pentecostalism in northern Mozambique, Premawardhana (2015) points to the scholarly failure to capture the intricate circularity of geographic or religious mobility and the tendency to make do with schematic and simplistic labels assuming unidirectional flow (for example, "urbanization," "Pentecostalization"). We agree with this critique, and our data has led us to consider return mobility as a fundamental manifestation of religious identity. Going beyond notions of "deconversion" (Streib 2014), we see return mobility in axiologically neutral terms as a form of accumulative engagement. Through the notion of familiarization, we emphasize how such past engagements could be rejected, yet cannot be unmade, contributing to our conceptualization of religious repertoires as a pool of available religious forms in which the exclusion of one form from active practice nonetheless keeps it within the realm of potential renewed engagement. Considering the common scholarly tendency to ignore religious forms once they have been excluded from affiliation or actual practice, we propose the religious repertoires model as a way of keeping past engagements in view, encompassing the arrangement or "management" of religious identities beyond the apparent realm of current practice.

Thinking in such terms allows us to view each person's religious identity as a comprehensive, and potentially highly dynamic, arrangement of interrelated elements. Religious forms may alternate in their intensity of practice and thus move up or down the vertical axis and along the horizontal axis, negotiating their role as center/pivot and periphery. In addition, new religious forms may be accumulated from the wide domain of unfamiliar forms through familiarization and, by crossing the familiarity threshold, join the range of familiar forms that inhabit a person's repertoire. As we began to see in the previous chapter, the religious pivot can be thought of as a vertical axis, a locus aimed at deepening familiarity and belonging within a single religious form. Affiliated practitioners become versed in the working of their institution, developing important ties with the leadership and the congregation and immersing themselves in its teachings and practices over time. Peripheral forms, by contrast, require little or no commitment and are therefore more flexible in their application. Unfettered by institutional obligations, these are often sites of unattached, even playful, exploration. At the same time, they may be linked to practical considerations, such as the need for prayer or healing away from the home church. Moreover, such secondary mobility may allow practitioners to send out their antenna and be on the lookout for new religious opportunities elsewhere. Inactive forms, while excluded from practice, are present as further potential elements for the practitioner to reintroduce and recall into activity, depending on circumstances, needs, and interests. Religious forms may "recede" into inactivity at certain points in time, seemingly disappearing from view and assuming a dormant form, only to reemerge when conditions have once more become favorable. As we have seen in our discussion on return mobility in the chapter on Kenya, such recession and reemergence may be associated with external pressures such as those linked to aggressive evangelism, marriage, and geographic relocation, which, in turn, may result in mobility that is superficial, partial, or unstable. While changes in personal conditions may have a bearing on re-engagement with once-dropped religious forms, the advantage of thinking in terms of a dynamic identity lies not in the conception of religious practitioners as seeking to maximize profit through the deployment of religious strategies, but rather in the recognition of the interrelatedness and complementarity of different practices. This point becomes apparent through subtle attentiveness to personal circumstances and to the balance between practical, social, and inclinational logics.

Conclusion

In this chapter, we laid out the foundation for a new model for capturing the dynamics of religious identity. With its emphasis on familiarity and de facto practice and its implied fluidity, the religious repertoires model helps us imagine how we can think about religious mobility, not as an anomaly but rather as an integral part of a vibrant identity, which creatively overflows institutional prescriptions. The model allows us to register how given religious forms meet in original and dynamic arrangements without imposing a reductionist or utilitarian perspective on the causes for such changeability.

Rather than looking at any single institutional (dis)affiliation, the religious repertoires model allows us to consider religious identity in terms of a comprehensive identity dynamic. This point can be understood in two ways. First, the model is comprehensive in that it tries to create a bridge between the institutional and the lived religion perspectives, while also taking into consideration social norms and expectations. Second, the model's comprehensiveness calls upon us to consider religious identity as situated and embedded in a broader set of relations. Thus, relations between practitioners and religious forms should not be studied in isolation, but rather through a prism of interrelations whereby changes in one element invite a realignment of the greater whole. In this respect, it is useful to consider the complementarity of elements as presented through the dual, vertical-horizontal axes. But while the two axes focus on the domain of active practice, the notion of familiarity invites us to probe even further and to adopt an integrative perspective that would consider inactive forms as participating in religious identity dynamics.

Combining familiarity with territory, we propose that practitioners tend to privilege practice within their repertoire, followed by appeal to other forms within their privileged territory, and are least likely to appeal to unfamiliar forms outside this territory. In this respect, the model sets aside the question of continuity across distinct religious worldviews. Rather than seeking signs of former practices and worldviews in the present, the model recognizes the ideological boundaries and mobility restrictions set by religious institutions themselves. Rather than adopting a syncretic or bricolage-based perspective, we recognize the integrity of predefined religious forms and look at the individual's back-and-forth journeying and bridge building – our butinage perspective – between these institutional points of reference (Birman 2001; McIntosh 2009; Birman 1996; Soares 2009). As the notion of territory implies social norms, it goes without saying that hypothetical territories for butinage would vary across religious landscapes, as demonstrated in the difference between the Swiss and the Kenyan examples. The Swiss tend to mistrust institutional religion and maintain a porous territory with an emphasis on peripheral practices, whereas Kenyan Christians largely maintain a strong emphasis on the boundaries of legitimate Christianity, while stressing the importance of maintaining a clear religious pivot and dismissing the secularist alternative.

9 Conclusion: The Peripatetic Practitioner

As we wrote this book, many conversations contributed to the refinement of our perspective. As we arrive at our conclusion, however, one in particular comes to mind. Early in our fieldwork in Kenya, we sat for an interview with Pastor Samuel, a popular youth pastor in one of Kenya's leading Presbyterian churches, in his Nairobi church office. Over a cup of sweet and milky Kenyan tea, we talked about Pentecostalization – a process that the Presbyterian Church of Kenya has experienced from up close[1] – and the appeal of up-and-coming Pentecostal churches to his Presbyterian congregants and, in particular, to the youth among them. While it was clear that the pastor was giving much consideration to these trends, he did not seem overly concerned: "We are losing some and gaining others," he said, referring to the substantial turnover at his church. But while he recognized the reality of religious mobility, Pastor Samuel seemed ill at ease with the idea of unidirectional conversion. He explained that the youth who are drifting out of the Presbyterian Church do so only temporarily or partially, adding that, at times, those who left reemerge years later, whether to fully renew their ties with the church or to ask him to perform their wedding ceremony in their new church. The pastor concluded that, based on those observations, our very conception of religious mobility needs to be revised:

> My view, and that is what I tell young people who leave this church and go to others, is that, if you look at it as changing church, I view it as expanding church. If you think about changing church, you almost bolt your doors to the Presbyterian Church and go to [the] Baptist, for example. You bolted your doors, the kind of view [that says] "I am no longer going there, now I'm going to this other place." But if you expand church, it means that now the Presbyterian's doors are open and the Nairobi Baptist doors are also open, so you have expanded. You can come here depending on which programs

> are going on, you can come here if and whatever, [and] the strength of the Baptist Church, you can access it as well. So that expansion of church, I find it to be a better mentality as compared to changing or closing one and opening the other. (Interview with Pastor Samuel, Nairobi 2011)

Pastor Samuel's insightful observation, and his notion of "expanding church," stayed with us throughout our fieldwork in Kenya and beyond. In his tone, we noted a progressive stance, insofar as he proposed updating rigid institutional categories regarding church affiliation in light of the actual practices that he observed all around him and especially among the church youth with whom he worked closely. In our work in Kenya, we observed this phenomenon in action: true, the appeal of Kenyan Pentecostalism has been palpable, but that was far from being the only direction of flow. The more personal stories we collected, the more we observed the truth of Pastor Samuel's observations. We spoke to people who, like the pastor's young congregants, open various religious horizons and do not "bolt their doors" in an exclusive way and often return to a denomination that they had supposedly left. We shared the pastor's concern that a dichotomist and exclusive view of religious identity based on the limited prism of membership may easily miss this dynamic richness. At the same time, the pastor presented us with a challenge: What does it mean to think about religious identity in terms of "expanding church," that is to say, as an accumulation of elements rather than exclusive belonging?

Like Pastor Samuel's ideas, the theoretical innovation of our perspective was not developed in a vacuum but responded to observable reality. We began this book's journey with a critique of a sedentary vision of the religious practitioner, as associated with Abrahamic notions of the model member and even with the rigidity of the religious fundamentalist. In the course of our inquiry, we pointed out the theoretical and empirical limits of such a prism, drawing particular attention to gaps between formal religious (self-)identifications and de facto practice, and exploring how we may register the actual subtlety of such mobility. Among our interviewees, we found a high degree of personal agency, which led us to propose that, even among deeply conservative practitioners, everyday religious practice and worldviews tend to be much richer and more diverse than is sometimes assumed. The vast majority of our interviewees, even those with a seemingly strict stance, have shown flexibility and notable openness to additional religious exposures.

As we thought about religion in motion, our approach brought to mind Appiah's (2018, 67) observation whereby "once you think of creedal identities in terms of mutable practices and communities rather than sets of immutable beliefs, religion becomes more verb than noun: the identity reveals as an activity, not a thing. And it's the nature of activities to bring change." These religion-in-motion and religion-as-verb elements were encapsulated by the butinage metaphor, which seeks to capture practitioners' trajectories as varied and dynamic – and in that sense is contrasted with rigid conceptions of the religious member. At the same time, our conceptual choice drew on a recognition of the loose, elastic, open-ended, and multifaceted nature of metaphors, which lend themselves to dynamic reinterpretation. Keeping our choice of terms intentionally open for added interpretations, we also reiterated the limitation of natural metaphors, which ought to be used mindfully and be well contained and guarded against the danger of the pareidoliac charm. A metaphor is a heuristic tool and not the thing itself, and as such, its reach is necessarily limited.

Gradually, and in close dialogue with our case studies, our Heraclitan metaphor became complemented by a number of general tools developed – in close dialogue with our data – in the third part of this book. This process eventually culminated in the presentation of our religious repertoires model, which introduced the concept of familiarity and focused on the interplay between four categories of practice: unfamiliar, familiar-yet-inactive, active-peripheral, and active-pivot. But while we believe in the inherent value of this model, the move from a general metaphorical approach toward the relative rigidity implied by a model was made with some trepidation. How much conceptual fixedness should we accommodate as part of a scheme aimed at capturing creative combinations of a dynamic identity?

In fact, the tension between the openness of the metaphor and our increasingly specific heuristic toolkit can itself be taken to represent a fundamental observation about the intertwinement of movement and fixedness. To use Gabriel Marcel's seemingly paradoxical suggestion, "a stable order can only be established on earth if man always remains acutely conscious that his condition is that of a traveller" (Marcel 1944, 7). Indeed, there is a need to understand the interplay between both mobility and stasis – or, to use the title of Tweed's (2006) book, both *Crossing and Dwelling* – for it is between these two stances that our lives receive their rhythm. As William James suggested, using a metaphor aptly akin to that of butinage, human consciousness is "like a bird's life … made of an alternation of flights and perchings" (James 1950, 243).[2] These ideas relate not only to the case of religion but can also be applied anywhere in the social sciences where people weave together fixedness and changeability. Cultivating awareness of social predispositions, we encourage other social scientists to experiment with alternative research perspectives, new scholarly suppositions, and even – wherever needed – new terminologies.

The interplay between stasis and motion takes us back to the ideas with which we started this work as related to the spirit and materiality of our time. In reading this book, the reader doubtless noted the signs of modernity and globalization woven into the discussion of our case studies: the development of religious branding and marketing practices; the dynamism of the international spread of some religious institutions and the relocation of practitioners; the use of information and communications technology (ICT) to reach out and reach in. On the level of the individual practitioner, we recognized the influence of social atomization and individualization of meaning-making, autonomy of faith, and, in some cases, creative picking and choosing. We noted that people may turn to religion as part of their response to fast-changing socioeconomic conditions and geographic displacement. In light of the breadth of our presentation, we may take a step back and ask, How, then, is religion changing, and what scholarly perspectives can help reinvigorate research in the face of its uncertain future?

Our findings offer a critique of conceptualizing religion as either fully institutionalized or fully personalized and seek a middle path between the two. As we have shown throughout the book, to conceive of religion in purely personal, free-flowing, meaning- or benefit-seeking terms has severe drawbacks. For one thing, such conceptions of a personal religion or "spirituality" represent Western ideas that took shape in response to specific understandings of religion. Indeed, in our study we noted that, outside Switzerland, the notion of spirituality was seldom used and, when applied, did not carry the Western emphasis on the personalization of the quest for ultimate meaning. In particular, a core idea to which we returned again and again has been that personal religious agency cannot be fully disentangled from social and institutional contexts. Indeed, the idea of a personal religiosity that fully transcends institutional binding forces goes against our basic finding whereby, mobile though the butineur may be, they remain wedded to the religious institution and communities in their life. This idea is further consistent with our concept of the "three logics," which recognizes that, alongside its ultimate meaning-making aspect, religion cannot be dissociated from its strong social and practical components. Attesting to the impossibility of fully isolating religion-as-meaning from the expectations and benefits of religion-as-community is the thirst for a (largely absent) community voiced by our Swiss interviewees: while they conveyed clear propensity for atomization and a spiritual quest for meaning, and were weary of religious congregations, they also admitted to religion's communal significance, often in contradiction to their own choices. Moreover, even those Swiss interviewees, many of whom identified themselves as spiritual-yet-irreligious, maintained their spiritual orientation in reference to given religious traditions.

The question remains, however, regarding the outcome of butinage. Although we admit to the limitations of a metaphor, further research drawing on the widespread existence of butinage as its premise may take the metaphor further and inquire into the "honey" – that is, the outcomes – of such dynamic religious identities in terms of individuals, religious institutions, and society at large. One possible outcome relates to the "pollination" of ideas and the transformation of religious institutions and of the religious landscape more broadly. While religious leaders may borrow techniques and ideas from each other, partially in response to competition within the religious landscape, it is interesting to apply the butinage framework to consider how institutional transformation passes through pollination of ideas and practices "from below." In our study, we encountered many instances in which itinerant lay practitioners brought into their religious communities practices that they had picked up elsewhere. Beyond the occasional cross-denominational borrowing of a hymn or a prayer, however, a perspective focused on butineurs as agents for the spread of ideas may shed new light on how large-scale transformative shifts within the religious landscape, such as the much-discussed process of Pentecostalization of mainline churches, echo the grassroots practices of lay practitioners rather than the other way around. Relatedly, research may dwell on the prominence of butinage as a way of fleshing out how popular approval of religious mobility as legitimate – some would say, a religious right – helps lay practitioners to negotiate their influence vis-à-vis their religious institutions. A possible byproduct of the ubiquity of butinage, therefore, may be the empowerment of lay believers, whose implicit threat of leaving and familiarity with multiple other religious forms can help negotiate greater institutional power.

Another type of "honey" produced by religious butinage, which takes us back to our starting point and to the discussion on the rigidity of fundamentalism, relates to the social and political realms. We see it in religious mobility related to invitation or social obligations, which we found to be widespread in all four case studies. For example, in Ghana, people are commonly invited to take part, as outsiders, in religious ceremonies. Such visits extend to religious leaders themselves, who visit other religious organizations for representational purposes in order to promote peace and unity within the nation and between religious groups, and to boost their own political capital. This mobility may take place even when it threatens a break with denominational norms, as was illustrated by the case of the funeral for Ghana's Ahmadi Amir. Even though in Switzerland, different from Ghana, these invitations appear to be more limited and narrowly revolve around extraordinary occasions such as weddings and funerals, in both countries social ties oblige a positive response. In some cases, such as that of Sonia, whom we discussed in the Swiss chapter and who observes Ramadan with her husband, a person may even partake in another religion's customs out of social solidarity. Such mobility thus sends out a message of unity – which, like honey, is both nourishing and adhesive. As such, the practice of butinage can be examined in terms of its implications for countering the inflammatory sociopolitical potential of religious cleavages. Indeed, some of the possible "honey" produced by butinage may take the shape of interreligious and cross-denominational tolerance and respect that counters extremist ideologies, as the passage between multiple religious forms in the course of a lifetime can foster understanding and overcome rigid exclusive identities in the context of religio-political tensions (Gez, Droz, and Maupeu 2020; Droz and Gez 2019).

Thus, if we examine "religious tribalism" (Lonsdale 1994), with its emphasis on strict dogmas of division, as linked to the exercise of power and symbolic violence, we can propose that the dynamism and diversity of butinage contributes to the decentralization of power away from institutional authorities and into the hands of lay practitioners. As such, religious butinage can be read as a popular mode of resistance and diffusion of tensions, a declaration of anti-sectarian convictions, and a reclaiming of peaceful individual agency. Researchers may thus consider the socioreligious role of butinage as a popular mode of political action (Bayart 1993) that seeks to counter and undercut tribalist divisiveness. In pursuing this line of observation, we suggest more research is needed on the apparent beneficial role of church visits, a practice that is widely regarded as legitimate and commonly associated with tolerant, ecumenical aspirations and even divinely sanctioned exploration.

At the same time, future studies might find the reverse, where by legitimizing multiple religious exposures, the practice of religious "to-ing and fro-ing" actually results in unidirectional gravitation toward radically anti-mobile, intolerant groups. Moreover, we must remember that religious tolerance, as manifesting in religious butinage, is not without its limits – hence the relative power of institutional boundaries, represented in this work through the concepts of monochrome butinage and territories. Religious practice is socially monitored and scrutinized, and mobility is often called upon to defend its claim for legitimacy. In this respect, we must be on guard against ideological extremism that uses religion to fortify exclusive identities and pit groups against one another. But while such formal ordinances and transcripts should not be ignored, both scholars and practitioners need to remember their incompleteness and not allow them to unfairly reinforce notions of insurmountable otherness in lieu of recognizing the commonness of lived human experience.

Appendix: Interview Guide*

Note: "religion" here is not defined by the researcher but is open to the interviewee's interpretation.

Interviewee's profile

Personal information: name, (approximate) age, gender; marital status (married, single, divorced, widow/er); occupation; education; social class as classified by the interviewee

1. Religious heritage

- What is (or was) the religion of your father?
- What is (or was) the religion of your mother?
- Have they always kept this affiliation? If not, which other affiliations have they had?
- In which religious tradition have you been brought up?

2. Religious practices and territories

- Religious self-identification: What is your religion? How do you practice it?
- Are you familiar with other places of worship? Which ones? How did you get to know them? When? With whom? What kind of engagement have you kept with each of these other places of

* For the Brazilian case study, we employed a parallel Portuguese version of the interview guide, and for the Swiss case study, we employed a parallel French version.

worship: occasional/long-standing participation, etc.? Do you still attend other places of worship? Why?
- Does your multiple practice go beyond participation in religious gatherings? How does it manifest? (If relevant: do you tithe and give offerings in a single place of worship or in several?)

3. Experiences and perceptions of butinage (for mobile butineurs)

- Are there, or have there been, particular reasons that drove you into attending different places of worship?
- What have you been taking from these experiences and teachings?
- Do you share your experiences of butinage with the people close to you (family, friends, partner, fellow believers, etc.)? What do they say about it? Do they themselves behave similarly, and why?

4. Potential religious territory

- Would you be willing to attend other places of worship? Which ones? What might drive you into going elsewhere?
- Are there any religions that you would never practice, or denominations that you would never set foot in? Which ones, and why?

5. Perspectives, tensions, and reaction by religious institutions

- Do you know other people who (like yourself) attend various places of worship? What do you make of such practices?
- Do you think that such practices give rise to any special difficulties or tensions? What might they be? How might such difficulties/tensions affect different people, and how may they cope with them?
- What do clergy in your place of worship teach concerning such movements? Which strategies do they employ in reaction to such practices?

6. Butinage *sur place*: objects and media

- Which (if any) are the objects or symbols you have in your possession that hold a religious significance for you?
- Which literature, if any, holds (or has held) religious importance for you?

- Do you listen to or watch religious programs? Which ones? How regularly do you do so? When and why do you do that?
- Do you use the internet to receive, send, or search for religious material? Do you participate in virtual religious (discussion) groups? What are you gaining from that?

Notes

1 Introduction: The Mobile Religious Practitioner

1 While such fundamentalism has come to be associated, certainly in the West, primarily with Islamist groups, one cannot ignore the rise of comparable religio-political projects within other world religions such as Christianity, Hinduism, Buddhism, and Judaism. Indeed, as is often noted, the very origin of the term actually dates back to a conservative Protestant strain that developed in the United States between the last third of the nineteenth century and the first quarter of the twentieth century. Following the historical 1925 Scopes Trial (the so-called Monkey Trial) and the ridicule to which it was exposed as a result, the movement then entered its "withdrawal stage" (Ruthven 2007, 15) of retreat from public view. It reemerged with thunder in the 1970s, concurrent to the emergence of other, non-Christian fundamentalist movements around the world, such as that associated with the Iranian Revolution of 1979 – a global trend that is still the subject of fierce scholarly debates. Remembering fundamentalism's Christian origin, the question might not be whether the term "fundamentalism" ought to be applied outside of Islamist movements as is particularly common in the West today, but rather, the question might be "the appropriateness of using the F-word in contexts outside its original Protestant setting" (Ruthven 2007, 4).

2 We use the term "identity" somewhat reluctantly, aware that it can be criticized for assuming the reification of the self through fixedness and sameness (Laplantine 1999). Indeed, the concept of identity's apparent tension with the dynamism implied by our *butinage* metaphor as presented later may lead one to avoid the term "identity," adopting an alternative terminology focused on personal religiosity or speaking instead, as Brubaker and Cooper (2000) do, about processes of "identification." However, we believe that the notion of identity is too entrenched and intuitive to be set

aside altogether. We thus use it in a qualified way, admitting its necessity as an object of study while insisting on dynamism and fluidity.

3 This marking of fundamentalism in terms of "fortifying borders" echoes the words of Marty and Appleby, for whom fundamentalism is associated with reaction against real or imagined foes who threaten drawing people into a "syncretistic, areligious, or irreligious cultural milieu" (Marty and Appleby 1993, 3).

4 Of course, while fundamentalism can be understood in terms of protest against the changes of modernity, fundamentalist thinking does not preclude religious mobility as such: as reactionary movements, fundamentalist groups support mobility in the form of renewed religious engagement and so-called return to the fundamentals by those affected by modernity's religiously corrosive pull.

5 As George Orwell commented in the 1930s, with reference to the stigmatization of tramps in London: "I have even read in a book of criminology that the tramp is an atavism, a throwback to the nomadic stage of humanity" (Orwell 2001, 203). Orwell went on to reject this view, saying that "of course a tramp is not a nomadic atavism – one might as well say that a commercial traveler is an atavism" (203–4).

6 As Asad suggests, "Geertz's treatment of religious belief, which lies at the core of his conception of religion, is a modern, privatized Christian one because and to the extent that it emphasizes the priority of belief as a state of mind rather than as a constituting activity in the world" (Asad 1993, 47; see also Robbins 2007, 14).

7 For example, see the debate surrounding the application of the idea of the division of society into classes, which closely followed the industrial revolution in Western Europe, to sub-Saharan Africa (Darbon and Toulabor 2014).

8 See, for example, Albrecht and Cornwall 1989; Albrecht, Cornwall, and Cunningham 1988; Roozen 1980; Thomas and Cooper 1978; Suchman 1992.

9 In this respect, the image of butinage is quite different from another image representing dynamic identity, that of the idle strolling associated with the concept of the "flâneur." Quite different from our butineur, the flâneur is a wandering observer of their own society. The term thus reflects a leisurely activity associated with the largely privileged experience of modern urbanism (Tester 1994).

10 Recognizing that religious groupings may not always assemble around clearly laid-out institutional structures and criticizing the Christian origin of the notion of denomination, we propose the more neutral notion of "religious forms" as a possible alternative. This alternative term can help to expand our scholarly frame of reference, making it possible to take

into account religious movements, such as African traditional religions (ATRs) and various new religious movements (NRMs), that defy strict denominational divisions. In addition, the notion of religious forms can help to defy the rigidity of formal institutional classifications and facilitate the consideration of local classificatory systems (for example, the importance of "born again" as a form of Christian classification in Kenya but not in Switzerland).

11 Later on in the book, in part III, we revisit these reflections and offer typologies of butineurs and butinage.
12 The International Grace of God Church (Igreja Internacional da Graça de Deus) split from the Universal Church of the Kingdom of God in 1980.
13 The religious repertoires model draws on Gez's (2014, 2018) doctoral thesis and monograph focused on religious mobility in Kenya.
14 The three logics draw on Gez's (2014, 2018) doctoral thesis and monograph focused on religious mobility in Kenya.

2 Religious Mobility: Current Debates

1 See, for example, Esposito, Fasching, and Lewis 2001, 431–2, 437–8; Horton 1971, 1975, 1982; Dubuisson 1998.
2 See, for example, Meintel 2003; Swatos and Gissurarson 1997; Heirich 1977; Suchman 1992.
3 Some notable early works include Starbuck 1899; Leuba 1896; James 1902; Coe 1916; Hall 1904. Already, however, the seeds were planted for looking at religious mobility in its wider social context (Jackson 1908).
4 The book's longevity continues despite certain flaws found in James's project, such as his choice of exemplars and his focus on dramatic narratives, the hypothetical and possibly stigmatizing nature of some of his concepts (such as the "sick soul"), and his almost exclusive focus on Western Christianity for his primary sources (Wulff 1991).
5 Some examples of early non-Pauline thinking are found in Strickland 1924; Nock 1933; Clark 1929. An early example of conversion among people with a "sound mind" can be found in Starbuck 1899.
6 Some of these early scholars include Hall 1904; Starbuck 1899. See Hood, Hill, and Spilka 2009; Richardson 1985.
7 Examples of the model's application to the case of prisoners of war include Schein 1961; Lifton 1961; Moloney 1955; Bauer 1957; Miller 1957. Examples of its application to the case of NRMs and cults include Enroth 1977; Sargant 1957; Glock and Bellah 1976; Barker 1983; Singer 1979.
8 See Kirkpatrick 1992, 1999; Granqvist and Kirkpatrick 2004; Granqvist 2003. Interestingly, such shifts also occur in conversion narratives themselves, for

example among Pentecostals, when religious conversion is framed in terms of healing from lack of parental affection (Rey 2019).

9 See Snow and Machalek 1984; Lofland and Stark 1965; Bromley and Shupe 1979; Snow and Phillips 1980; Lofland and Skonovd 1981; Long and Hadden 1983; Kox, Meeus, and Hart 1991.

10 See Roof 1978; Houghland and Wood 1980; Albrecht, Cornwall, and Cunningham 1988; Cornwall 1987; Kirkpatrick and Shaver 1990; Long and Hadden 1983.

11 Note Snow and Machalek's (1984) observation that, even though, in their view, "it is not evident that only the more radical type of change should be conceptualized as conversion" (170), "the notion of radical change remains at the core of all conceptions of conversion" (169).

12 See Rambo 1999. Such bias is evident, for instance, in the way in which the theoretical framework of the "brainwashing" model has attracted "a disproportionate share of those who believe cults are a menace to them, their families or other citizens" (Long and Hadden 1983, 4). Similarly, as Ralph Hood and his colleagues argue with regard to the study of fundamentalist religious groups, empirical issues pertaining to such studies may be clouded by value-laden differences between investigators and subjects (Hood, Hill, and Williamson 2005).

13 As Jean Comaroff and John Comaroff (1991) have shown with regard to the work of Christian missionaries among the Tswana people in South Africa, the very application of the terminology of conversion may connote Western colonial imposition of paradigms of thought.

14 See Stromberg 1993; Beckford 1978; Lofland and Skonovd 1981; Preston 1981; Snow 1976; Snow and Machalek 1984. Also note Bourdieu's (1986) more general critique of life history narratives.

15 Some examples include Lambek 2008; Janson and Meyer 2016.

16 In fact, contestations against the idea that religions correspond to any single, "pure" strand of tradition is traceable to antiquity (Leopold and Jensen 2004; Borgeaud 2004).

17 The spiritual head of a *terreiro*, the highest position in the Afro-Brazilian spiritual hierarchy. The term "*terreiro*" (ground, site) refers to the site of gathering for Afro-Brazilians associated with Candomblé.

18 A follower of *Batuque* – an Afro-Brazilian religion common in the south of Brazil and especially in the city of Porto Alegre.

19 *Saravá* is an Afro-Brazilian term for the life force.

20 As Bourdieu reminds us, "nothing is simpler, and in a sense, more 'natural,' than imposing a problematic ... The imposition effect applied in the guise of 'neutrality' is all the more pernicious in that publication of such imposed opinions helps to impose them and give them a social existence" (Bourdieu 1999, 619–20).

21 As Droz explains, additional conversions are a "particular type of conversion, since they suppose neither the abjuration of previous faith nor a simple change of liturgy ... [T]he 'born again' can stay Anglican or Methodist, Lutheran or Presbyterian, without this affiliation constituting an obstacle to their conversion" (Droz 2002b, 93; our translation). Also see Boyer 1998, 2009; Oro 1991; Birman 1996; Soares 2009.
22 Interestingly, Goffman suggests that one possible reason for participating in an underlife is an attempt to reduce deprivation. It follows that secondary adjustments might be picked up most adamantly by those with the least to gain from complying with their normative role.
23 See Adams, Clemens, and Orloff 2005; North 1981; Evans, Rueschemeyer, and Skocpol 1985; March and Olsen 1989; Streeck and Thelen 2005; Unger 1987; Sabel 1994.
24 Of course, the word "lived" should not be read in the past tense but in the passive voice – lived religion is a living religion, experienced and enacted by active actors.
25 In chapter 6, we further engage with the concept of "spirituality," which shares certain commonalities with that of lived religion.
26 See Hervieu-Léger 2000; Lövheim 2007.
27 See, for example, Travisano 1970; Gordon 1974; Suchman 1992; Rambo 1993; Scobie 1973. Thus, for instance, Snow and Machalek (1984, 170) identify "at least" four types of religious change, including "alternation" (Travisano 1970), "consolidation" (Gordon 1974), "regeneration" (Clark 1929), and a radical "road to Damascus" transformation. Some less embellished terminological choices include "religious change" (Granqvist 2003), "religious transit" (De Almeida and Monteiro 2001), or – a term routinely employed throughout the present work – "religious mobility." In the French literature, we find yet more terminological ideas, such as "*religieux à la carte*" (Schlegel 1995), "*religieux flottant*," "*des éclats de religion*" or "*religion diffuse*" (Champion 2003, 1993), "*religieux en vadrouille*" (Desroche 1965), "*nouvelle sensibilité mystique-ésotérique*," "*sacralité non religieuse*," or, again, "*nouvelle réalité syncrétique*" (Mardones 1994), "*nébuleuse mystique ésotérique*" or "*crédules diffus*" (Champion, Hervieu-Léger, and Hourmant 1990).
28 Note that this challenge has also been posed by Durkheim in the context of his decision to define religion through the category of the sacred (Durkheim 1968).

Introduction to Part II: Methodology

1 These ties have in part been explored in our edited volume dedicated to religious connections between sub-Saharan Africa and Latin America (Chanson et al. 2014).
2 The division of fieldwork within the research team is presented in the introduction to each of the coming chapters.

3 Neighborliness as a Driver for Mobility in Brazil

1 Project StAR (Structures anthropologiques du religieux: Butinage et voisinage) was financed by the Swiss National Science Foundation and based at the Graduate Institute of International and Development Studies in Geneva (2010–15). Led by Principal Investigator Yvan Droz, it involved the four authors of this book.

2 The survey was conducted by the IBGE and is titled "Sinopse do censo demográfico: 2010"; it was published in 2011 in Rio de Janeiro. See https://biblioteca.ibge.gov.br/visualizacao/livros/liv49230.pdf.

3 *Terreiro* and *centro* designate places of worship associated with Afro-Brazilian religions. The former is associated with Candomblé, while the latter is associated with Macumba and Umbanda.

4 The Kenyan Case: Dynamism and Precariousness

1 In the Kikuyu Bantu language, the closest translation of the notion of conversion – *kirira ne magongona* – implies a shift in ritual liturgy and sacrifices. Above all, the concept has been intertwined with quests for therapy by afflicted individuals and families, and evokes a sense of spatial relocation (Droz 2002b, 86n11).

2 In this brief presentation, we refer primarily to the Kenyan hinterland and refrain from delving into the country's coastal area, whose unique history – in which Islam has played, and continues to play, an important role – diverges from the dominance of Kenyan Christianity. See, for example, McIntosh 2009.

3 Article 78 of the 1963 constitution declares, among other things, that "except with his own consent (or, if he is a minor, the consent of his guardian), no person attending a place of education shall be required to receive religious instruction or to take part in or attend a religious ceremony or observance if that instruction, ceremony or observance relates to a religion other than his own." Article 32 of the 2010 constitution declares, among other things, that "every person has the right, either individually or in community with others, in public or in private, to manifest any religion or belief through worship, practice, teaching or observance, including observance of a day of worship," and that "a person shall not be compelled to act, or engage in any act, that is contrary to the person's belief or religion."

4 According to the 2019 census, out of a total population size of 47,564,296, the majority (85.5 per cent) are Christians, with Protestants, Catholics, and Evangelical churches accounting for 33.4, 20.6, and 20.4 per cent, respectively. The country's second largest religion is Islam, with Muslims

accounting for 11 per cent of the total population (Kenya National Bureau of Statistics 2019, 12, 422).

5 In both categories, Nigeria ranked second, with 76 percent and 48 percent respectively. The countries participating in the study included the United States, Brazil, Chile, Guatemala, Kenya, Nigeria, South Africa, the Philippines, South Korea, and parts of India.

6 However, according to a Kenyan TV news item, "close to 80 percent of churches in Kenya are unregistered" (NTV Kenya 2012b). This assessment is claimed to have come from the Registrar General's office.

7 According to sources cited by Gifford (1994, 519), Kenya has shown an astounding growth in the number of missionaries. In 1989, it had 1,225 American Protestant missionaries, and in 1993, it had 1,337. Considering foreign Protestant missionaries as a whole (as opposed to Americans only), Kenya allegedly had 1,150 in 1978; 1,850 in 1986; and 2,321 in 1993.

8 The survey, conducted among members of the church's Buruburu branch, had 55.3 percent of respondents arguing that their congregation is not in fact Pentecostal (Chelule 2012). Nairobi Pentecostal Church is also known as Christ Is the Answer Ministries (CITAM), but this latter name is less commonly used.

9 Parsitau and Mwaura, in their article on the Deliverance Church in Kenya, similarly suggest that "the church was started by young people and about 80% of the church is currently constituted by young people" (Parsitau and Mwaura 2010, 6).

10 Sheng is an urban Kiswahili slang, most popular in Nairobi (Ferrari 2012).

11 While widely used, the term has also been subject to critique. For example, Aguilar (1995) avoids the term – speaking, instead, of "local religious traditions." In explaining his choice, he cites Shaw's (1990, 339) assertion whereby the term "African traditional religions" is "a product of the paradigmatic status accorded in religious studies to the Judeo-Christian tradition and of the associated view of religion as text." While we accept this critique, which is in line with our own, this debate is secondary to our key focus.

12 For example, in 2013, the *Daily Nation* published a cover story titled "Preaching to the Converted: The Rise of Atheism in Modern Kenya" (Okeyo 2013). Painting a complex picture, the article concluded that, in Kenya today, atheism is fast growing.

13 See the section "Religious Identity in Context and Motion" in chapter 8 of this volume.

14 Allegedly, Rose did not qualify as a member because she did not participate regularly in home fellowship or "cell group" meetings. As she explained, she does not participate in those activities because there are no such group meetings in her immediate neighborhood and attending a group in another

part of town would require her to return home alone after dark using public transportation, which might compromise her personal safety.

15 An exception to that rule can be seen, for example, in the case of Alicia, a Pentecostal in her mid-thirties. Even though we met at her Kisumu church, where she is an engaged women's leader, Alicia still felt a sense of belonging to her two "previous" churches, one back in her village and another in Nairobi. When it comes to giving tithe, she divides a tenth of her salary in three, donates a third to her Kisumu church and sends the remaining two thirds through her mobile phone to her two "former" congregations.

16 See chapter 8, "From Religious Mobility to Dynamic Religious Identities."

17 We opt for the notion of "return mobility" over that of "deconversion" (Streib 2014) and "disaffiliation" (Gooren 2010).

18 This finding emerged even though return mobility was never included in our formal interview guide. It was only in the latter period of our Kenyan fieldwork, as preliminary analysis of our data showed such a tendency, that we began to explicitly ask our interviewees about continued ties with religious forms that they had once left.

19 Indicative of the size of existing literature on geographic return mobility, an academic bibliography on the subject, prepared by Jørgen Carling, Elin Berstad Mortensen, and Jennifer Wu (2011), located over 1,100 titles published since 1960.

20 At the same time, however, the fact that women tend to be more practicing and more prominent in taking care of the children may create an interesting tension. In a minority of cases, husband and wife continue attending separate churches, or it is the husband who follows his wife to her church.

21 In our research in Kenya, we met a number of "church zappers," whose religious exposure is carried out primarily on their own through the consumption of televangelism and other religious media. While this choice might be justified in terms of convenience, virtually all the church zappers we spoke to admitted to having experienced problems in their congregations. For them, zapping might merely involve a reclusive period, during which the congregant-turned-spectator observes from a safe distance (Gez 2018; Gez and Droz 2017).

22 One may introduce a nuanced distinction between rumors, defined as "claims of fact – about people, groups, events, and institutions – that have not been shown to be true, but that move from one person to another and hence have credibility not because direct evidence is known to support them, but because other people seem to believe them" (Sunstein 2009, 6), and scandals, which represent the public explosion of rumors that have been validated by clear evidence. However, for the sake of simplicity, and

as this discussion is secondary to our interest in religious mobility, we avoid developing it.

23 For a critique of the term, see Crisp and Cowton (1994).

24 M-Pesa is a popular system for transferring money using cell phones. The derogatory term "M-Pesa pastors" derives from the emphasis, by some pastors and especially televangelists who subscribe to the prosperity gospel, on M-Pesa as a way for believers to send money to the church/pastor in exchange for blessings (Parsitau 2014, 246, 262, 285).

25 Winners' Chapel is a Nigerian church advocating prosperity teachings. In Kenya, it has an ambivalent reputation – many believe that it is successful in contributing to congregants' socioeconomic ascension, even as they suspect that the church draws its powers by being in league with evil powers.

26 It is worth mentioning that, in Ghana, similar rumors crop up about pastors from Nigeria. It is also alleged that some Ghanaian pastors owe their spiritual power to ungodly rituals performed in Nigeria.

27 In Kenya, it is largely considered unthinkable to sell a plot where a relative is buried: it would imply disowning one's deceased ancestors (Droz 2011).

28 This phenomenon is not necessarily new, as Valeer Neckebrouck (1983) shows.

29 At the same time, schisms may also occur because founding a new ministry serves as a way for the founder to achieve self-accomplishment (Droz 2000a).

5 Mobility Intertwined: Migration, Kinship, and Education in Ghana

1 See, for example, Van Dijk 2004; Warner and Wittner 1998; Williams 1988; Warner 2000; Ebaugh and Saltzman Chafetz 2000; Sabar 2004; Van Dijk 1997; Adogame 2003, 2004.

2 This presentation is somewhat simplistic because the very transnationalization of religious congregations goes hand in hand with significant changes in religious practice and discourse. Ethnographic studies by Fancello (2006), Daswani (2015), and Rey (2019), for instance, document such transnationalization processes with regard to Ghanaian churches in Europe.

3 Such family ruptures add an interesting dimension to the common allusion to kinship terminologies within religious circles and within Pentecostal-charismatic circles in particular – whereby the church assumes the role of a spiritual foster family (see, for example, Sharma 2012; Bonsu and Belk 2010).

4 A Muslim who has completed a pilgrim to Mecca.

5 Kofuridua is a town situated between Accra and Kumasi in southern Ghana.

6 Fufu is a popular meal made using pounded cassava and plantain.

7 Like many other taxi drivers in Accra, Kofi did not own the car he drove, but rented it on a daily basis. Rental rates may reach 80 cedis per day (2014),

which is more than half of a driver's average daily income in Accra. Thus, owning a car is a significant step toward financial independence.

8 The equivalent of about 80 to 120 euros.

9 *Adinkra* are symbols often associated with Akan proverbs or moral values. They are worn on a person's clothes (for example, for funerals) and include brass or gold figures and other artistic creations. They now serve as an expression of Akan culture. Houses, shops, or pieces of furniture may also be decorated with *adinkra* symbols.

10 *Gye Nyame*, which literally means "except for God," is one of the most popular and widespread *adinkra* symbols in Ghana. It has an inherently trans-religious character as it speaks to Muslims, Christians, and Traditionalists. It is therefore an illustration of the cultural "bridges" that transcend religious boundaries within Akan society.

6 Religion and Mobility in Switzerland: A Most Private Affair

1 The questionnaires were administered from 2008 to 2009.

2 The authors also considered alternative medicine, such as Reiki and chromatology, as religious "resources" at the disposal of believers.

3 Exit is a Swiss association that assists people to end their lives by physician-assisted suicide. Its website can be found at https://exit.ch/en/.

4 Such division was demonstrated by Karl Polanyi (1944) with regard to the economy and by Michel Foucault (1972, 1976) with regard to madness and sexuality.

5 One appealing attempt at reconciling the two terms is proposed by Peter Hill et al. (2000). According to their suggestion, spirituality necessarily involves a search for the sacred, broadly defined by individuals themselves. Religion may or may not involve a similar objective and is necessarily complemented by two additional components not shared by spirituality: (1) a search for nonsacred goals (for example, identity, belonging, meaning, health, or wellness); and (2) a prescription of means and methods by which to search for the sacred that receives validation from an identifiable group. As Schlehofer, Omoto, and Adelman (2008) positively comment, this conceptual approach may help harmonize, rather than polarize, the two terms.

6 *Le secret* refers to a therapeutic practice in which a person recites – often over the phone – secret prayers transmitted over generations, which are supposed to cure burns and skin disease. It is widely known in the Catholic cantons of Switzerland and France (Jenny 2008).

7 Such a critical approach toward religious institutions is by no means new. Its most famous antecedent, perhaps, is the Christian Reformation, with

its emphasis on establishing a personal, less institutionally dependent, relationship with God (Gauchet 1985; Tillich 1952, 160–3).

8 In such cases, we could not identify a preferred pattern of gender-based intergenerational identification.

7 Between Bees and Flowers

1 See chapter 8, "From Religious Mobility to Dynamic Religious Identities."

2 The issue of how to classify a religious form is also driven by the degree of specificity that one is interested in obtaining. In our research in Kenya, following our interlocutors' emphasis on their attachment to their denominations as a whole rather than to specific congregations, we categorically regarded all branches within the same denomination as a single religious form, but that might not be the case elsewhere.

3 See chapter 4, "The Kenyan Case: Dynamism and Precariousness."

4 Wijsen further reminds us that this strand of pragmatism has long been considered in the study of African religiosity. If it had been common in traditional African practices, with their emphasis on magic as practical spirituality, it became entrenched through the work of missionaries, who offered converts access to gains such as education, health, and social status. Wijsen further suggests that this same line of thinking may be used to explain present-day attraction to the prosperity gospel (Wijsen 2007, 81).

5 Over the years, Allport's original approach has been revised and updated. Of particular relevance to the present discussion is the introduction of a third "quest orientation," contrasted with the rigid closed-mindedness associated with intrinsic orientation (Batson 1976; Batson and Ventis 1982).

6 The idea was in part inspired by Henri Gooren's (2010) work on religious mobility through the prism of "conversion careers," in which he recognized the difficulties of determining reasons for mobility and identified five factors that may have a bearing on religious mobility throughout the life cycle: personal, social, institutional, cultural, and contingency.

7 We were unable to determine the precise origin of the term. However, having seen it in use in various non-Kenyan sources, we suspect that it has been popularized in the country through the activities of foreign, possibly American, (tel)evangelists.

8 From Religious Mobility to Dynamic Religious Identities

1 Aristotle, *Metaphysics, Books 1–9,* trans. Hugh Tredennick. Loeb Classical Library 271 (Cambridge, MA: Harvard University Press, 1933), 4.5.14 (1010a10–15).

2 Aristotle, *Generation of Animals*, trans. A.L. Peck. Loeb Classical Library 366 (Cambridge, MA: Harvard University Press, 1942), 2.1, 735a9ff.

3 Note in particular the debate over first and second actuality (Kosman 1969).

4 Due to this tendency, scholars should be especially attentive in "gleaning" peripheral practices from interviewees' narratives.

5 Our use of the term "religious repertoires" as a general model for dynamic religious identity is different from Justin Thomas McDaniel's (2011) use of the same terminology in his exploration of Buddhism in modern-day Thailand, and was developed independently of McDaniel's work.

6 See, for example, Fisher 2012; Lamont 1992; Silber 2003; Steinberg 1999; Swidler 2001a, 2001b, 1986; Tilly 1979; Traugott 1995; Larsen 2004; Fine 2004; Mizrachi, Drori, and Anspach 2007.

7 In her later work, Swidler (2001a) abandons the image of the toolkit, arguing that it misleadingly insinuates the work of an active agent, consciously and intentionally employing cultural elements. However, Swidler continues to maintain the concept of repertoire, which was used interchangeably with toolkit in her earlier (1986) publication on the topic.

8 Interesting to our case, Swidler (1986) offers the example of religious traditions, which she sees as a toolkit offering diverse lines of (at times contradictory) potential action. As she explains, "all real cultures contain diverse, often conflicting symbols, rituals, stories, and guides to action. The reader of the Bible can find a passage to justify almost any act, and traditional wisdom usually comes in paired adages counselling opposite behaviors" (277). For more examples on the application of the concept of cultural repertoires to religious or spiritual settings, consider John Larsen (2004) and Gareth Fisher (2012).

9 While recognizing that actors are predisposed by their habitus to a certain collective repertoire, little has been done to map out actors' personal profiles and precise range of competences and preferences. At times, it is not completely clear whether the term "repertoire," as used by Swidler and others, refers to that which is potentially available to all participants within a given culture or to the particular pieces mastered by individual actors. Moreover, as little was written on the place of the individual practitioner vis-à-vis the general cultural repertoire, some theoretical questions remain unresolved. As Gary Alan Fine suggests with regard to Swidler's concept of "cultural toolkit," "unexplored is the question of how tools are placed in and taken out of that kit. At what point do individuals acquire the knowledge of the use of these tools, and when do individuals discard those tools that they had previously relied upon successfully?" (Fine 2004, 3).

10 See Stromberg 1993; Wuthnow 2011; Beckford 1978; Lofland and Skonovd 1981; Snow and Machalek 1984; Preston 1981.

11 Charles Camic (1986) indicates how the human propensity toward habits, central to the works of such luminaries as Weber and Durkheim, has fallen out of favor since the mid-twentieth century. This change might be understood in the context of sociology's battle against behaviorist psychology.

9 Conclusion: The Peripatetic Practitioner

1 The Pentecostalization of the Presbyterian Church of Kenya manifested in iconoclast actions that, in the early 2000s, saw the destruction of the stained glass windows of its flagship St. Andrew's Church in Nairobi for supposedly featuring Masonic symbols (Gifford 2009, 206–11).

2 We thank Devaka Premawardhana for bringing this beautiful image to our attention.

Bibliography

Adam, Michel, ed. 2015. *Indian Africa: Minorities of Indian-Pakistani Origin in Eastern Africa.* Dar es Salaam: Mkuki na Noyta. First published 2010 in French by Karthala (Paris).

Adams, Julia, Elisabeth S. Clemens, and Ann S. Orloff, eds. 2005. *Remaking Modernity: Politics, History and Sociology.* Durham, NC: Duke University Press.

Adler, Jerry. 2005. "In Search of the Spiritual." *Newsweek,* August 8, 2005, 46–64.

Adogame, Afe. 2003. "Betwixt Identity and Security: African New Religious Movements and the Politics of Religious Networking in Europe." *Nova Religio: The Journal of Alternative and Emergent Religions* 7 (2): 24–41. https://doi.org/10.1525/nr.2003.7.2.24.

– 2004. "Engaging the Rhetoric of Spiritual Warfare: The Public Face of Aladura in Diaspora." *Journal of Religion in Africa* 34 (4): 493–522. https://doi.org/10.1163/1570066042564392.

Afrobarometer. 2011. Round 5 Afrobarometer: Survey in Kenya. Institute for Development Studies (IDS), University of Nairobi & Michigan State University (MSU). https://afrobarometer.org/data/kenya-round-5-data-updated-july-2015.

Aguilar, Mario I. 1995. "African Conversion from a World Religion: Religious Diversification by the Waso Boorana in Kenya." *Africa* 65 (4): 525–44. https://doi.org/10.2307/1161131.

Ahmad, Attiya. 2017. *Everyday Conversions: Islam, Domestic Work, and South Asian Migrant Women in Kuwait.* Durham, NC: Duke University Press.

Albrecht, Stan L., and Marie Cornwall. 1989. "Life Events and Religious Change." *Review of Religious Research* 31 (1): 23–38. https://doi.org/10.2307/3511021.

Albrecht, Stan L., Marie Cornwall, and Perry H. Cunningham. 1988. "Religious Leave-Taking: Disengagement and Disaffiliation among Mormons." In *Falling from the Faith: The Causes and Consequences of Religious*

Apostasy, edited by David G. Bromley, 67–80. Beverly Hills, CA: SAGE Publications.

Allport, Gordon W. 1966. "The Religious Context of Prejudice." *Journal for the Scientific Study of Religion* 5 (3): 447–57. https://doi.org/10.2307/1384172.

Allport, Gordon W., and Michael J. Ross. 1967. "Personal Religious Orientation and Prejudice." *Journal of Personality and Social Psychology* 5 (4): 432–43. https://doi.org/10.1037/h0021212.

Almond, Gabriel A., R. Scott Appleby, and Emmanuel Sivan. 2003. *Strong Religion: The Rise of Fundamentalisms around the World*. Chicago: University of Chicago Press.

Ammerman, Nancy T. 2003. "Religious Identities and Religious Institutions." In *Handbook of the Sociology of Religion*, edited by Michele Dillon, 207–24. Cambridge: Cambridge University Press.

Anderson, Allan. 2004. *An Introduction to Pentecostalism: Global Charismatic Christianity*. Cambridge: Cambridge University Press.

– 2010. "Varieties, Taxonomies, and Definitions." In *Studying Global Pentecostalism: Theories and Methods*, edited by Allan Anderson, Michael Bergunder, André Droogers, and Cornelis van der Laan, 13–29. Berkeley: University of California Press.

Anderson, Allan, Michael Bergunder, André Droogers, and Cornelis van der Laan. 2010. "Introduction." In *Studying Global Pentecostalism: Theories and Methods*, edited by Allan Anderson, Michael Bergunder, André Droogers, and Cornelis van der Laan, 1–12. Berkeley: University of California Press.

Anderson, Benedict. 1983. *Imagined Communities: Reflections on the Origin and Spread of Nationalism*. London: Verso.

Appiah, Kwame A. 2018. *The Lies That Bind: Rethinking Identity*. New York: Liveright Publishing.

Asad, Talal. 1993. *Genealogies of Religion: Discipline and Reasons of Power in Christianity and Islam*. Baltimore, MD: Johns Hopkins University Press.

– 2003. *Formations of the Secular: Christianity, Islam, Modernity*. Stanford, CA: Stanford University Press.

Austin-Broos, Diane. 2003. "The Anthropology of Conversion: An Introduction." In *The Anthropology of Religious Conversion*, edited by Andrew Buckser and Stephen D. Glazier, 1–12. Lanham, MD: Rowman & Littlefield.

Barker, Eileen. 1983. "New Religious Movements in Britain: The Context and the Membership." *Social Compass* 30 (1): 33–48. https://doi.org/10.1177/003776868303000103.

Barth, Fredrik. 1983. *Sohar: Culture and Society in an Omani Town*. Baltimore, MD: Johns Hopkins University Press.

– 1984. "Problems in Conceptualizing Cultural Pluralism, with Illustrations from Sohar, Oman." In *The Prospects for Plural Societies: 1982 Proceedings of the American Ethnological Society*, edited by David Maybury-Lewis, 77–87. Washington, DC: American Ethnological Society.

Bastide, Roger. 1955. "Le principe de coupure et le comportement afro-brésilien." In *Anais do XXXI Congresse internacional de Americanistas 1954*, 493–503. São Paulo: Anhembi.

– 1960. *Les religions africaines au Brésil.* Paris: PUF.

Batson, Daniel C. 1976. "Religion as Prosocial: Agent or Double Agent?" *Journal for the Scientific Study of Religion* 15 (1): 29–45. https://doi.org/102307/1384312.

Batson, Daniel C., and Larry W. Ventis. 1982. *The Religious Experience: A Social-Psychological Perspective.* New York: Oxford University Press.

Bauer, Raymond A. 1957. "Brainwashing: Psychology or Demonology?" *Journal of Social Issues* 13 (3): 41–7. https://doi.org/10.1111/j.1540-4560.1957.tb02269.x.

Bayart, Jean-François, ed. 1993. *Religion et modernité politique en Afrique noire. Dieu pour tous et chacun pour soi.* Paris: Karthala.

Becker, Howard S. 1960. "Notes on the Concept of Commitment." *American Journal of Sociology* 66 (1): 32–40. https://doi.org/10.1086/222820.

Beckford, James A. 1978. "Accounting for Conversion." *British Journal of Sociology* 29 (2): 249–62. https://doi.org/10.2307/589892.

Bellah, Robert. 2011. *Religion in Human Evolution: From the Paleolithic to the Axial Age.* Cambridge, MA: Belknap Press of Harvard University Press.

Bellah, Robert, Richard Madsen, William M. Sullivan, Ann Swidler, and Steven M. Tipton. 1985. *Habits of the Heart: Individualism and Commitment in American Life.* Berkeley: University of California Press.

Bellah, Robert, and Steven M. Tipton, eds. 2006. *The Robert Bellah Reader.* Durham, NC: Duke University Press.

Berger, Peter L. 1967a. *Philosophische Vertiefung des Physikunterrichts.* Braunschweig, DE: F. Vieweg.

– 1967b. *The Sacred Canopy: Elements of a Sociological Theory of Religion.* Garden City, NY: Doubleday.

Berk, Gerald, and Denis Galvan. 2009. "How People Experience and Change Institutions: A Field Guide to Creative Syncretism." *Theory and Society* 38 (6): 543–80. https://doi.org/10.1007/s11186-009-9095-3.

Bibby, Reginald W. 1997. "Going, Going, Gone: The Impact of Geographical Mobility on Religious Involvement." *Review of Religious Research* 38 (4): 289–307. https://doi.org/10.2307/3512192.

Birman, Patricia. 1996. "Cultos de possessao e pentecostalismo no Brasil. Passagens." *Religião & Sociedade* 17 (1–2): 90–109.

– 2001. "Conexões políticas e bricolagens religioas: questões sobre o pentecostalismo a partir de alguns contrapontos." In *Fiéis & Cidadãos.*

Percursos de Sincretismo no Brasil, edited by Pierre Sanchis, 59–86. Rio de Janeiro: UERJ.

Bloor, David. 2001. "Wittgenstein and the Priority of Practice." In *The Practical Turn in Contemporary Theory*, edited by Theodore R. Schatzki, Karin Knorr Cetina, and Eike von Savigny. London: Routledge and Kegan Paul.

Bocquier, Philippe, Alfred T.A. Otieno, Anne A. Khasakhala, and Samuel Owuor. 2009. *Urban Integration in Africa: A Socio-Demographic Survey of Nairobi*. Dakar: CODESRIA.

Bonsu, Samuel K., and Russell W. Belk. 2010. "Marketing a New African God: Pentecostalism and Material Salvation in Ghana." *International Journal of Nonprofit and Voluntary Sector Marketing* 15 (4): 305–23. https://doi.org/10.1002/nvsm.398.

Borgeaud, Philippe. 2004. *Aux origines de l'histoire des religions*. Paris: Seuil.

Bourdieu, Pierre. 1980. *Le sens pratique*. Paris: Minuit.

– 1986. "Habitus, code et codification." *Actes de la recherche en sciences sociales* 64 (septembre): 40–4. https://doi.org/10.3406/arss.1986.2335.

– 1999. "Understanding." In *The Weight of the World: Social Suffering in Contemporary Society*, edited by Pierre Bourdieu et al., translated by Priscilla Parkhurst Ferguson, 607–26. Stanford, CA: Polity Press.

Bourdieu, Pierre, Jean-Claude Chamboredon, and Jean-Claude Passeron. 1973. *Le métier de sociologue*. La Haye et Paris: Mouton. First published 1969.

Bowlby, John. 1969. *Attachment and Loss*. Vol. 1, *Attachment*. New York: Basic Books.

– 1973. *Attachment and Loss*. Vol. 2, *Separation Anxiety and Anger*. New York: Basic Books.

– 1980. *Attachment and Loss*. Vol. 3, *Loss*. New York: Basic Books.

Boyer, Véronique. 1998. "Le récit de Lessa. Des cultes de possession aux Églises pentecôtistes." *L'Homme* 38 (148): 119–38. https://doi.org/10.3406/hom.1998.370579.

– 2009. *L'expansion évangélique et migration en Amazonie brésilienne*. Paris: Karthala.

Bromley, David G., and Anson D. Shupe. 1979. "'Just a Few Years Seem Like a Lifetime': A Role Theory Approach to Participation in Religious Movements." In *Research in Social Movements, Conflicts, and Change*, vol. 2, edited by Louis Kriesberg, 159–85. Greenwich, CT: JAI Press.

Brubaker, Rogers, and Frederick Cooper. 2000. "Beyond 'Identity.'" *Theory and Society* 29 (1): 1–47. https://doi.org/10.1023/A:1007068714468.

Buckser, Andrew, and Stephen D. Glazier, eds. 2003. *The Anthropology of Religious Conversion*. Lanham, MD: Rowman & Littlefield.

Camic, Charles. 1986. "The Matter of Habit." *American Journal of Sociology* 91 (5): 1039–87. https://doi.org/10.1086/228386.

Campiche, Roland J., avec la collaboration de Raphaël Broquet, Alfred Dubach, and Jörg Stolz, eds. 2004. *Les deux visages de la religion. Fascination et désenchantement.* Genève, CH: Labor et Fides.

Campiche, Roland J., Alfred Dubach, Claude Bovay, Michael Krüggeler, and Peter Voll. 1992. *Croire en Suisse(s). Analyse des résultats de l'enquête menée en 1988/1989 sur la religion des Suisses.* Lausanne, CH: L'Age d'homme.

Canclini, Néstor Garcia. 1998. *Culturas Híbridas. Estratégias para entrar e sair da modernidade.* São Paulo, BR: Edusp.

Carling, Jørgen, Elin Berstad Mortensen, and Jennifer Wu. 2011. *A Systematic Bibliography on Return Migration.* Oslo, NO: Peace Research Institute Oslo (PRIO).

Centre intercantonal d'information sur les croyances (CIC). 2004. *Rapport annuel 2004.* Genève, CH: CIC. https://www.cic-info.ch/wp/wp-content/uploads/2004.pdf.

Chamel, Jean. 2018. "'Tout est lié'; Ethnographie d'un réseau d'intellectuels engagés de l'écologie (France-Suisse): de l'effrondrement systémique à l'écospiritualité holiste et monise." PhD, Faculté de théologie et de sciences des religions, Université de Lausanne. https://serval.unil.ch/en/notice/serval:BIB_1784208FEA8D.

Champion, Françoise. 1993. "Religieux flottant, éclectisme et syncrétisme." In *Le fait religieux,* edited by Jean Delumeau, 741–72. Paris: Fayard.

– 2003. "La religion n'est plus ce qu'elle était." *La Revue du MAUSS* 2 (22): 171–80.

Champion, Françoise, Danièle Hervieu-Léger, and Louis Hourmant, eds. 1990. *De l'émotion en religion: renouveaux et traditions.* Paris: Centurion.

Chanson, Philippe. 2011. *Variations métisses. Dix métaphores pour penser le métissage. Anthropologie prospective,* tome 8. Louvain-la-Neuve, BE: Academia-Bruylant.

Chanson, Philippe, Yvan Droz, Yonatan N. Gez, and Edio Soares, eds. 2014. *Mobilité religieuse. Retours croisés des Afriques aux Amériques.* Paris: Karthala.

Chelule, Esther. 2012. "Pentecostalism and Being Born-Again: A Case Study of Nairobi Pentecostal Church (NPC)/Christ Is The Answer Ministries (CITAM) Buruburu, Nairobi." Paper presented at the conference *Mobilité religieuse en Afrique de l'Est / Religious Mobility in Eastern Africa,* CUEA, Nairobi, April 24–26, 2012.

Chen, Carolyn. 2005. "A Self of One's Own: Taiwanese Immigrant Women and Religious Conversion." *Gender and Society* 19 (3): 336–57. https://doi.org/10.1177/0891243204273125.

Clark, Elmer T. 1929. *The Psychology of Religious Awakening.* New York: Macmillan.

Coe, George Albert. 1916. *Psychology of Religion.* Chicago: University of Chicago Press.

Coffey, Amanda. 1999. *The Ethnographic Self: Fieldwork and the Representation of Identity*. London: Sage Publications.

Cohen, Anthony P. 1982. "Belonging: The Experience of Culture." In *Belonging: Identity and Social Organisation in British Rural Cultures*, edited by Anthony P. Cohen. Manchester, UK: Manchester University Press.

Coleman, James William. 2001. *The New Buddhism: The Western Transformation of an Ancient Tradition*. New York: Oxford University Press.

Collins, Randall. 2004. *Interaction Ritual Chains*. Princeton, NJ: Princeton University Press.

Comaroff, Jean, and John Comaroff. 1991. *Of Revelation and Revolution*. Vol. 1, *Christianity, Colonialism, and Consciousness in South Africa*. Chicago: University of Chicago Press.

– 2015. *Theory from the South: Or, How Euro-America Is Evolving Toward Africa*. New York: Routledge.

Corbin Dwyer, Sonya, and Jennifer L. Buckle. 2009. "The Space Between: On Being an Insider-Outsider in Qualitative Research." *International Journal of Qualitative Methods* 8 (1): 54–63. https://doi.org/10.1177/160940690900800105.

Cordell, Dennis D., Joel Gregory, and Victor Piché. 1996. *Hoe and Wage: A Social History of a Circular Migration System in West Africa*. African Modernization and Development Series, edited by Paul Lovejoy. Boulder, CO: Westview Press.

Cornwall, Marie. 1987. "The Social Base of Religion: A Study of Factors Influencing Religious Belief and Commitment." *Review of Religious Research* 29 (1): 44–56. https://doi.org/10.2307/3511951.

Corten, André, and Ruth Marshall-Fratani, eds. 2001. *Between Babel and Pentecost: Transnational Pentecostalism in Africa and Latin America*. London: Hurst.

Crisp, Roger, and Christopher Cowton. 1994. "Hypocrisy and Moral Seriousness." *American Philosophical Quarterly* 31 (4): 343–9. https://doi.org/10.2307/20009796.

Cuénod, Jean-Noël. 1992. "Chacun fait son marché." *Tribune de Genève*, October 16, 1992.

Cullity, Garrett. 1995. "Moral Free Riding." *Philosophy and Public Affairs* 24 (1): 3–34. https://doi.org/10.1111/j.1088-4963.1995.tb00020.x.

Da Matta, Roberto. 1983. *Carnavals, bandits et héros. Ambiguïtés de la société brésilienne*. Collection Esprit. Paris: Seuil.

Darbon, Dominique, and Comi Toulabor, eds. 2014. *L'invention des classes moyennes africaines*. Paris: Karthala.

Daswani, Girish. 2013. "On Christianity and Ethics: Rupture as Ethical Practice in Ghanaian Pentecostalism." *American Ethnologist* 40 (3): 467–79. https://doi.org/10.1111/amet.12033.

– 2015. *Looking Back, Moving Forward: Transformation and Ethical Practice in the Ghanaian Church of Pentecost.* Toronto: University of Toronto Press.

Davie, Grace. 1990. "Believing without Belonging: Is This the Future of Religion in Britain?" *Social Compass* 37 (4): 455–69. https://doi.org/10.1177/003776890037004004.

– 2007. "Vicarious Religion: A Methodological Challenge." In *Everyday Religion: Observing Modern Religious Lives,* edited by Nancy T. Ammerman, 21–36. Oxford: Oxford University Press.

Day, Abby. 2011. *Believing in Belonging: Belief and Social Identity in the Modern World.* Oxford: Oxford University Press.

De Almeida, Ronaldo. 2004. "Religião na metrópole paulista." *Revista Brasileira de Ciências Sociais* 19 (56): 15–27. https://doi.org/10.1590/S0102-69092004000300002.

De Almeida, Ronaldo, and Paula Monteiro. 2001. "Trânsito Religioso no Brasil." *Revista São Paulo em Perspectiva* 15 (3): 17–35. https://doi.org/10.1590/S0102-88392001000300012.

Debray, Régis. 2005. *Les communions humaines. Pour en finir avec "la religion."* Paris: Fayard.

De Certeau, Michel. 1980. *L'invention du quotidien.* Tome 1, *Arts de faire.* Paris: UGE.

Desroche, Henri. 1965. *Socialismes et sociologie religieuse.* Paris: Éditions Cujas.

Dilger, Hansjörg, and Dorothea Schulz. 2013. "Politics of Religious Schooling: Christian and Muslim Engagements with Education in Africa." *Journal of Religion in Africa* 43 (4): 365–78. https://doi.org/10.1163/15700666-12341262.

Dobbelaere, Karel, and Liliane Voyé. 1992. "D'une religion instituée à une religion recomposée." In *Belges, heureux et satisfaits. Les valeurs des Belges dans les années 90,* edited by Liliane Voyé, Bernadette Bawin-Legros, Jan Kerkhofs, and Karel Dobbelaere. Bruxelles: De Boeck.

Donahue, Michael J. 1985. "Intrinsic and Extrinsic Religiousness: Review and Meta-Analysis." *Journal of Personality and Social Psychology* 48 (2): 400–19. https://doi.org/10.1037/0022-3514.48.2.400.

Drewal, Henry John, ed. 2008. *Sacred Waters: Arts for Mami Wata and Other Divinities in Africa and the Diaspora.* Bloomington: Indiana University Press.

Droz, Yvan. 1999. *Migrations Kikuyus. Des pratiques sociales à l'imaginaire; Ethos, réalisation de soi et millénarisme.* Neuchâtel et Paris: Institut d'ethnologie & Maison des sciences de l'homme.

– 2000a. "Les origines vernaculaires du Réveil pentecôtiste kenyan: mobilité sociale et politique." In *Imaginaires politiques et pentecôtisme: Afrique/Amérique latine,* edited by André Corten and André Mary, 81–101. Paris: Karthala.

– 2000b. "Prologue: une 'grand-messe' à Nairobi." In *Imaginaires politiques et pentecôtisme: Afrique/Amérique latine,* edited by André Corten and André Mary, 35–8. Paris: Karthala.

– 2002a. "Cultiver le champ du possible. Circulation familiale, transhumance personnelle et archipel vertical en pays kikuyu." In *Constructing Risk, Threat, Catastrophe: Anthropological Perspectives*, edited by Christian Giordano and Andrea Boscoboinik, 145–57. Fribourg, CH: Éditions universitaires de Fribourg.

– 2002b. "Esquisse d'une anthropologie de la conversion. Pratiques religieuses et organisation sociale en pays kikuyu." In *Convocations thérapeutiques du sacré*, edited by Raymond Massé and Jean Benoist, 81–103. Paris: Karthala.

– 2004. "Retour au Mont des Oliviers. Les formes du pentecôtisme kenyan." In *L'effervescence religieuse en Afrique*, edited by Gilles Séraphin, 17–42. Paris: Karthala.

– 2011. "Transformations of Death among the Kikuyu of Kenya: From Hyenas to Tombs." In *Funerals in Africa: Exploration of a Social Phenomenon*, edited by Michael Jindra and Joël Noret, 69–87. New York: Berghahn.

– 2016. "Les métamorphoses de la mobilité: du schème migratoire au butinage religieux." In *Religion, guérison et forces occultes en Afrique. Le regard du jésuite Éric de Rosny*, edited by Gilles Séraphin, 113–26. Paris: Karthala.

Droz, Yvan, and Yonatan N. Gez. 2015. "A God Trap: Seed Planting, Gift Logic and the Prosperity Gospel." In *Pastures of Plenty: Tracing Religio-Scapes of Prosperity Gospel in Africa and Beyond*, edited by Andreas Heuser, 295–307. Frankfurt am Main, DE: Peter Lang.

– 2019. "Pentecôtisation du christianisme et butinage religieux au Kenya: entre fondamentalisme et mode populaire d'action politico-religieuse." *Canadian Journal of African Studies/Revue canadienne des études africaines* 53 (2): 317–35. https://doi.org/10.1080/00083968.2019.1577146.

Droz, Yvan, Yonatan N. Gez, Carmen Delgado Luchner, and Hervé Maupeu. 2019. "Pentecostalism and Alternative Paths for Self-Accomplishment in Kenya." In *Religion and Human Security in Africa*, edited by Ezra Chitando and Joram Tarusarira, 114–27. London: Routledge.

Droz, Yvan, and Beat Sottas. 1997. "Partir ou rester? Partir et rester. Migrations des Kikuyus au Kenya." *L'Homme* 37 (142): 69–88. https://doi.org/10.3406/hom.1997.370248.

Duany, Jorge. 2002. "Mobile Livelihoods: The Sociocultural Practices of Circular Migrants between Puerto Rico and the United States." *The International Migration Review* 36 (2): 355–88. https://doi.org/10.1111/j.1747-7379.2002.tb00085.x

Dubuisson, Daniel. 1998. *L'Occident et la religion. Mythes, science et idéologie.* Bruxelles: Ed. Complexe.

Durkheim, Émile. 1915. *The Elementary Forms of the Religious Life.* Translated by Joseph Ward Swain. London: George Allen & Unwin.

– 1968. *Les formes élémentaires de la vie religieuse. Le système totémique en Australie.* Paris: PUF. First published 1912.

Ebaugh, Helen Rose, and Janet Saltzman Chafetz, eds. 2000. *Religion and the New Immigrants: Continuities and Adaptations in Immigrant Congregations.* Walnut Creek, CA: AltaMira.

Edgell, Penny. 2012. "A Cultural Sociology of Religion: New Directions." *Annual Review of Sociology* 38: 247–65. https://doi.org/10.1146/annurev-soc-071811-145424.

Ellis, Stephen. 1989. "Tuning In to Pavement Radio." *African Affairs* 88 (352): 321–30. https://doi.org/10.1093/oxfordjournals.afraf.a098185.

– 2011. *Season of Rains: Africa in the World.* London: C. Hurst.

Ellis, Stephen, and Gerrie ter Haar. 2004. *Worlds of Power: Religious Thought and Political Practice in Africa.* London: Hurst.

Englund, Harri. 2007. "Pentecostalism beyond Belief: Trust and Democracy in a Malawian Township." *Africa: Journal of the International African Institute* 77 (4): 477–99. https://doi.org/10.3366/afr.2007.77.4.477.

Enroth, Ronald M. 1977. *Youth, Brainwashing, and the Extremist Cults.* Grand Rapids, MI: Zondervan.

Esposito, John L., Darrell J. Fasching, and Todd Thornton Lewis. 2001. *World Religions Today.* New York: Oxford University Press.

Evans, Peter B., Dietrich Rueschemeyer, and Theda Skocpol, eds. 1985. *Bringing the State Back In.* Cambridge: Cambridge University Press.

Fabian, Johannes. 1985. "Religious Pluralism: An Ethnographic Approach." In *Theoretical Explanations in African Religion,* edited by Wim Van Binsbergen and Matthew Schoffeleers, 138–63. London: Routledge and Kegan Paul.

Fancello, Sandra. 2006. *Les aventuriers du pentecôtisme ghanéen. Nation, conversion et délivrance en Afrique de l'Ouest.* Paris: IRD – Karthala.

Fancello, Sandra, and André Mary, eds. 2010. *Chrétiens africains en Europe. Prophétismes, pentecôtismes et politiques des nations.* Paris: Karthala.

Fauré, Yves-André. 2012. "*Jeitinho* and Other Related Phenomena in Contemporary Brazil." In *Neopatrimonialism in Africa and Beyond,* edited by Daniel C. Bach and Mamoudou Gazibo, 169–85. New York: Routledge.

Ferrari, Aurélia. 2012. *Émergence d'une langue urbaine le sheng de Nairobi.* Collection Afrique et langage. Louvain Paris: Peeters.

Fine, Gary A. 2004. "Adolescence as Cultural Toolkit: High School Debate and the Repertoires of Childhood and Adulthood." *The Sociological Quarterly* 45 (1): 1–20. https://doi.org/10.1111/j.1533-8525.2004.tb02395.x.

Finke, Roger, and Rodney Stark. 1992. *The Churching of America, 1776–1990: Winners and Losers in Our Religious Economy.* New Brunswick, NJ: Rutgers University Press.

Fisher, Gareth. 2012. "Religion as Repertoire: Resourcing the Past in a Beijing Buddhist Temple." *Modern China* 38 (3): 346–76. https://doi.org/10.1177/0097700411417327.

Foucault, Michel. 1972. *Histoire de la folie à l'âge classique.* Paris: Gallimard.

– 1976. *Histoire de la sexualité. La volonté de savoir.* Paris: Gallimard.

– 1984. "Pourquoi étudier le pouvoir: la question du sujet." In *Michel Foucault. Un parcours philosophique,* edited by Hubert Dreyfus and Paul Rabinow, 297–308. Paris: Gallimard. First published 1982.

Fountain, Philip. 2013. "The Myth of Religious NGOs: Development Studies and the Return of Religion." *International Development Policy* 4 (1): 9–30. https://doi.org/10.4000/poldev.1361.

Freston, Paul. 1995. "Pentecostalism in Brazil: A Brief History." *Religion* 25 (2): 119–33. https://doi.org/10.1006/reli.1995.0012.

– 2004. *Evangelicals and Politics in Asia, Africa and Latin America.* Cambridge: Cambridge University Press.

Gathogo, Julius. 2011. "The Challenge of Money and Wealth in Some East African Pentecostal Churches." *Studia Historiae Ecclesiasticae* 37 (2): 133–51. http://hdl.handle.net/10500/5124.

Gauchet, Marcel. 1985. *Le désenchantement du monde. Une histoire politique de la religion.* Paris: Gallimard.

Geertz, Clifford. 1973. *The Interpretation of Cultures.* New York: Basic Books.

– 2002. "Religion as a Cultural System." In *A Reader in the Anthropology of Religion,* edited by Michael Lambek, 61–82. Oxford: Blackwell Publishers. First published 1966.

Gellner, Ernest. 1974. *Legitimation of Belief.* Cambridge: Cambridge University Press.

– 1983. *Nations and Nationalism.* Ithaca, NY: Cornell University Press.

Gez, Yonatan N. 2014. "Religious Identity and Mobility in Nairobi: A 'Religious Repertoire' Approach." PhD, Development Studies, The Graduate Institute of International and Development Studies (IHEID), Geneva.

– 2018. *Traditional Churches, Born Again Christianity, and Pentecostalism: Religious Mobility and Religious Repertoires in Urban Kenya.* Cham, CH: Palgrave Macmillan.

Gez, Yonatan N., and Yvan Droz. 2015. "Negotiation and Erosion of Born Again Prestige in Nairobi." *Nova Religio* 18 (3): 18–37. https://doi.org/10.1525/nr.2015.18.3.18.

– 2017. "The Sheep-Stealing Dilemma: The Ambiguities of Church Visits in Kenya." *Journal of Religion in Africa* 47 (2): 163–89. https://doi.org/10.1163/15700666-12340103.

– 2019. "'It's All under Christianity': Religious Territories in Kenya." *Journal of Africana Religions* 7 (1): 37–61. https://doi.org/10.5325/jafrireli.7.1.0037.

Gez, Yonatan N., Yvan Droz, and Hervé Maupeu. 2020. "Religious Tribalism, Local Morality and Violence in Christian Kenya." In *Themes in Religion and Human Security in Africa,* edited by Ezra Chitando and Joram Tarusarira, 102–120. London: Routledge.

Gez, Yonatan N., Yvan Droz, Edio Soares, and Jeanne Rey. 2017. "From Converts to Itinerants: Religious *Butinage* as Dynamic Identity." *Current Anthropology* 58 (2): 141–59. https://doi.org/10.1086/690836.

Gifford, Paul. 1994. "Some Recent Developments in African Christianity." *African Affairs* 93 (373): 513–34. https://doi.org/10.1093/oxfordjournals.afraf.a098757.

– 2004a. *Ghana's New Christianity: Pentecostalism in a Globalising African Economy.* London: C. Hurst.

– 2004b. "Persistence and Change in Contemporary African Religion." *Social Compass* 51 (2): 169–76. https://doi.org/10.1177/0037768604043004.

– 2009. *Christianity, Politics and Public Life in Kenya.* London: Hurst.

Glaser, Barney G., and Anselm L. Strauss. 1967. *The Discovery of Grounded Theory: Strategies for Qualitative Research.* Chicago: Aldine.

Glock, Charles Y., and Robert N. Bellah, eds. 1976. *The New Religious Consciousness.* Berkeley: University of California Press.

Goffman, Erving. 1959. *The Presentation of Self in Everyday Life.* Garden City, NY: Anchor Books.

– 1961. *Asylums: Essays on the Social Situation of Mental Patients and Other Inmates.* New York: Anchor Books.

– 1967. *Interaction Ritual: Essays on Face-to-Face Behavior.* Garden City, NY: Anchor Books.

Gois, Antônio, and Hélio Schwartsman. 2011. "Sobe total de evangélicos sem vínculos com igrejas (POF, IBGE)." *Folha de São Paulo,* agosto 15, 2011.

Gooren, Henri. 2007. "Reassessing Conventional Approaches to Conversion: Toward a New Synthesis." *Journal for the Scientific Study of Religion* 46 (3): 337–53. https://doi.org/10.1111/j.1468-5906.2007.00362.x.

– 2010. *Religious Conversion and Disaffiliation: Tracing Patterns of Change in Faith Practices.* New York: Palgrave Macmillan.

– 2014. "Anthropology of Religious Conversion." In *The Oxford Handbook of Religious Conversion,* edited by Lewis R. Rambo and Charles E. Farhadian, 84–116. Oxford: Oxford University Press.

Gordon, David F. 1974. "The Jesus People: An Identity Synthesis." *Urban Life and Culture* 3 (2): 159–78. https://doi.org/10.1177/089124167400300202.

Graham, C.K. 1971. *The History of Education in Ghana: From the Earliest Times to the Declaration of Independence.* Abingdon, UK: Frank Cass.

Granqvist, Pehr. 2003. "Attachment Theory and Religious Conversions: A Review and a Resolution of the Classic and Contemporary Paradigm Chasm." *Review of Religious Research* 45 (2): 172–87. https://doi.org/10.2307/3512581.

Granqvist, Pehr, and Lee A. Kirkpatrick. 2004. "Religious Conversion and Perceived Childhood Attachment: A Meta-Analysis." *International Journal for the Psychology of Religion* 14 (4): 223–50. https://doi.org/10.1207/s15327582 ijpr1404_1.

Graveling, Elizabeth. 2010. “Marshalling the Powers: The Challenge of Everyday Religion for Development.” In *Development and Politics from Below: Exploring Religious Spaces in the African State*, edited by Barbara Bompani and Maria Frahm-Arp, 197–217. Basingstoke, UK: Palgrave Macmillan.

Griffith, R. Marie. 1997. *God’s Daughters: Evangelical Women and the Power of Submission*. Berkeley: University of California Press.

Hall, Granville Stanley. 1904. *Adolescence: Its Psychology and Its Relations to Physiology, Anthropology, Sociology, Sex, Crime, Religion and Education*. New York: Appleton.

Haynes, Jeff. 1995. *Religion, Fundamentalism and Ethnicity A Global Perspective*. United Nations Research Institute for Social Development (UNRISD) paper. Geneva: UNRISD.

Headland, Thomas N., Kenneth L. Pike, and Marvin Harris, eds. 1990. *Emics and Etics: The Insider/Outsider Debate*. Newbury Park, CA: Sage.

Heirich, Max. 1977. “Change of Heart: A Test of Some Widely Held Theories about Religious Conversion.” *American Journal of Sociology* 83 (3): 653–80. https://doi.org/10.1086/226598.

Hermans, Hubert J.M., and Harry J.G. Kempen. 1993. *The Dialogical Self: Meaning as Movement*. San Diego, CA: Academic Press.

Hervieu-Léger, Danièle. 1999. *Le Pèlerin et le converti. La religion en mouvement*. Paris: Flammarion.

– 2000. *Religion as a Chain of Memory*. Translated by Simon Lee. New Brunswick, NJ: Rutgers University Press.

– 2001a. “Crise de l’universel et planétarisation culturelle: les paradoxes de la ‘mondialisation’ religieuse.” In *La globalisation du religieux*, edited by Jean-Pierre Bastian, 87–98. Paris: L’Harmattan.

– 2001b. “Quelques paradoxes de la modernité religieuse. Crise de l’universel, planétarisation culturelle et renforcements communautaires.” *Futuribles* 260 (janvier): 99–109.

Heuser, Andreas, ed. 2015. *“Pastures of Plenty”: Tracing Religio-Scapes of Prosperity Gospel in Africa and Beyond*. Frankfurt am Main, DE: Peter Lang.

Hill, Peter C., Kenneth I. Pargament, Ralph W. Hood Jr., Michael E. McCullough, James P. Swyers, David B. Larson, and Brian J. Zinnbauer. 2000. “Conceptualizing Religion and Spirituality: Points of Commonality, Points of Departure.” *Journal for the Theory of Social Behaviour* 30 (1): 51–77. https://doi.org/10.1111/1468-5914.00119.

Hobsbawm, Eric, and Terence O. Ranger, eds. 1983. *The Invention of Tradition*. Cambridge: Cambridge University Press.

Hood, Ralph W. Jr., Peter C. Hill, and Bernard Spilka. 2009. *The Psychology of Religion: An Empirical Approach*. 4th ed. New York: Guilford Press.

Hood, Ralph W. Jr., Peter C. Hill, and W. Paul Williamson. 2005. *The Psychology of Religious Fundamentalism.* New York: Guilford Press.

Horton, Robin. 1971. "African Conversion." *Africa* 41 (2): 85–108. https://doi.org/10.2307/1159421.

– 1975. "On the Rationality of Conversion." *Africa* 45 (3–4): 219–35; 372–99. https://doi.org/10.2307/1159632.

– 1982. "Tradition and Modernity Revisited." In *Rationality and Relativism,* edited by Martin Hollis and Steven Lukes, 201–60. Oxford: B. Blackwell.

Houghland, James G. Jr., and James R. Wood. 1980. "Correlates of Participation in Local Churches." *Sociological Focus* 13 (4): 343–58. https://doi.org/10.1080/00380237.1980.10570371.

Hull, Brooks B., and Jody Lipford. 2010. "Free Riding, Market Structure, and Church Member Donations in South California." *Review of Religious Research* 52 (2): 172–87. http://hdl.handle.net/2027.42/78447.

Hunter, James D. 1983. *American Evangelicalism: Conservative Religion and the Quandary of Modernity.* New Brunswick, NJ: Rutgers University Press.

Huntington, Samuel P. 1996. *The Clash of Civilizations and the Remaking of World Order.* New York: Simon & Schuster.

Hyman, Corine, and Paul J. Handal. 2006. "Definitions and Evaluation of Religion and Spirituality Items by Religious Professionals: A Pilot Study." *Journal of Religion and Health* 45: 264–82. https://doi.org/10.1007/s10943-006-9015-z.

Iannaccone, Laurence R. 1991. "The Consequences of Religious Market Structure: Adam Smith and the Economics of Religion." *Rationality and Society* 3 (2): 156–77. https://doi.org/10.1177/1043463191003002002.

Iannaccone, Laurence R., Roger Finke, and Rodney Stark. 1997. "Deregulating Religion: The Economics of Church and State." *Economic Inquiry* 35 (2): 350–64. https://doi.org/10.1111/j.1465-7295.1997.tb01915.x.

Ingram, Larry C. 1982. "Underlife in a Baptist Church." *Review of Religious Research* 24 (2): 138–52. https://doi.org/10.2307/3511103.

Jackson, G. 1908. *The Fact of Conversion: The Cole Lectures for 1908.* New York: Revell.

James, William. 1902. *The Varieties of Religious Experience: A Study in Human Nature.* New York: Longmans, Green.

– 1950. *The Principles of Psychology.* vol. 1. New York: Dover.

Janson, Marloes. 2016. "Unity through Diversity: A Case Study of Chrislam in Lagos." *Africa* 86 (4): 646–72. https://doi.org/10.1017/S0001972016000607.

Janson, Marloes, and Birgit Meyer. 2016. "Introduction: Towards a Framework for the Study of Christian-Muslim Encounters in Africa." *Africa* 86 (4): 615–19. https://doi.org/10.1017/S0001972016000553.

Jenkins, Philip. 2002. *The Next Christendom: The Coming of Global Christianity.* New York: Oxford University Press.

Jenny, Magali. 2008. *Guérisseurs, rebouteux et faiseurs de secret en Suisse Romande.* Lausanne, CH: Éditions Favre.

Jewsiewicki, Bogumil. 2003. *Mami Wata. La peinture urbaine au Congo.* Paris: Gallimard.

Kaba, Lansiné. 2000. "Islam in West Africa: Radicalism and the New Ethic of Disagreement, 1960–1990." In *The History of Islam in Africa*, edited by Nehemia Levtzion and Randall L. Pouwels, 189–208. Athens: Ohio University Press.

Kale, Sudhir H. 2004. "Spirituality, Religion, and Globalization." *Journal of Macromarketing* 24 (2): 92–107. https://doi.org/10.1177/0276146704269296.

Kavulla, Travis R. 2008. "'Our Enemies Are God's Enemies': The Religion and Politics of Bishop Margaret Wanjiru, MP." *Journal of Eastern African Studies* 2 (2): 254–63. https://doi.org/10.1080/17531050802058369.

Kenya National Bureau of Statistics. 2019. *The 2019 Kenya Population and Housing Census.* Vol. 4, *Distribution of Population by Socio-Economic Characteristics.* Nairobi: Kenya National Bureau of Statistics. https://africacheck.org/wp-content/uploads/2020/06/VOLUME-IV-KPHC-2019.pdf.

Keupp, Heiner, Thomas Ahbe, Wolfgang Gmür, Renate Höfer, Beate Mitzscherlich, Wolfgang Kraus, and Florian Straus. 1999. *Identitätskonstruktionen. Das Patchwork der Identitäten in der Spätmoderne.* Reinbek, DE: Rowohlt-Taschenbuch-Verlag.

Kinuthia, Njoroge. 2013. "Seen Lip Twister Mwende, Lately?" *The Standard*, April 10, 2013, 17.

Kirkpatrick, Lee A. 1992. "An Attachment-Theory Approach to the Psychology of Religion." *International Journal for the Psychology of Religion* 2 (1): 3–28. https://doi.org/10.1207/s15327582ijpr0201_2.

– 1999. "Attachment and Religious Representations and Behavior." In *Handbook of Attachment Theory and Research*, edited by Jude Cassidy and Phillip R. Shaver, 803–22. New York: Guilford.

Kirkpatrick, Lee A., and Ralph W. Hood Jr. 1990. "Intrinsic-Extrinsic Religious Orientation: The Boon or Bane of Contemporary Psychology of Religion?" *Journal for the Scientific Study of Religion* 29 (4): 442–62. https://doi.org/10.2307/1387311.

Kirkpatrick, Lee A., and Phillip R. Shaver. 1990. "Attachment Theory and Religion: Childhood Attachments, Religious Beliefs, and Conversion." *Journal for the Scientific Study of Religion* 29 (3): 315–34. https://doi.org/10.2307/1386461.

Kirsch, Thomas G. 2004. "Restaging the Will to Believe: Religious Pluralism, Anti-Syncretism, and the Problem of Belief." *American Anthropologist* 106 (4): 699–709. https://doi.org/10.1525/aa.2004.106.4.699.

Kosman, L.A. 1969. "Aristotle's Definition of Motion." *Phronesis* 14 (1): 40–62. https://doi.org/10.1163/156852869X00037.

Kox, Willem, Wim Meeus, and Harm 't Hart. 1991. "Religious Conversion of Adolescents: Testing the Lofland and Stark Model of Religious Conversion." *Sociological Analysis* 52 (3): 227–40. https://doi.org/10.2307/3711359.

Krause, Kristine. 2006. "'The Double Face of Subjectivity': A Case Study in a Psychiatric Hospital (Ghana)." In *Multiple Medical Realities: Patients and Healers in Biomedical, Alternative and Traditional Medicine,* edited by Helle Johannessen and Imre Lázár, 54–71. New York: Berghahn.

Lambek, Michael. 2002. *The Weight of the Past: Living with History in Mahajanga, Madagascar.* New York: Palgrave Macmillan.

– 2008. "Provincializing God? Provocations from an Anthropology of Religion." In *Religion: Beyond a Concept,* edited by Hent de Vries, 120–38. New York: Fordham University Press.

– ed. 2010. *Ordinary Ethics: Anthropology, Language and Action.* New York: Fordham University Press.

Lambert, Yves. 1994. "Un paysage religieux en profonde évolution." In *Les valeurs des Français,* edited by Hélène Riffault, 123–62. Paris: PUF.

Lamont, Michèle. 1992. *Money, Morals and Manners: The Culture of the French and American Upper Middle Classes.* Chicago: University of Chicago Press.

Lang, Kurt, and Gladys Engel Lang. 1961. *Collective Dynamics.* New York: Crowell.

Langewiesche, Katrin. 2003. *Mobilité religieuse. Changements religieux au Burkina Faso.* Münster, DE: LIT Verlag.

Laplantine, François. 1999. *Je, nous et les autres: être humain au-delà des appartenances.* Paris: Le Pommier.

– 2003. "Penser anthropologiquement la religion." *Anthropologie et sociétés* 27 (1): 11–33. https://doi.org/10.7202/007000ar.

Larbi, Emmanuel Kingsley. 2001. *Pentecostalism: The Eddies of Ghanaian Christianity.* Accra, GH: Centre for Pentecostal and Charismatic Studies.

Larkin, Brian. 2016. "Entangled Religions: Response to J.D.Y. Peel." *Africa* 86 (4): 633–9. https://doi.org/10.1017/S0001972016000589.

Larsen, John A. 2004. "Finding Meaning in First Episode Psychosis: Experience, Agency, and the Cultural Repertoire." *Medical Anthropology Quarterly* 18 (4): 447–71. https://doi.org/10.1525/maq.2004.18.4.447.

Leopold, Anita Maria, and Jeppe Sinding Jensen, eds. 2004. *Syncretism in Religion: A Reader.* London: Equinox.

Leuba, James H. 1896. "A Study in the Psychology of Religious Phenomena." *American Journal of Psychology* 7 (3): 309–85. https://doi.org/10.2307/1411387.

Levtzion, Nehemia, and Randall L. Pouwels. 2000. "Patterns of Islamization and Varieties of Religious Experience among Muslims of Africa." In *The History of Islam in Africa,* edited by Nehemia Levtzion and Randall L. Pouwels, 1–20. Athens: Ohio University Press.

Lifton, Robert J. 1961. *Thought Reform and the Psychology of Totalism: A Study of "Brainwashing" in China.* New York: Norton.

Lindquist, Galina, and Simon Coleman. 2008. "Introduction: Against Belief?" *Social Analysis* 52 (1): 1–18. https://doi.org/10.3167/sa.2008.520101.

Lippy, Charles H. 1994. *Being Religious, American Style: A History of Popular Religiosity in the United States.* Westport, CT: Praeger.

Lofland, John, and Norman Skonovd. 1981. "Conversion Motifs." *Journal for the Scientific Study of Religion* 20 (4): 373–85. https://doi.org/10.2307/1386185.

Lofland, John, and Rodney Stark. 1965. "Becoming a World-Saver: A Theory of Conversion to a Deviant Perspective." *American Sociological Review* 30 (6): 862–75. https://doi.org/10.2307/2090965.

Long, Theodore E., and Jeffrey K. Hadden. 1983. "Religious Conversion and the Concept of Socialization: Integrating the Brainwashing and Drift Models." *Journal for the Scientific Study of Religion* 22 (1): 1–14. https://doi.org/10.2307/1385588.

Lonsdale, John. 1994. "Moral Ethnicity and Political Tribalism." In *Inventions and Boundaries: Historical and Anthropological Approaches to the Study of Ethnicity and Nationalism: Papers from the Researcher Training Course Held at Sandbjerg Manor, 23 to 29 May 1993*, edited by Preben Kaarsholm and Jan Hultin, 131–50. Roskilde, DK: International Development Studies, Roskilde University.

– 2002. "Kikuyu Christianities: A History of Intimate Diversity." In *Christianity and the African Imagination: Essays in Honour of Adrian Hastings*, edited by David Maxwell with Ingrid Lawrie, 157–97. Leiden, NL: Brill.

Lövheim, Mia. 2007. "Virtually Boundless? Youth Negotiating Tradition in Cyberspace." In *Everyday Religion: Observing Modern Religious Lives*, edited by Nancy T. Ammerman, 83–100. New York: Oxford University Press.

Mahmood, Saba. 2005. *Politics of Piety: The Islamic Revival and the Feminist Subject.* Princeton, NJ: Princeton University Press.

Marcel, Gabriel. 1944. *Homo viator: Prolégomènes à une métaphysique de l'espérance.* Collection Philosophie de l'esprit. Paris: Aubier-Montaigne.

March, James G., and Johan P. Olsen. 1989. *Rediscovering Institutions: The Organizational Basis of Politics.* New York: Free Press.

Marcus, George E. 1995. "Ethnography in/of the World System: The Emergence of Multi-Sited Ethnography." *Annual Review of Anthropology* 24: 95–117. https://doi.org/10.1146/annurev.an.24.100195.000523.

Mardones, José Maria. 1994. *Para comprender las nuevas formas de la religión: la reconfiguración postcristina de la religión.* Estella (Navarra): Verbo divino.

Marler, Penny Long, and C. Kirk Hadaway. 2002. "'Being Religious' or 'Being Spiritual' in America: A Zero-Sum Proposition." *Journal for the Scientific Study of Religion* 41 (2): 289–300. https://doi.org/10.1111/1468-5906.00117.

Marshall, Ruth. 2009. *Political Spiritualities: The Pentecostal Revolution in Nigeria.* Chicago: University of Chicago Press.

– 2016. "Destroying Arguments and Captivating Thoughts: Spiritual Warfare Prayer as Global Praxis." *Journal of Religious and Political Practice* 2 (1): 92–113. https://doi.org/10.1080/20566093.2016.1085243.

Marty, Martin Emil, and R. Scott Appleby, eds. 1993. *Fundamentalisms and the State: Remaking Polities, Economies, and Militance.* The Fundamentalism Project. Chicago: University of Chicago Press.

Mary, André. 1998. "La diabolisation du sorcier et le réveil de Satan." *Religiologiques* 18: non paginé. http://www.religiologiques.uqam.ca/18/18texte/18mary.html.

Maupeu, Hervé. 1991. "Une opposition en régime autoritaire: L'exemple du Réveil Est-Africain au Kenya." *Canadian Journal of African Studies/Revue canadienne d'études africaines* 25 (2): 257–72. https://doi.org/10.1080/00083968.1991.10803891.

– 2014. "La politique du butinage religieux et le butinage religieux en politique: le cas de Mungiki (Kenya)." In *Mobilité religieuse. Retours croisés des Afriques aux Amériques,* edited by Philippe Chanson, Yvan Droz, Yonatan N. Gez, and Edio Soares, 71–94. Paris: Karthala.

Mavuno Church. 2010. "Why Are Christians Hypocrites?" Sermon series "Doubt Is Good." *Blog Mavuno,* September 19, 2010. https://mavuno.wordpress.com/2010/09/20/why-are-christians-hypocrites/ (audio recording removed).

Maxwell, David. 2002. "Christianity and the African Imagination." In *Christianity and the African Imagination: Essays in Honour of Adrian Hastings,* edited by David Maxwell with Ingrid Lawrie. Leiden, NL: Brill.

McDaniel, Justin. 2011. *The Lovelorn Ghost and the Magical Monk: Practicing Buddhism in Modern Thailand.* New York: Columbia University Press.

McDonald, David, ed. 2000. *On Borders: Perspectives on International Migration in Southern Africa.* Cape Town, SA: St. Martin's Press.

McGuire, Meredith B. 2008. *Lived Religion: Faith and Practice in Everyday Life.* New York: Oxford University Press.

McIntosh, Janet. 2009. *The Edge of Islam: Power, Personhood, and Ethnoreligious Boundaries on the Kenya Coast.* Durham, NC: Duke University Press.

– 2019. "Polyontologism: When 'Syncretism' Does Not Suffice." *Journal of Africana Religions* 7 (1): 112–20. https://doi.org/10.5325/jafrireli.7.1.0112.

Meintel, Deirdre. 2003. "La stabilité dans le flou: Parcours religieux et identités de spiritualistes." *Anthropologie et sociétés* 27 (1): 35–63. https://doi.org/10.7202/007001ar.

– 2007. "When There Is No Conversion: Spiritualists and Personal Religious Change." *Anthropologica* 49, no. 1 (2007): 149–62. https://www.jstor.org/stable/25605339.

Meyer, Birgit. 1998. "'Make a Complete Break with the Past': Memory and Post-Colonial Modernity in Ghanaian Pentecostalist Discourse." *Journal of Religion in Africa* 28 (3): 316–49. https://doi.org/10.1163/157006698X00044.

Miller, James G. 1957. "Brainwashing: Present and Future." *Journal of Social Issues* 13 (3): 48–55. https://doi.org/10.1111/j.1540-4560.1957.tb02270.x..

Mizrachi, Nissim, Israel Drori, and Renee R. Anspach. 2007. "Repertories of Trust: The Practice of Trust in a Multinational Organization amid Political Conflict." *American Sociological Review* 72 (1): 143–65. https://doi.org/10.1177/000312240707200107.

Moloney, James C. 1955. "Psychic Self-Abandon and Extortion of Confessions." *International Journal of Psychoanalysis* 36 (1): 53–60.

Monnier, Laurent, and Yvan Droz. 2004. "Propos." In *Côté jardin, côté cour. Anthropologie de la maison africaine*, edited by Yvan Droz and Laurent Monnier, 11–39. Paris: Presses Universitaires de France.

Morgan, Lewis Henry. 1877. *Ancient Society, or, Researches in the Lines of Human Progress from Savagery through Barbarism to Civilization.* New York: Henry Holt.

Mudimbe, V.Y. 1988. *The Invention of Africa: Gnosis, Philosophy, and the Order of Knowledge.* Bloomington: Indiana University Press; James Currey.

Müller, Louise. 2013. *Religion and Chieftaincy in Ghana.* Berlin: LIT Verlag.

Murra, John. 1981. "Socio-Political and Demographic Aspects of Multi-Altitude Land Use in the Andes." In *L'homme et son environnement à haute altitude/ Environmental and Human Population Problems at High Altitude,* edited by Centre national de la recherche scientifique (CNRS), 129–35. Paris: CNRS.

Ndegwa, Alex. 2007. "Over 6000 Churches Awaiting Registration." *The Standard,* September 4, 2007, 6.

Neckebrouck, Valeer. 1983. *Le peuple affligé. Les déterminants de la fissiparité dans un mouvement religieux au Kenya central.* Immensee, CH: Nouvelle revue de science missionnaire.

Needham, Rodney. 1972. *Belief, Language, and Experience.* Chicago: University of Chicago Press.

Newbold, Bruce. 2001. "Counting Migrants and Migrations: Comparing Lifetime and Fixed-Interval Return and Onward Migration." *Economic Geography* 77 (1): 23–40. https://doi.org/10.1111/j.1944-8287.2001.tb00154.x.

Nock, Arthur Darby 1933. *Conversion: The Old and the New in Religion from Alexander the Great to Augustine of Hippo.* Oxford: Clarendon Press.

Norris, Pippa, and Ronald Inglehart. 2004. *Sacred and Secular: Religion and Politics Worldwide.* Cambridge: Cambridge University Press.

North, Douglass C. 1981. *Structure and Change in Economic History.* New York: Norton.

NTV Kenya. 2012a. The Gospel Ltd.: Fire Ministries Comes under Fire. *NTV Kenya,* July 20, 2012. Accessed July 20, 2012. http://www.youtube.com/watch?v=RZ8PhVZj7Vw (since removed).

NTV Kenya. 2012b. The Gospel Ltd.: part 4. *NTV Kenya,* July 23, 2012. Accessed December 14, 2013. http://www.youtube.com/watch?v=QVd7I71KrxU (since removed).

Obadare, Ebenezer. 2016. "The Muslim Response to the Pentecostal Surge in Nigeria: Prayer and the Rise of Charismatic Islam." *Journal of Religious and Political Practice* 2 (1): 75–91. https://doi.org/10.1080/20566093.2016.1085240.

Oduor, Peter. 2013. "The Kenyan Church and the Gospel of Prosperity." *Daily Nation – DN2*, February 13, 2013, 2–3.

Okeyo, Verah 2013. "Preaching to the Converted: The Rise of Atheism in Modern Kenya." *Daily Nation – DN2*, July 3, 2013, 2–3.

Olando, Martin. 2012. "Yes! Bishops, Pastors Should Be Vetted." Readers Dialogue. *The Standard*, November 20, 2012, 16. https://www.standardmedia.co.ke/article/2000071047/yes-bishops-pastors-should-be-vetted.

Olivier de Sardan, Jean-Pierre. 1995. "La politique du terrain. Sur la production des données en anthropologie." *Enquête* 1:71–109. https://doi.org/10.4000/enquete.263.

Oro, Ari Pedro. 1991. "Mobilidade religiosa dos católicos no Sul do Brasil." *Revista Eclesiástica Brasileira* 51 (202): 309–31.

– 2009. *Festa de Nossa Senhora dos Navegantes em Porto Alegre. Sincretismo entre Maria e Iemanjá*. Porto Alegre, BR: Editora da Cidade.

Orsi, Robert. 1997. "Everyday Miracles: The Study of Lived Religion." In *Lived Religion in America: Toward a History of Practice*, edited by David D. Hall, 3–21. Princeton, NJ: Princeton University Press.

– 2012. "Afterword: Everyday Religion and the Contemporary World: The Un-Modern, or What Was Supposed to Have Disappeared But Did Not." In *Ordinary Lives and Grand Schemes: An Anthropology of Everyday Religion*, edited by Samuli Schielke and Liza Debevec, 146–61. New York: Berghahn Books.

Orwell, George. 2001. *Down and Out in Paris and London*. London: V. Gollancz. First published 1933.

Otto, Rudolf. 1923. *Aufsätze, das Numinose betreffend*. Gotha, DE: L. Klotz.

Owusu-Ansah, David. 2000. "Prayer, Amulets, and Healing." In *The History of Islam in Africa*, edited by Nehemia Levtzion and Randall L. Pouwels, 477–88. Athens: Ohio University Press.

Pargament, Kenneth I. 1997. *The Psychology of Religion and Coping: Theory, Research, Practice*. New York: Guilford Press.

– 1999. "The Psychology of Religion and Spirituality? Yes and No." *International Journal for the Psychology of Religion* 9 (1): 3–16. https://doi.org/10.1207/s15327582ijpr0901_2.

Parsitau, Damaris Seleina. 2008. "From the Fringes to the Centre: Rethinking the Role of Religion in the Public Sphere in Kenya." Paper presented at CODESRIA: 12th General Assembly, Governing the African Public Sphere, Yaoundé, Cameroun, December 7–11, 2008.

– 2014. "The Civic and Public Roles of Neo-Pentecostal Churches in Kenya (1970–2010)." PhD diss., Dept. of Philosophy and Religious Studies, Kenyatta University.

Parsitau, Damaris Seleina, and Philomena Njeri Mwaura. 2010. "God in the City: Pentecostalism as an Urban Phenomenon in Kenya." *Studia Historiae Ecclesiasticae* 36 (2): 95–112. http://uir.unisa.ac.za/bitstream/handle/10500/4631/Parsitau-Mwaura-SHEXXXVI_2_-October2010.pdf.

Peel, John D.Y. 2015. *Christianity, Islam, and Orisa-Religion: Three Traditions in Comparison and Interaction.* Oakland: University of California Press.

Peterson, Derek R. 2004. *Creative Writing: Translation, Bookkeeping, and the Work of Imagination in Colonial Kenya.* Social History of Africa Series. Portsmouth, NH: Heinemann.

Pew Research Center. 2006. "Spirit and Power: A 10-Country Survey of Pentecostals." Washington, DC: The Pew Forum on Religion & Public Life. https://www.pewforum.org/2006/10/05/spirit-and-power/.

Piot, Charles. 2010. *Nostalgia for the Future: West Africa after the Cold War.* Chicago: University of Chicago Press.

Polanyi, Karl. 1944. *The Great Transformation.* New York: Farrar & Rinehart.

Pouillon, Jean. 1979. "Remarques sur le verbe 'croire.'" In *La fonction symbolique. Essais d'anthropologie,* edited by Michel Izard and Pierre Smith, 43–51. Paris: Gallimard.

Prandi, Carlo. 2000. "The Reciprocal Relationship of Syncretism and Fundamentalism from the Early History of Religion to Modernity." In *Research in the Social Scientific Study of Religion,* vol. 11, edited by Joanne Marie Greer and David O. Moberg, 23–35. Stamford, CT: JAI Press.

Premawardhana, Devaka. 2015. "Conversion and Convertibility in Northern Mozambique." In *What Is Existential Anthropology,* edited by Michael Jackson and Albert Piette, 30–57. New York: Berghahn Books.

– 2018. *Faith in Flux: Pentecostalism and Mobility in Rural Mozambique.* Philadelphia: University of Pennsylvania Press.

Preston, David L. 1981. "Becoming a Zen Practitioner." *Sociological Analysis: A Journal in the Sociology of Religion* 42 (1): 47–55. https://doi.org/10.2307/3709701.

Pye, Michael. 1971. "Syncretism and Ambiguity." *Numen* 18 (2): 83–93. https://doi.org/10.1163/156852771X00026.

Rambo, Lewis R. 1993. *Understanding Religious Conversion.* New Haven, CT: Hall University Press.

– 1999. "Theories of Conversion: Understanding and Interpreting Religious Change." *Social Compass* 46 (3): 259–71. https://doi.org/10.1177/003776899046003003.

– 2003. "Anthropology and the Study of Conversion." In *The Anthropology of Religious Conversion,* edited by Andrew Buckser and Stephen D. Glazier, 211–22. Lanham, MD: Rowman &Littlefield.

Ranger, Terence. 1993. "The Local and the Global in Southern African Religious History." In *Conversion to Christianity: Historical and Anthropological*

Perspectives on a Great Transformation, edited by. R. W. Hefner, 65–98. Berkeley: University of California Press.

Rey, Alain et al. 1998. *Le Robert. Dictionnaire historique de la langue française*. Paris: Le Robert.

Rey, Jeanne. 2013a. "Mermaids and Spirit Spouses: Rituals as Technologies of Gender in Transnational African Pentecostal Spaces." *Religion and Gender* 3 (1): 60–75. https://doi.org/10.1163/18785417-00301005.

– 2013b. "Migrations africaines et pentecôtisme en Suisse: des dispositifs rituels au commerce de l'onction." Thèse de doctorat en Anthropologie/Sociologie soutenue à l'Institut de Hautes Études Internationales et du Développement, Genève.

– 2014. "L'onction dans le (néo)pentecôtisme: histoire et trajectoire transatlantique (Amérique, Afrique, Europe)." In *Mobilité religieuse. Retours croisés des Afriques aux Amériques*, edited by Philippe Chanson, Yvan Droz, Yonatan N. Gez, and Edio Soares, 213–27. Paris: Karthala.

– 2015. "Missing Prosperity: Economies of Blessings in Ghana and the Diaspora." In *Pastures of Plenty: Tracing Religio-Scapes of Prosperity Gospel in Africa and Beyond*, edited by Andreas Heuser, 339–53. Frankfurt am Main, DE: Peter Lang.

– 2018. "Migration Policies and Uncertainty: Prayer as (Un)Political Activism among African Pentecostals in Switzerland." *African Diaspora* 10 (1–2): 28–45. https://doi.org/10.1163/18725465-01001006.

– 2019. *Migration africaine et pentecôtismes en Suisse. Dispositifs rituels, pouvoirs, mobilités*. Paris: Karthala.

Richardson, James T., ed. 1978. *Conversion Careers: In and Out of the New Religions*. Sage Contemporary Social Scientist Issues Series No. 47. Beverly Hills, CA: Sage Publications.

– 1985. "The Active vs. Passive Convert: Paradigm Conflict in Conversion/Recruitment Research." *Journal for the Scientific Study of Religion* 24 (2): 163–79. https://doi.org/10.2307/1386340.

– 1998. "Conversion." In *Encyclopedia of Religion and Society*, edited by William H. Swatos Jr. Walnut Creek, CA: AltaMira.

Richardson, James T., and Mary Stewart. 1977. "Conversion Process Models and the Jesus Movement." *American Behavioral Scientist* 20 (6): 819–38. https://doi.org/10.1177/000276427702000603.

Robbins, Joel. 2007. "Continuity Thinking and the Problem of Christian Culture: Belief, Time, and the Anthropology of Christianity." *Current Anthropology* 48 (1): 5–38. https://doi.org/10.1086/508690.

Roberts, Bryan R. 1968. "Protestant Groups and Coping with Urban Life in Guatemala City." *American Journal of Sociology* 73 (6): 753–67. https://doi.org/10.1086/224568.

Roberts, Nathaniel. 2016. *To Be Cared For: The Power of Conversion and Foreignness of Belonging in an Indian Slum*. Oakland: University of California Press.

Roof, Wade C. 1978. *Community and Commitment: Religious Plausibility in a Liberal Protestant Church*. New York: Elsevier.

– 1993. *Generation of Seekers: The Spiritual Journeys of the Baby-Boomer Generation*. San Francisco: HarperCollins.

– 2001. *Spiritual Marketplace: Baby Boomers and the Remaking of American Religion*. Princeton, NJ: Princeton University Press.

Roozen, David R. 1980. "Church Dropouts: Changing Patterns of Disengagement and Re-Entry." *Review of Religious Research* 21 (4): 427–50. https://doi.org/10.2307/3510682.

Rosa, João Guimarães. 1963. *The Devil to Pay in the Backlands*. Translated by James L. Taylor and Harriet de Onís. New York: Alfred A. Knopf. First published 1956.

Ruthven, Malise. 2007. *Fundamentalism: A Very Short Introduction*. Very Short Introductions Series. Oxford: Oxford University Press.

Sabar, Galia. 2004. "African Christianity in the Jewish State: Adaptation, Accommodation and Legitimization of Migrant Workers' Churches, 1990–2003." *Journal of Religion in Africa* 34 (4): 407–37. https://doi.org/10.1163/1570066042564400.

Sabel, Charles, F. 1994. "Learning by Monitoring: The Institutions of Economic Development." In *Handbook of Economic Sociology*, edited by Neil Smelser and Richard Swedberg, 137–65. Princeton, NJ: Princeton University Press; Russell Sage Foundation.

Sargant, W. 1957. *Battle for the Mind: A Physiology of Conversion and Brainwashing*. London: Heinemann.

Schein, E.H. 1961. *Coercive Persuasion: A Socio-Psychological Analysis of the "Brain washing" of American Civilian Prisoners by the Chinese Communists*. New York: Norton.

Schielke, Samuli. 2012. "Being a Non-Believer in a Time of Islamic Revival: Trajectories of Doubt and Certainty in Contemporary Egypt." *International Journal of Middle East Studies* 44 (2): 301–20. https://doi.org/10.1017/S0020743812000062.

Schielke, Samuli, and Liza Debevec. 2012a. "Introduction." In *Ordinary Lives and Grand Schemes: An Anthropology of Everyday Religion*, edited by Samuli Schielke and Liza Debevec, 1–16. New York: Berghahn Books.

–, eds. 2012b. *Ordinary Lives and Grand Schemes: An Anthropology of Everyday Religion*. New York: Berghahn Books.

Schlegel, Jean-Louis. 1995. *Religions à la carte*. Paris: Hachette.

Schlehofer, Michèle M., Allen M. Omoto, and Janice R. Adelman. 2008. "How Do 'Religion' and 'Spirituality' Differ? Lay Definitions among Older Adults." *Journal for the Scientific Study of Religion* 47 (3): 411–25. https://doi.org/10.1111/j.1468-5906.2008.00418.x.

Schnapper, Dominique. 2001. "De l'État-nation au monde transnational. Du sens et de l'utilité du concept de diaspora." *Revue européenne des migrations internationales* 17 (2): 9–36. https://doi.org/10.3406/remi.2001.1777.

Schneiders, Sandra M. 2003. "Religion vs. Spirituality: A Contemporary Conundrum." *Spiritus: A Journal of Christian Spirituality* 3 (2): 163–85. https://doi.org/10.1353/scs.2003.0040.

Scobie, G.E.W. 1973. "Types of Religious Conversion." *Journal of Behavioral Science* 1: 265–71.

Scott, Allie B. 1997. "Categorizing Definitions of Religion and Spirituality in the Psychological Literature: A Content Analytic Approach." Unpublished manuscript.

Sen, Amartya. 2006. *Identity and Violence: The Illusion of Destiny.* London: Penguin Books.

Sharma, Sonya. 2012. "'The Church Is ... My Family': Exploring the Interrelationship between Familial and Religious Practices and Spaces." *Environment and Planning* 44 (4): 816–31. https://doi.org/10.1068/a4447.

Shaw, Rosalind. 1990. "The Invention of 'African Religion.'" *Religion* 20 (4): 339–53. https://doi.org/10.1016/0048-721X(90)90116-N.

Shaw, Rosalind, and Charles Stewart. 1994. "Introduction: Problematizing Syncretism." In *Syncretism/Anti-Syncretism: The Politics of Religious Synthesis,* edited by Charles Stewart and Rosalind Shaw, 1–26. London: Routledge.

Sheldrake, Philip. 1992. *Spirituality and History: Questions of Interpretation and Method.* New York: Crossroads.

Silber, Ilana F. 2003. "Pragmatic Sociology as Cultural Sociology: Beyond Repertoire Theory?" *European Journal of Social Theory* 6 (4): 427–49. https://doi.org/10.1177/13684310030064004.

Singer, Margaret. 1979. "Coming Out of Cults." *Psychology Today* 12: 72–82. https://culteducation.com/group/1153-margaret-thaler-singer-ph-d/17913-coming-out-of-the-cults.html.

Skinner, David. 2013.. "Conversion to Islam and the Promotion of 'Modern' Islamic Schools in Ghana." *Journal of Religion in Africa* 43 (4): 426–50. https://doi.org/10.1163/15700666-12341264.

Smilde, David. 2007. *Reason to Believe: Cultural Agency in Latin American Evangelicalism.* Berkeley: University of California Press.

Snow, David A. 1976. "The Nichiren Shoshu Buddhist Movement in America: A Sociological Examination of its Value Orientation, Recruitment Efforts and Spread." PhD diss., University of California, Los Angeles.

Snow, David A., and Richard Machalek. 1984. "The Sociology of Conversion." *Annual Review of Sociology* 10: 167–90. https://doi.org/10.1146/annurev.so.10.080184.001123.

Snow, David A., and Cynthia L. Phillips. 1980. "The Lofland-Stark Conversion Model: A Critical Reassessment." *Social Problems* 27 (4): 430–47. https://doi.org/10.2307/800171.

Soares, Benjamin. 2016. "Reflections on Muslim-Christian Encounters in West Africa." *Africa* 86 (4): 673–97. https://doi.org/10.1017/S0001972016000619.

Soares, Edio. 2007. "Butinage religieux. 'Manières de faire' en religion à Paranaguá-mirim (Brésil)." Thèse de doctorat, Institut universitaire d'études du développement, Genève.

– 2009. *Le butinage religieux. Pratiques et pratiquants au Brésil.* Genève; Paris: Institut de hautes études internationales et du développement; Karthala.

Sperber, Dan. 1982. "Les croyances apparemment irrationnelles." In *Le savoir des anthropologues*, edited by Dan Sperber, 49–85. Paris: Hermann.

Starbuck, Edwin Diller. 1899. *The Psychology of Religion: An Empirical Study of the Growth of Religious Consciousness.* New York: Charles Scribner's Sons.

Stark, Rodney, Eva Hamberg, and Alan S. Miller. 2005. "Exploring Spirituality and Unchurched Religions in America, Sweden, and Japan." *Journal of Contemporary Religion* 20 (1): 3–23. https://doi.org/10.1080/1353790052000313882.

Steinberg, Marc W. 1999. "The Talk and Back Talk of Collective Action: A Dialogic Analysis of Repertoires of Discourse among Nineteenth-Century English Cotton Spinners." *American Journal of Sociology* 105 (3): 736–80. https://doi.org/10.1086/210359.

Stewart, Charles. 1999. "Syncretism and Its Synonyms: Reflections on Cultural Mixture." *Diacritics* 29 (3): 40–62. https://doi.org/10.1353/dia.1999.0023.

Stifoss-Hanssen, Hans. 2009. "Religion and Spirituality: What a European Ear Hears." *International Journal for the Psychology of Religion* 9 (1): 25–33. https://doi.org/10.1207/s15327582ijpr0901_4.

Stoll, David. 1993. "Introduction: Rethinking Protestantism in Latin America." In *Rethinking Protestantism in Latin America*, edited by Virginia Garrard-Burnett and David Stoll. Philadelphia, PA: Temple University Press.

Stolz, Jörg, Judith Könemann, Mallory Schneuwly Purdie, Thomas Englberger, and Michael Krüggeler. 2015. *Religion et spiritualité à l'ère de l'ego. Profils de l'institutionnel, de l'alternatif, du distancié et du séculier.* Collection Religions et modernités. Genève: Labor et Fides.

Streeck, Wolfgang, and Kathleen Thelen, eds. 2005. *Beyond Continuity: Institutional Change in Advanced Political Economies.* Oxford: Oxford University Press.

Streib, Heinz. 2014. "Deconversion." In *The Oxford Handbook of Religious Conversion*, edited by Lewis Ray Rambo and Charles E. Farhadian, 271–96. New York: Oxford University Press.

Strickland, Francis L. 1924. *Psychology of Religious Experience.* New York: Abingdon Press.

Stromberg, Peter G. 1993. *Language and Self-Transformation: A Study of the Christian Conversion Narrative.* Cambridge: Cambridge University Press.

Suchman, Mark C. 1992. "Analyzing the Determinants of Everyday Conversion." *Sociological Analysis* 53 (S): S15–S33. https://doi.org/10.2307/3711248.

Sunstein, Cass R. 2009. *On Rumors: How Falsehoods Spread, Why We Believe Them, What Can Be Done.* New York: Farrar, Straus and Giroux.

Swatos, William H., and Loftur Reimar Gissurarson. 1997. *Icelandic Spiritualism: Mediumship and Modernity in Iceland.* New Brunswick, NJ: Transaction.

Swidler, Ann. 1986. "Culture in Action: Symbols and Strategies." *American Sociological Review* 51 (2): 273–86. https://doi.org/10.2307/2095521.

– 2001a. *Talk of Love: How Culture Matters.* Chicago: University of Chicago Press.

– 2001b. "What Anchors Cultural Practices." In *The Practical Turn,* edited by Theodore R. Schatzki, Karin Knorr Cetina, and Eike von Savigny. London: Routledge; Kegan Paul.

Tarot, Camille. 1999. *De Durkheim à Mauss, l'invention du symbolique. Sociologie et sciences des religions.* Paris: La Découverte/M.A.U.S.S.

Ter Haar, Gerrie. 2011. "Religion and Development: Introducing a New Debate." In *Religion and Development: Ways of Transforming the World,* edited by Gerrie ter Haar, 3–27. London: Hurst.

Tester, Keith. 1994. *The Flâneur.* London: Routledge.

Thomas, L. Eugene, and Pamela E. Cooper. 1978. "Measurement and Incidence of Mystical Experience: An Exploratory Study." *Journal for the Scientific Study of Religion* 17 (4): 433–7. https://doi.org/10.2307/1385407.

Tillich, Paul. 1952. *The Courage to Be.* New Haven, CT: Yale University Press.

Tilly, Charles. 1979. "Repertoires of Contention in America and Britain, 1750–1830." In *The Dynamics of Social Movements,* edited by John D. McCarthy and Mayer Zald. Cambridge, MA: Winthrop Publishers.

Togarasei, Lovemore. 2005. "Modern Pentecostalism as an Urban Phenomenon: The Case of the Family of God Church in Zimbabwe." *Exchange: Journal of Missiological and Ecumenical Research* 34 (4): 349–75. https://doi.org/10.1163/157254305774851484.

To the Editor. 2012. "The Time Has Come to Start Auditing Churches." *Daily Nation (Sunday Nation)*, August 5, 2012, 14.

Traugott, Mark, ed. 1995. *Repertoires and Cycles of Collective Action.* Durham, NC: Duke University Press Books.

Travisano, Richard. 1970. "Alternation and Conversion as Qualitatively Different Transformations." In *Social Psychology through Symbolic Interaction,* edited by Gregory P. Stone and Harvey A. Farberman, 594–606. Waltham, MA: Ginn-Blaisdell.

Turner, Robert P., David Lukoff, Ruth Tiffany Barnhouse, and Francis G. Lu. 1995. "Religious or Spiritual Problem: A Culturally Sensitive Diagnostic Category in the DSM-IV." *Journal of Nervous and Mental Disease* 183 (7): 435–44. https://doi.org/10.1097/00005053-199507000-00003.

Turner, Victor. 1982. *From Ritual to Theatre: The Human Seriousness of Play*. New York: Performing Arts Journal Publications.

Tweed, Thomas A. 2006. *Crossing and Dwelling: A Theory of Religion*. Cambridge, MA: Harvard University Press.

Tylor, Edward Burnett. 1871. *Primitive Culture*. London: John Murray.

Unger, Roberto M. 1987. *Social Theory: Its Situation and Its Task*. Cambridge: Cambridge University Press.

Van Dijk, Rijk. 1997. "From Camp to Encompassment: Discourses of Transsubjectivity in the Ghanaian Pentecostal Diaspora." *Journal of Religion in Africa* 27 (1–4): 135–59. https://doi.org/10.1163/157006697X00090.

– 2001. "Contesting Silence: The Ban on Drumming and the Musical Politics of Pentecostalism in Ghana." *Ghana Studies* 4: 31–64. http://hdl.handle.net/1887/9516.

– 2004. "Negotiating Marriage: Questions of Morality and Legitimacy in the Ghanaian Pentecostal Diaspora." *Journal of Religion in Africa* 34 (4): 438–67. https://doi.org/10.1163/1570066042564383.

Van Gennep, Arnold. 1909. *Les rites de passages*. Paris: Éditions A. & J. Picard.

Velho, Otavio. 2003. *Circuitos Infinitos*. São Paulo: Editora Attar.

Vincett, Giselle, and Linda Woodhead. 2009. "Spirituality." In *Religions in the Modern World: Traditions and Transformations*, edited by Linda Woodhead, Hiroko Kawanami, and Christopher Partridge, 319–38. New York: Routledge.

Voas, David, and Alasdair Crockett. 2005. "Religion in Britain: Neither Believing nor Belonging." *Sociology* 39 (1): 11–28. https://doi.org/10.1177/0038038505048998.

Wafula, Elizabeth Were. 2003. "Inter-Denominational Mobility of the Faithful among Churches in Nairobi." Master's thesis, University of Nairobi.

Ward, Graham. 2006. "The Future of Religion." *Journal of the American Academy of Religion* 74 (1): 179–86. https://doi.org/10.1093/jaarel/lfj024.

Warner, R. Stephen. 2000. "Religion and New (Post-1965) Immigrants: Some Principles Drawn from Field Research." *American Studies* 41 (2–3): 267–86.

Warner, R. Stephen, and Judith G. Wittner, eds. 1998. *Gatherings in Diaspora: Religious Communities and the New Immigration*. Philadelphia, PA: Temple University Press.

Wijsen, Frans. 2007. *Seeds of Conflict in a Haven of Peace: From Religious Studies to Interreligious Studies in Africa*. Amsterdam: Rodopi.

Williams, Raymond Brady. 1988. *Religions of Immigrants from India and Pakistan: New Threads in the American Tapestry*. Cambridge: Cambridge University Press.

Wilson, Rob. 2009. *Be Always Converting, Be Always Converted: An American Poetics*. Cambridge, MA: Harvard University Press.

Wittgenstein, Ludwig. 1922. *Tractatus Logico-Philosophicus*. London: Routledge & Kegan Paul.

Wuaku, Albert Kafui. 2009. "Hinduizing from the Top, Indigenizing from Below: Localizing Krishna Rituals in Southern Ghana." *Journal of Religion in Africa* 39 (4): 403–28. https://doi.org/10.1163/002242009X12537559494232.

Wulff, David M. 1991. *Psychology of Religion: Classic and Contemporary Views*. New York: John Wiley & Sons.

Wuthnow, Robert J. 2011. "Taking Talk Seriously: Religious Discourse as Social Practice." *Journal for the Scientific Study of Religion* 50 (1): 1–21. https://doi.org/10.1111/j.1468-5906.2010.01549.x.

Zinnbauer, Brian J., Kenneth I. Pargament, Brenda Cole, Mark S. Rye, Eric M. Butter, Timothy G. Belavich, Kathleen M. Hipp, Allie B. Scott, and Jill L. Kadar. 1997. "Religion and Spirituality: Unfuzzying the Fuzzy." *Journal for the Scientific Study of Religion* 36 (4): 549–64. https://doi.org/10.2307/1387689.

Zinnbauer, Brian J., Kenneth I. Pargament, and Allie B. Scott. 1999. "The Emerging Meanings of Religiousness and Spirituality: Problems and Prospects." *Journal of Personality* 67 (6): 889–919. https://doi.org/10.1111/1467-6494.00077.

www.ingramcontent.com/pod-product-compliance
Lightning Source LLC
LaVergne TN
LVHW090157080826
844660LV00013B/847/J